A VERY CANADIAN COUP

A VERY CANADIAN COUP

The Rise and Demise of
Prime Minister Mackenzie Bowell,
1894–1896

TED GLENN

DUNDURN
PRESS

Copyright © Ted Glenn, 2022

All rights reserved. No part of this publication may be reproduced, stored in a retrieval system, or transmitted in any form or by any means, electronic, mechanical, photocopying, recording, or otherwise (except for brief passages for purpose of review) without the prior permission of Dundurn Press. Permission to photocopy should be requested from Access Copyright.

Publisher: Kwame Scott Fraser | Acquiring editor: Kathryn Lane | Editor: Laurie Miller
Cover designer: Karen Alexiou
Cover image: Library and Archives Canada, PA-025851

Library and Archives Canada Cataloguing in Publication

Title: A very Canadian coup : the rise and demise of Prime Minister Mackenzie Bowell, 1894-1896 / Ted Glenn.
Names: Glenn, Ted, author.
Description: Includes index.
Identifiers: Canadiana (print) 20220276110 | Canadiana (ebook) 20220276196 | ISBN 9781459750180 (softcover) | ISBN 9781459750197 (PDF) | ISBN 9781459750203 (EPUB)
Subjects: LCSH: Bowell, Mackenzie, Sir, 1823-1917. | LCSH: Prime ministers—Canada—History—19th century. | CSH: Manitoba School Question. | CSH: Canada—Politics and government—1878-1896.
Classification: LCC FC525 .G54 2022 | DDC 971.05/5—dc23

We acknowledge the support of the Canada Council for the Arts and the Ontario Arts Council for our publishing program. We also acknowledge the financial support of the Government of Ontario, through the Ontario Book Publishing Tax Credit and Ontario Creates, and the Government of Canada.

Care has been taken to trace the ownership of copyright material used in this book. The author and the publisher welcome any information enabling them to rectify any references or credits in subsequent editions.

The publisher is not responsible for websites or their content unless they are owned by the publisher.

Printed and bound in Canada.

Dundurn Press
1382 Queen Street East
Toronto, Ontario, Canada M4L 1C9
dundurn.com, @dundurnpress

For Dad

Contents

Cast ix
Timeline xvii
Introduction 1
   1 Sans Souci 3
   2 Black Day 9
   3 Halifax 33
   4 Ides 45
   5 Blazing Heather 71
   6 Friendly Negotiations 99
   7 Coup 119
   8 Anew 147
   9 Coda 171
Notes 175
Sources 179
Image Credits 199
Index 201
About the Author 207

Cast

ABERDEEN, LADY ISHBEL MARJORIBANKS (1857–1939). Wife of Governor General Lord Aberdeen, president of the International Council of Women, and founder and organizer of the National Council of Women of Canada. Her *Canadian Journal, 1893–1898* is one of the most important primary documents for Canadian politics of the 1890s, providing particular insight into the life and times of Canada's Sixth Ministry.

ABERDEEN, LORD JOHN HAMILTON GORDON (1847–1934). Aberdeen served briefly as Lord Lieutenant of Ireland in 1886, prior to his appointment as Canadian Governor General in 1893. He was served by four Canadian prime ministers — Thompson, Bowell, Tupper, and Laurier. He and his wife, Ishbel, purchased Coldstream Ranch in British Columbia's Okanagan Valley in 1891 and oversaw the development of one of the region's first commercial orchard operations.

ANGERS, AUGUSTE-RÉAL (1837–1919). After six tumultuous years in provincial politics, Angers was appointed to the Quebec Superior Court in 1880 where he served until his return to politics as Lieutenant Governor of Quebec in 1887. At the height of the Mercier affair in 1891, Angers unceremoniously dismissed the Quebec premier, strengthening his reputation for decisiveness and action. In December 1892, Prime Minister Thompson appointed Angers to the Senate and made him minister of agriculture. Angers resigned from the Dominion cabinet in July 1895 to protest Bowell's decision to delay introduction of remedial legislation.

CARON, ADOLPHE (1843–1908). A graduate of McGill law (where he studied under John Abbott), the always-debonaire Caron was first elected to the House of Commons in 1873 and represented three different Quebec ridings until 1900. An able organizer, Caron was appointed minister of militia and defence in 1880 and in that capacity led the Canadian government's efforts to put down the Northwest Rebellion in 1885. Caron was moved to postmaster general under Abbott, a position he retained until Tupper became prime minister in May 1896. Caron, along with fellow Quebec minister Ouimet, briefly resigned from cabinet in July 1895 to protest Bowell's proposed delay in introducing remedial legislation.

CLARKE WALLACE, NATHANIEL (1844–1901). Long-time member for York West, Clarke Wallace was also grand master of the Loyal Orange Association of British North America and president of the Triennial Council of the Orangemen of the World. Appointed to cabinet by Prime Minister Thompson in December 1892, Clarke Wallace was seen as Bowell's successor as unofficial Orange representative in the Dominion cabinet. He resigned his post in December 1895 to protest Bowell's plans to proceed with remedial legislation in the upcoming legislative session.

COOK, FRED (1858–1943). Journalist and parliamentary correspondent with the *Montreal Star, Toronto Empire, Toronto Mail, Mail and Empire, Globe, Globe and Mail,* and *London Times* before a long career in municipal politics, including two terms as mayor of Ottawa.

DALY, THOMAS (1852–1911). A two-term mayor of Brandon, Daly was elected to the House of Commons in 1887 for Selkirk and promoted to minister of the interior in 1892, the first "westerner" appointed to cabinet. Daly travelled with Bowell during his 1895 trip across British Columbia, the Northwest Territories, and Manitoba.

DICKEY, ARTHUR (1854–1900). In 1888, Dickey succeeded Sir Charles Tupper as member for Cumberland in the House of Commons. He was appointed secretary of state in Bowell's Sixth Ministry, with subsequent promotions to the militia and defense and justice portfolios under Bowell and then attorney general in Tupper's Seventh Ministry. In the fall of 1895, Dickey encouraged Tupper Sr. to return to Canada and seek the prime ministership. He was one of the seven "bolters" who forced Bowell to resign and make way for Tupper in 1896.

DRUMMOND, GEORGE (1829-1910). A successful businessman and Conservative booster from Montreal, Drummond was summoned to the Senate by Prime Minister Macdonald in 1888. With Donald Smith, Drummond helped convince Charlie Tupper to rescind his resignation from cabinet in March 1895.

EWART, JOHN (1852-1933). The Winnipeg-based lawyer represented Manitoba's Roman Catholic minority in a series of cases concerning the Manitoba schools question and in negotiations with the Dominion government over the content of Bill C-58, the Bowell administration's proposed remedial legislation.

FOSTER, GEORGE (1847-1931). First elected to the House of Commons in 1882, Foster was promoted to minister of marine and fisheries in 1885 and then to finance in 1888 — a position he held through the Abbott, Thompson, Bowell, and Tupper administrations. A strong temperance advocate, Foster's leadership ambitions were derailed by his marriage to a divorcee, an inexcusable indiscretion in conservative 1890s Ottawa. Foster was one of seven "bolters" who forced Bowell to resign in 1896 and make way for Sir Charles Tupper to assume the premiership.

GREENWAY, THOMAS (1838-1908). Greenway was a three-term Manitoba premier (1888 to 1900). He and his government are perhaps best remembered for the legislation introduced in 1890 to abolish Manitoba's separate school system.

HAGGART, JOHN (1836-1913). One of the longest-serving members of the House of Commons, Haggart was first elected in 1872 for Perth and promoted to cabinet in 1888. Prime Minister Abbott promoted Haggart to minister of railways and canals and made him senior cabinet minister responsible for Ontario in 1892. Haggart's leadership ambitions were thwarted by numerous scandals, including the Canadian Pacific Schedule B contract scandal in British Columbia, the Tay Canal scandal in Perth, and the scandal involving an overpaid typist in the department of postmaster general, Miss Jane

Craig. Haggart was one of the seven "bolters" who forced Bowell to resign and make way for Sir Charles Tupper to succeed him in 1896.

IVES, WILLIAM (1841–1899). A successful, albeit controversial, businessman from the Eastern Townships, Ives was elected to the House of Commons in 1878. He was promoted to cabinet as one of two English-language representatives from Quebec in December 1892, a position formerly held by his father-in-law, John Henry Pope. Ives was one of the seven "bolters" who forced Bowell to resign in 1896 to make way for Sir Charles Tupper.

LAURIER, WILFRID (1841–1919). The longest-serving member of the House of Commons and Canada's first French Canadian prime minister, Laurier led a spirited opposition to Bill C-58, the Bowell administration's proposed remedial legislation, in the winter and early spring of 1895–96. Laurier and his Liberals defeated Prime Minister Tupper and his Conservatives in the June 1896 general election, ending nearly eighteen years of Conservative rule.

MAGURN, ARNOTT (1861–1923). Long-time journalist, editor and parliamentary correspondent with the *Montreal Herald*, the *Globe*, and the *Manitoba Free Press*.

McCARTHY, D'ALTON (1836–1898). A respected lawyer from Barrie, Ontario, McCarthy was an important legal advisor to John A. Macdonald in the 1880s on issues ranging from elections to the constitution to federal-provincial relations. McCarthy's 1890 speech in Portage la Prairie is credited with helping fan the flames of anti-French sentiment that led the Greenway government to abolish Manitoba's separate school system and make English the sole official language in the province. McCarthy represented the Greenway government in the Manitoba Roman Catholic minority's appeal to the Dominion cabinet.

MONTAGUE, DR. WALTER (1858–1915). A practising medical doctor, Montague wrested the Ontario federal riding of Haldimand away from its Liberal incumbent in 1890. He was promoted to cabinet by Bowell in December 1894 upon the insistence of senior Ontario cabinet minister John Haggart. Montague was one of the seven "bolters" who forced Bowell to resign in 1896 to make way for Sir Charles Tupper.

OUIMET, JOSEPH-ALDRIC (1847-1916). A Montreal-based lawyer, Ouimet came to prominence as lieutenant colonel of Montreal's 65th Battalion in the Northwest Rebellion. He was made Speaker of the House of Commons for his efforts, and then promoted to minister of public works in 1891 by Prime Minister Abbott. Following Angers's lead in July 1895, Ouimet and Alphonse Caron tendered — but then quickly rescinded — their resignations when Prime Minister Bowell refused to pass remedial legislation in the Fifth Session of Canada's Seventh Parliament.

SANFORD, WILLIAM (1838-1899). A wealthy clothing manufacturer and retail magnate from Hamilton, Sanford was appointed to the Senate by Prime Minister Macdonald in 1887. Prime Minister Thompson and his family were Sanford's guests at Sans Souci in the summer of 1894. Sanford accompanied Thompson's body home on the *Blenheim*.

SIFTON, CLIFFORD (1861-1929). Sifton was elected to the Manitoba legislature in 1888 and appointed attorney general in Thomas Greenway's Liberal government in 1891. Often viewed as the power behind the Greenway throne, Sifton deftly managed Manitoba's resistance to Dominion remediation efforts and served as one of two provincial delegates to meet with the Smith Commission in the spring of 1896.

SMITH, DONALD, FIRST BARON STRATHCONA (1820-1914). Businessman, philanthropist, politician, and diplomat — there weren't many events in Canada's first fifty years that Smith didn't play a part in. During the life of Canada's Sixth Ministry, Smith was a member of Parliament for Montreal West and led efforts in the spring of 1896 to negotiate a settlement with the Greenway government of the Manitoba schools question.

SMITH, FRANK (1822-1901). A successful businessman and Conservative bagman from Toronto, Smith was appointed by Macdonald to the Senate in 1871 and to cabinet in 1882. There, he served as unofficial representative of Canadian Irish Catholics. Smith brokered the deal that saw Bowell agree to resign in favour of Sir Charles Tupper in January 1896.

TACHÉ, ALEXANDRE-ANTONIN (1823–1894). Long-time Archbishop of Saint-Boniface, Taché led the resistance to Manitoba's efforts to abolish that province's separate schools. He asked Lieutenant Governor Schultz to withhold assent of the legislation, requested that Prime Minister Macdonald disallow the legislation, and petitioned the Dominion cabinet for remedial action.

TAYLOR, GEORGE (1840–1919). The member for Leeds South since 1882, Taylor served as Conservative whip during the fifth and sixth sessions of Canada's Seventh Parliament. He played a key role in helping organize Ontario Conservatives against Bowell's efforts to introduce remedial legislation.

THOMPSON, ANNIE (1842–1913). Wife of Prime Minister John Thompson.

THOMPSON, JOHN SPARROW DAVID (1845–1894). Thompson was Nova Scotia attorney general from 1878 to 1882 and then, briefly, premier. After going down to defeat in the general election of 1882, Thompson served as puisne justice on the Nova Scotia Supreme Court until 1885, when Prime Minister Macdonald appointed him minister of justice in the Dominion cabinet. Religious intolerance prevented the Catholic convert from succeeding Macdonald when he died in June 1891. A successful parliamentary record, and an extraordinary string of by-election wins, though, allowed Thompson to assume the premiership unopposed when Prime Minister Abbott was forced to retire because of poor health in 1892. Thompson died at Windsor Castle in December 1894.

TUPPER, CHARLES HIBBERT (1855–1927). Second son of Sir Charles Tupper, Charlie studied law at Harvard and then established a successful practice in Halifax with future prime minister Robert Borden. Charlie was elected to the House of Commons in 1882 and promoted to cabinet as minister of marine and fisheries in 1887, a position he retained until his promotion to the justice portfolio in December 1894. Following the 1896 election, Charlie's leadership ambitions were scuttled by his father's decision to serve as leader of the opposition. With a long history of resigning (or threatening to resign) when things didn't go his way, Charlie Tupper was one of the seven "bolters" who forced Bowell to resign in 1896 to make way for his father to become prime minister.

TUPPER, SIR CHARLES (1821–1915). A former premier of Nova Scotia, a Father of Confederation, and a long-time Dominion cabinet minister under John A. Macdonald, Tupper Sr. was appointed Canadian high commissioner to the United Kingdom in 1883, a position he retained until his re-election to the House of Commons in February 1896. Appointed prime minister on May 1, 1896, Tupper lost the general election on June 23, 1896. At sixty-eight days, Tupper's is the shortest tenure of any Canadian prime minister's.

Timeline

MARCH 31, 1890	Royal Assent is granted to two pieces of Manitoba legislation — *An Act Respecting the Department of Education* and *An Act Respecting Public Schools* — which abolish the province's separate school system and establish a public, non-sectarian system.
OCTOBER 27, 1890	First constitutional challenge of Manitoba legislation to abolish separate schools fails in *Barrett v. City of Winnipeg*.
NOVEMBER 24, 1890	Manitoba Court dismisses *Barrett* appeal.
FEBRUARY 2, 1891	Manitoba Court of Queen's Bench upholds Manitoba Court ruling in *Barrett*.
MARCH 5, 1891	Prime Minister John A. Macdonald leads Conservative Party to fourth-straight general election victory.
JUNE 6, 1891	John A. Macdonald dies in Ottawa.
JUNE 12, 1891	Senator John Abbott becomes prime minister.
OCTOBER 28, 1891	Appeal to Supreme Court of Canada reverses Manitoba Court of Queen's Bench decision in *Barrett* and declares Manitoba school laws unconstitutional.

JULY 30, 1892	Canada's highest court at the time, the Judicial Committee of the Privy Council (JCPC) in London, overrules Supreme Court of Canada in *Barrett* and finds that separate school rights had not been prejudicially affected by the Manitoba legislation of 1890.
NOVEMBER 23, 1892	Justice Minister John Thompson becomes prime minister when Abbott resigns due to poor health.
JANUARY 1893	Dominion cabinet begins hearing appeal from Manitoba's Roman Catholic minority. Shortly after, Prime Minister Thompson suspends hearings and refers the matter to the Supreme Court in a reference case known as *Brophy*.
FEBRUARY 20, 1894	Supreme Court rules in *Brophy* that no constitutional rights had been affected by the Manitoba schools legislation, and that without any infringement of rights, there were no grounds for appeal to the Dominion cabinet on this issue.
DECEMBER 12, 1894	Prime Minister John Thompson dies while lunching at Windsor Castle.
DECEMBER 13, 1894	Senator Mackenzie Bowell asked to form Canada's Sixth Ministry.
JANUARY 3, 1895	State funeral for Prime Minister John Thompson in Halifax, Nova Scotia.
JANUARY 29, 1895	JCPC overturns Supreme Court in *Brophy*, ruling that denominational school rights did exist in 1870 and were protected under section 22 of the *Manitoba Act*. As such, the Roman Catholic

Timeline

	minority did have a right to appeal to the Dominion cabinet and Parliament did have the authority to legislate remediation.
FEBRUARY 16, 1895	Dominion cabinet decides to continue the hearings from Manitoba's Roman Catholic minority that Thompson had initiated in December 1893.
MARCH 4–7, 1895	Appeal of Manitoba's Roman Catholic minority to the Dominion cabinet, where John Ewart represents the minority and D'Alton McCarthy the Manitoba government.
MARCH 5, 1895	Dominion cabinet issues an order in council committing to put $2.5 million for a loan to the Winnipeg–Hudson Bay railway project before Parliament in the coming session.
MACH 17–20, 1895	Dominion cabinet meets to decide on the Roman Catholic appeal.
MARCH 21, 1895	Governor General Lord Aberdeen signs orders in council directing the Manitoba government to restore Roman Catholic minority rights to denominational schooling and empowering Parliament to pass such a law if Manitoba failed to pass such remedial legislation.
	Charlie Tupper threatens to resign when he discovers that Bowell and the rest of Canada's Sixth Ministry have decided not to dissolve Parliament and go to the polls on the question of whether to proceed with remediation.
APRIL 18, 1895	Lord Aberdeen opens the Fifth Session of Canada's Seventh Parliament, promising that

	Parliament would pass remedial legislation if Manitoba did not.
JUNE 17, 1895	Attorney General Clifford Sifton informs the Manitoba legislature that the Greenway government would not be carrying out the Dominion remedial order.
JULY 4, 1895	Dominion cabinet decides to push passage of remedial legislation to a future session. Quebec cabinet minister Auguste-Réal Angers resigns his post as minister of agriculture in protest; fellow Quebecers Adolphe Caron and Joseph-Aldric Ouimet tender their resignations as well.
JULY 11, 1895	Bowell and Foster convince Caron and Ouimet to rescind their resignations and resume their cabinet positions.
JULY 20, 1895	Senate debates the *Lake Manitoba Railway Act* and the *Winnipeg and Great Northern Railway Act*, key parts of William Mackenzie and Donald Mann's plan for their Canadian Northern Railway.
JULY 22, 1895	Lord Aberdeen prorogues the Fifth Session of Canada's Seventh Parliament.
JULY 27, 1895	Bowell issues "friendly negotiations" memo to Manitoba premier Thomas Greenway, then departs Ottawa with the Aberdeens to conduct "friendly negotiations" himself.
JULY 27–SEPT. 15, 1895	Bowell tours reserves and residential schools across British Columbia, the Northwest Territories, and Manitoba. Fails to conduct

Timeline

	"friendly negotiations" with Greenway or any other member of the Manitoba government.
NOVEMBER 1, 1895	In a letter to Sir Charles Tupper, Minister of Militia and Defense Arthur Dickey invites the high commissioner to "come out as first minister," refresh the Conservative ranks, and "form a powerful government that would sweep the country."
NOVEMBER 4, 1895	Dominion cabinet decides to proceed with remedial legislation in the upcoming session. Haggart threatens to resign and take four Ontario cabinet ministers with him.
NOVEMBER 7, 1895	In a letter to his father, Charlie Hibbert Tupper assures Tupper Sr. that "if you could visit Canada on some excuse the party would run up and form under you."
DECEMBER 16, 1895	Tupper Sr. arrives back in Ottawa and immediately meets with conspirators.
DECEMBER 17, 1895	British Columbia's six-member Conservative caucus revolt ends with promotion of putative leader E.G. Prior to a full cabinet position.
DECEMBER 21, 1895	Manitoba premier Greenway officially rejects Dominion order to re-establish separate schools.
JANUARY 2, 1896	Lord Aberdeen opens Sixth Session of Canada's Seventh Parliament with a promise to introduce remedial legislation.
JANUARY 3, 1896	Minister of Railways and Canals John Haggart and Minister without Portfolio Walter Montague

	meet with Bowell and tell him that he risks losing the government's majority if he proceeds with remedial legislation.
JANUARY 4, 1896	In the morning, Bowell informs Charlie Tupper he plans to resign. In the afternoon, Bowell and Tupper Sr. meet to discuss Bowell's resignation. Meeting ends abruptly when the resignations of seven cabinet ministers are submitted.
JANUARY 6, 1896	A day after meeting with Lord Aberdeen, Bowell tries to reconstruct his cabinet.
JANUARY 8, 1896	The *Globe* publishes interview with Sir Charles Tupper, in which he turns up the heat on Bowell to resign.
	Bowell attempts to hand Aberdeen his letter of resignation; Aberdeen refuses to accept it and asks Bowell to continue his reconstruction efforts.
JANUARY 12, 1896	Bowell and Tupper Sr. meet again, but fail to come to terms.
JANUARY 13, 1896	Senator Frank Smith negotiates a deal between Bowell and Tupper Sr. after rumours that Lord Aberdeen was about to ask Wilfrid Laurier to form a government.
JANUARY 15, 1896	The final, reconstructed version of Canada's Sixth Ministry announced in Parliament. Manitoba premier Thomas Greenway's Liberal government elected to third-straight majority.
FEBRUARY 2, 1896	Sir Charles Tupper elected to the House of Commons in Cape Breton by-election.

Timeline

FEBRUARY 11, 1896	Bill C-58, *The Remedial Act (Manitoba)*, introduced for first reading in the House of Commons.
MARCH 3–20, 1896	Second reading and debate on Bill C-58.
MARCH 25–APR. 2, 1896	In Winnipeg, the Smith Commission meets with Manitoba representatives, Attorney General Clifford Sifton and Provincial Secretary John Cameron.
APRIL 6, 1896	Clause-by-clause review of Bill C-58 begins.
APRIL 15, 1896	Bill C-58 withdrawn.
APRIL 27, 1896	Mackenzie Bowell resigns; Sir Charles Tupper asked to form Canada's Seventh Ministry.
JUNE 23, 1896	Wilfrid Laurier leads Liberal Party to majority victory in general election.
NOVEMBER 16, 1896	Laurier-Greenway Compromise resolving the Manitoba schools question announced.

Introduction

Prime Minister John A. Macdonald died in June 1891 — just three months after leading his Conservative Party to a fourth-straight general election majority. Religious intolerance, however, prevented the Old Man's most capable heir, the Roman Catholic justice minister John Thompson, from succeeding him, and forced a reluctant compromise candidate, Senator John Abbott, to assume the reins of office from the Red Chamber while Thompson led the government in the Commons.

Abbott and Thompson were a good team. They cleaned up several scandals inherited from Macdonald and forced the resignation of two senior ministers caught up therein — Hector Langevin and Joseph-Adolphe Chapleau. Voters were impressed. In a remarkable string of by-elections that began in December 1891, nineteen Conservatives wrested seats away from Liberal incumbents and twenty-one of twenty-three Conservatives retained their positions. The victories proved to Protestant Conservatives that Thompson could win elections regardless of his religion. Not surprisingly, when poor health forced Abbott to resign in November 1892, no one opposed Thompson's ascension to office.

Thompson died two years later. By that point in the beleaguered life of Canada's Seventh Parliament, the Governor General, Lord Aberdeen, thought it best to appoint a caretaker administration until a general election could be held in the spring of 1895 and voters could provide a fresh mandate to either a reconstructed Conservative Party or Wilfrid Laurier's Liberals.

Aberdeen's choice of caretaker was another senator, Mackenzie Bowell. But Canada's fifth prime minister didn't make it to the polls. A month after he was appointed to the job, the Manitoba schools question derailed plans for a spring election, and high dudgeon and palace intrigue set the stage for one of the most dramatic events in Canadian political history: the bloodless coup that deposed Bowell and installed Charles Tupper as prime minister in the spring of 1896.

Only a handful of studies have examined Bowell's sixteen months in office, and only one of note in the past fifty years. In large part, the lack of attention is because the historical record for this period is thin and unreliable. Bowell himself didn't write much — he told Lady Aberdeen his "inability to write letters" was due to his being "a printer in his young days" — and the memorials left by contemporaries are either heavily sanitized (Tupper Sr.), highly subjective (Lady Aberdeen), or politically expedient (Foster). What's left — and where this book attempts to make a new contribution to a better understanding of the period — are the elements of the record scattered throughout newspapers of the day.

The most important sources for this book were the stories filed by parliamentary correspondents Fred Cook (for the *Toronto Empire*), Arnott Magurn (for the *Toronto Globe*), and Robert MacLeod (for the *Ottawa Citizen*). Compared to the highly partisan editorials found on other pages of their papers, these investigative reports reflect the intimate, long-standing relationships these journalists had with key players of the period and often include exclusive interviews with them, both on and off the record. I have used these stories, together with more traditional sources like Lady Aberdeen's diary, Hansard, and the limited correspondence that does exist, to create what I think is a fair representation of the life and times of Prime Minister Mackenzie Bowell and Canada's Sixth Ministry. Quotation marks are used when conversations are attributable to a specific source (e.g., Fred Cook's account of Bowell receiving news of Thompson's death) and left out where the content of the conversation is known but exact dialogue is not (e.g., when Bowell informs Annie Thompson of her husband's death). To streamline the text, all attribution, and any additional explananda, are included in the Sources.

1
Sans Souci

Naiad

William Sanford loved to entertain. Each summer, the senator and his wife, Harriet, welcomed scores of family and friends to their cottage on Sans Souci Island in the eastern end of Lake Rosseau. They spent the days touring the Muskokas on Sanford's ninety-eight-foot steam yacht, the *Naiad,* and the evenings gathered 'round roaring campfires telling tales and singing.

"Mack, did you know Edward Blake?" Sanford asked fellow senator Mackenzie Bowell, a guest at Sans Souci in August 1894. Sanford had heard the story before. In fact, most lounging in the *Naiad's* plush cabin after lunch had. But no one tired of hearing it.

"I rather did," Bowell said. The seventy-one-year-old leaned back and settled in against the mullion bar between the open windows. "Yes, I suppose I'm the only man ever lived that took Edward Blake down, once on the floor of the House and once in the lobby."

"Metaphorically speaking, eh?" Sanford looked down the table and gave John Thompson and his wife, Annie, a wink and a nod. Canada's fourth prime minister and his family were also guests of the Sanfords that summer.

They were staying at Lorelei, the Sanfords' quaint guest cottage across the bay from Sans Souci.

"Not by a jugful! No, flopped him fair on his back." Bowell brought his hand down flat on the table with a bang. "Yes, Blake got gibing me a bit one night after the House adjourned, and I said: 'Now, a little more of that and I'll take you down right here.' He allowed that I couldn't do that. I insisted that I could. And then" — Bowell snapped forward, snatched his arms around his imaginary foe — "the big elephant came at me!" Everyone jerked back and laughed.

"Oh, I never was a very big man, but what there was of me was hard as nails." Bowell patted his bicep and leaned back against the mullion again with a big grin.

"And that was it?" Sanford nudged Faith Fenton's elbow and winked. The country's most famous female reporter was also staying at Sans Souci that week. She was on assignment for the *Toronto Empire*, writing an exclusive on the notoriously private prime minister.

Bowell continued. "Well, I downed him, but it wasn't exactly easy. He chased me 'round the table, but Blake never could run in anything but an election." Thompson shook his head, pulled his kerchief from his pocket, and wiped the tears streaming from his eyes. Sir John was at his heaviest that summer — he'd topped the scales at Port Carling earlier in the week at over two hundred — and his body fairly bounced from the laughter.

Bowell paused again. He'd dined out on the Blake story for years and knew exactly when to deliver the *coup de grâce*. "A few days afterwards I met Blake in the lobby. He started to come at me like a bull at a toreador. 'Now, look out, old fellow,' I said, 'I'll down you again.' 'You can't do it,' Blake said, crisply. 'But by jingo, I will.' So I ducked and grabbed him under the hips somewhere. I heaved him as high as I could and came down on top of him. George, I cracked a rib, nearly broke a finger, and didn't get over that flop for a month!"

The *Naiad* got under way again after lunch, the breeze providing welcome respite from the heat and humidity of the late August afternoon. Sir John

Sans Souci

resumed his seat in the bow of the yacht and Sanford took up his station at the helm ten feet behind. Bowell, Fenton, and Thompson's two adult sons, John and Joe, sprawled beneath the canopy next to the cabin. Everyone else was inside napping.

"When we reach the head of Lake Joseph, where shall we be?" Sir John called back from his perch.

"We shall be precisely at the head of Lake Joseph," Joe replied promptly.

Not to be outdone by his younger brother, John added, "Port Cockburn is a little summering place at the head of Lake Joseph, and when we reach it we shall be within twelve miles east of Parry Sound." Sir John nodded slowly, pleased with the boys' attention to detail.

"Is there any outlet between these lakes and Georgian Bay?" Sir John continued.

"Only one, and that is in Lake Muskoka; but it is full of rapids and is unnavigable," Joe explained. John gave him a shove.

"And the only way to get the *Naiad* or any other steamer out of the Muskoka lakes is to put her on board a few flatcars," Sanford added.

A couple of miles out of Port Sandfield, the *Naiad* emerged from a narrow channel and onto a stretch of open water where two canoes came into view. From a distance, they appeared abandoned, but as Sanford brought the *Naiad* closer, four female paddlers popped their heads up to see who was approaching.

"Would you like a lift?" Sanford called as the *Naiad* coasted closer. The young women said they'd been out since morning and would be ever so grateful.

The Thompson boys tied the canoes to the stern of the yacht and Sanford escorted the rescuees to the foredeck where one of the women spied Sir John's gold-braided captain's cap. It was a custom Sanford insisted upon while the prime minister was on board. Sanford himself wore the first mate's silver braids.

"Thank you so much," the woman said to Sir John. "It was so good of you to take us in; we had undertaken too long a row and were getting so tired."

"I appreciate that, but it is not me who deserves the thanks," Sir John replied.

The woman looked puzzled.

"Do you sail these lakes many months of the year?" one of the other women asked Sanford.

"Only through July and August," Sanford replied. "It is a very short season, but of course it is very pleasant."

The first woman tried to engage Thompson again.

"You have such a pretty yacht," she said. Thompson explained it wasn't his, but Sanford's.

"Oh," she said. Still confused, she walked back to the seats beneath the canopy and joined Bowell, Fenton, and the Thompson boys.

"Just who is that?" the woman asked.

Fenton explained it was the prime minister, Sir John Thompson. Bowell winked at the boys and told the woman the gold-braided cap should have given it away: it was, after all, the prime minister's official insignia.

The sun was setting by the time the *Naiad* chugged south of Tobin Island, a couple of miles west of Sans Souci. The crew had set the running lights and were handing out blankets to insulate against the cool evening air. On one of the smaller islands just past Tobin, a massive bonfire was blazing onshore. The merrymakers recognized the *Naiad*'s lights and called out for Sanford and his guests to come and join the festivities. Sanford manoeuvred to drop anchor while a landing party rowed out to ferry everyone to shore. Sir John and Annie elected to stay on board and protect the *Naiad* against the pirates they claimed were lurking in the shadows. The two sat conspiratorially on the bow, one blanket across their laps, another pulled around their shoulders, the bonfire crackling away in the distance and the stars twinkling in the late summer sky.

The wharf and trail to the party were festooned with Chinese lanterns. Children ran back and forth throwing cedar branches onto the fire and squealed when showers of sparks erupted skyward. Someone pulled out a mandolin and strummed out the first few bars of "Down upon the Swanee River" and everyone soon joined in.

Sans Souci

When the bonfire burned low, Sanford rounded up his revellers and returned to the *Naiad*. Everyone was sleepy, chilled, and ready for bed. Back on Sans Souci, the crew helped Thompson and his family into their skiffs for the final leg back to Lorelei, three hundred yards across the bay. As the boats pulled away, Fenton, Bowell, and the Sanfords waved and called out good night. "*Bonne nuit!*" came the reply, as the Thompsons glided through the darkness toward the distant lanterns.

Sir John S.D. Thompson with family and friends on Sans Souci, August 1894. Standing, left to right: Senator Mackenzie Bowell, Frankie Thompson, Babe Thompson, Emma Sanford (wife of Jackson, who took this picture), Senator William Sanford, Faith Fenton. Seated, left to right: Prime Minister Sir John Thompson, Joseph Thompson, Annie Thompson, Mary Thompson, John Thompson.

2
Black Day

News

At 11:45 a.m., John Carleton bolted up the back staircase of East Block and down the narrow hall to his boss's office. He didn't bother knocking. Mackenzie Bowell, the minister of trade and commerce and acting prime minister, was seated behind the desk chatting with his old friend Sandford Fleming about the state of negotiations on the proposed Pacific cable that would link Australia, Canada, and Great Britain. Carleton handed Bowell a short telegram: "11:36 am, Dec 12, 1894. Reported from Windsor Castle that Sir John Thompson expired after meeting of Privy Council …"

Bowell stopped, stunned. Fleming and Carleton could see the blood drain from his face, even behind the grey beard.

Fleming asked what the news was.

"It can't be true." Bowell shook his head, turned the telegram over, looking for more. "It has got to be mere newspaper rumour." Fleming reached across the desk and took the cable.

John Payne, Bowell's private secretary, had slipped into the office behind Carleton. "It may be rumour," Payne said, "but the message is authentic — I can confirm it's CPR."

"I'm not going to give it credit until it's confirmed," Bowell said, shaking his head.

Fleming stood up. "I'll wire Hosmer in Montreal to confirm the authority of the dispatch," he said and left. Carleton and Payne followed.

The office was quiet for a few minutes, then came a tap on the door. Payne stuck his head in. "Fred Cook for you, Mack."

Bowell didn't respond; Payne showed the *Empire*'s Ottawa correspondent in.

"Can you confirm it?" Cook asked, sliding into Sanford's chair.

"No, nothing official. Just the same newspaper rumours you've been reading," Bowell said. He was looking out the window at the rain. It was coming down in sheets.

Two more men came into Bowell's office — George Foster, the minister of finance, and John Costigan, the secretary of state.

"Is this terrible news true?" Foster asked.

Bowell kept shaking his head. "I can't believe it," he said, looking back to the telegram, "but it seems to be authentic."

"I can't believe for the third time in three years the Dominion is mourning the loss of a premier, our party the loss of a chief," Foster said. "And while the first two were heavy blows, this has got to be the heaviest. Macdonald and Abbott were loved, but they were old, well past their allotted spans of life. It's like the sun falling out of the sky at midday."

The room fell silent again. The rain fell harder, shading the midday light to a dull grey.

Payne returned a few minutes later with two more telegrams, the first from Governor General Lord Aberdeen from his residence in Montreal, the second from Sir Charles Tupper, Canada's high commissioner to Great Britain in London. Bowell asked Payne to read them out.

> Mr. Hosmer, CPR Telegraphs, and also the North Western's office inform me that they have just received the following most distressing intelligence by cablegram from Windsor Castle: "Reported from Windsor Castle that Sir John Thompson expired after meeting of Privy Council." Let

me offer, and exchange with you and other members of the Government, expressions of deep grief and condolence concerning this irreparable loss.
ABERDEEN

Deeply regret to say Sir John died suddenly at Windsor castle to-day at luncheon, after the ceremony of swearing-in.
TUPPER

The telegrams dashed whatever hope remained in the room. Bowell took the papers from Payne and laid them on the desk, gently smoothing out the edges over and over. The tears ran down his cheeks into his beard. Everyone in the room felt lost, wasted.

Payne stood silent by the door. Bowell looked up at one point and tried to talk, but his voice failed. Payne understood the task at hand, though: get the ministers of Thompson's now-defunct Fifth Ministry back to Ottawa. Charlie Tupper was on the West Coast, John Haggart and James Patterson were on tour in southwestern Ontario, Joseph-Aldric Ouimet and Auguste-Réal Angers were in Montreal, and Adolphe Caron was in New York.

"Poor Annie," Bowell finally got out, still shaking his head. "Who can we get to take the news to her?"

"Mack, it's your duty," Foster said.

"Oh God, I can't do it," Bowell said, burying his face in his hands again.

"It's clearly the duty of some member of the Ministry to tell her," Costigan added.

"She's already heard," Douglas Stewart said. Thompson's private secretary for the past decade had slipped into the room and sat slumped on the settee.

"What do you mean?" Foster asked.

"When I first heard, I ran over to reassure Annie it was just another rumour, like when news arrived last year of Sir John's demise at the Bering Sea conference. But a reporter beat me to it. Some fool called over to ask if the news was true. She hadn't heard yet." Stewart rubbed his face.

"How is she?" Bowell asked.

"As you can imagine," Stewart replied. "She won't stop sobbing."

The room went quiet again.

"She asked if you'd come to discuss funeral arrangements," Stewart finally said.

Bowell relented. "Of course."

At five to one, the Grand Trunk special pulled into Wingham in the middle of a downpour. The four men onboard the official government car *Ottawa* — railway minister John Haggart, Minister of Militia James Patterson, Senator Donald Ferguson, and newly elected Ontario MP Dr. Walter Montague — were exhausted. They'd been on the road a week already; a whistle-stop tour with three stops a day to prop up support for a Conservative government in power since '78 and facing stiff competition from the Liberal Party and its surging leader, Wilfrid Laurier.

Eleven grim-faced men were waiting on the wooden platform for them in the pouring rain. When the train stopped, the reception committee moved to climb aboard. Hugh Morphy, the president of the local Young Men's Conservative Association, came on first and stuck his head into the sitting room.

"Have you heard the news?"

"What news?" Patterson asked.

"There are reports Sir John Thompson died at Windsor."

"Impossible!" Haggart said.

Morphy pulled a soggy telegram from an inside pocket and handed it to Patterson.

"'Reported Sir John Thompson died at Windsor to-day,'" Patterson read out. "'Report confirmed.'"

The men went silent while the rain pummelled the car roof. In a minute or two, Patterson and Haggart got up, clambered down the ladder, and hustled across the platform into the station. Patterson got the first telegram off to Bowell: "If anyone has official word of the news it would be Bowell." Haggart had the station master cable Grand Trunk

Black Day

headquarters in Montreal to inform them the *Ottawa* would return to Ottawa at once. He also sent word to St. Marys and Galt cancelling the remainder of the tour.

The ministers returned to their car and waited while the minutes churned. A quarter of an hour, half an hour, an hour — still no word from Bowell. Patterson had the station master send another cable.

"Perhaps the message was 'Sir John had *dined* at Windsor Castle' not 'Sir John had *died* at Windsor Castle,'" Ferguson said hopefully.

They'd reached the point where they couldn't wait any longer if they wanted to make Ottawa that evening, when the station master came on board. He read out a United Press cable describing how Thompson died at Windsor Palace. But still nothing from Bowell. Haggart told the conductor to get under way.

The train steamed into Elora at two thirty in the morning, where a cable from Bowell was waiting: "It is true. Official dispatch received from Tupper. Return to Ottawa immediately." Another cable from Thomas Daly, the minister of the interior, read: "Our Chief was taken ill at luncheon immediately after being sworn in a member of the Privy Council and expired before medical aid arrived."

At Elora, the men went into the station to send condolences to Annie Thompson:

> Accept our most profound sympathy at your great bereavement and the country's irreparable loss. May God sustain you in your affliction.
>
> I have no words to express my profound sorrow at the news I have just heard. May God sustain you in your bereavement.
>
> I cannot tell you how deeply I sympathize with you in your hour of so great a sorrow.

The *Ottawa* waited long enough for those on board to speak with the handful of reporters who'd gathered on the platform.

"We've known for years that Sir John Thompson's health was not the best," Patterson said. "Doctors in London said he was suffering from Bright's disease. But even though Mr. Haggart and I knew what we did his death has come upon us like a thunderclap."

"I simply can't tell you how deeply pained we are [sic] this terrible news," Haggart added.

"We have no words to express our feelings," Patterson continued. "We were all his close personal friends, bound to him not merely by ties of party, but by the strongest ties of personal affection."

Haggart went on. "Sir John was a truly great man, possessing one of the clearest intellects it has ever been my good fortune to meet, and a heart as warm beneath a reserved exterior as ever beat. He was a true Canadian. No more honourable man ever held a place of public trust in the country, and the country never lost a truer friend or abler statesman that it has lost today."

As the ministers started to climb back on board, Ferguson hung back. "I believe him, now that he is gone, to have been possessed of one of the greatest intellects of the age. Canada has never seen a greater more honest or more upright man than Sir John Thompson."

Mackenzie Bowell sat next to Annie Thompson on her living room sofa, George Foster and Douglas Stewart across in chairs. Bowell tried his best to console Annie. Both struggled to find any words. So, they just sat quiet, Annie sobbing gently.

Annie eventually asked Mack if he knew anything more about what happened. Bowell said Sir Charles had sent some additional telegrams with the details — but was she sure she wanted to hear them now? Annie said she needed to know.

Well, you know your husband. He arrived at Paddington Station a half-hour early because he didn't want to miss the train to Windsor Castle. He waited on the platform with Lord Breadalbane, the chief steward of the Queen's household; Lord Ripon, the colonial secretary; and a dozen or so other members of the Privy Council.

Black Day

The train pulled into Windsor around one and the ministers were taken by carriage to the council chamber for the ceremony where Sir John was sworn in as imperial privy councillor. Ripon said Sir John looked tired, but no more than he'd looked for the past couple of weeks while in London.

The ceremony itself took just fifteen minutes and then the group adjourned to the Octagon Dining Room for lunch. Sir John sat between one of Queen Victoria's ladies-in-waiting and Lord Pelham Clinton, the Master of the Queen's Household. A few minutes later he fainted. Breadalbane sent for the Queen's physician, a Dr. Reid, and then he and Pelham carried Sir John into an adjoining room and laid him on a chaise by the window. Breadalbane got some water and told Pelham to fetch some brandy.

Pelham and Ripon came back with the brandy, by which time Sir John was conscious again. He took the drink from Ripon. Everyone thought Sir John had revived.

But you know your husband. He was distressed at the thought of having made a scene. He told Breadalbane, "It seems too weak and foolish to faint like this," but Breadalbane told him, "One does not faint on purpose; pray do not distress yourself about the matter."

Dr. Reid arrived about then and Sir John said he'd "only had a slight heart attack." Reid examined him and said he had to rest, doctor's orders. But you know Sir John; he insisted on returning to lunch so there wasn't any more of a scene. Breadalbane said he wouldn't hear of it and made him lie down a spell longer. But Sir John was insistent, and Breadalbane said he looked to have recovered, so he rose and offered John his arm for support. Sir John, of course, refused. "I am all right now, thank you," he said. But, of course, he wasn't.

They'd just sat back down to lunch again, Reid beside him now, when Sir John suddenly slumped over again. Reid got a hold of him and gently laid him out on the floor. He felt for a pulse but there was none. Reid said it was his heart.

Annie asked where her poor pet was now. Bowell said he'd been moved to a makeshift mortuary in Clarence Tower. Queen Victoria herself had commanded a requiem mass be held there late last evening.

And his body? Bowell said the Queen had asked Sir Charles Tupper to accompany Sir John back to the Lady Chapel of St. James Church in London for the embalming.

Tupper? Annie sat straight up. She'd been leery of Tupper since he'd taken all praise for negotiating the U.S. fisheries treaty six years earlier, leaving no recognition for her dear pet, who was clearly the brains behind the operation. Bowell said Tupper had already told Ripon he'd accompany Sir John home. He was, after all, the Dominion government's official representative in Britain.

Annie sat quietly for a moment and then asked where Helena was. Her second-eldest daughter was supposed to be on her way to Paris with William Sanford, who was going to get her settled into school while Sir John was busy with colonial matters in London. Bowell said they were on their way back to London now and that the Sanfords had promised to escort Helena back to Canada with Sir John's body.

By six forty-five that evening, Bowell was exhausted. He headed back to his permanent suite at the Russell House and found Fred Cook waiting for him in the lobby when he stepped through the doors.

"Any news this evening, Senator?" Cook asked.

"Nothing. Perhaps in the morning," Bowell said.

"Anything else you'd like to add about Sir John?"

Bowell stopped for a moment and collected his thoughts.

"My first acquaintance with Sir John Thompson dates from the time when he joined the Government of our lamented chieftain, Sir John Macdonald, now more than nine years ago. Since that time, I have been with him constantly, and our relations were of the most intimate and cordial character. We scarcely ever differed in opinion on questions of public policy. He was an ardent and devoted lover of his country. He was possessed with the strongest possible attachment to the crown, believing that the destiny of Canada and its future greatness depended on the closest possible relations with the motherland.

Black Day

"In private and social life, he was a prince. There was an apparent air of reserve about him, but beneath it, there was a generous temperament and an affability of manner which those not intimate with him could hardly realize. During the number of years we have been associated, it has been my good fortune never to have had an unkind or disagreeable word with him."

"Thank you, Senator — and have a good evening."

Rt. Hon. Sir John Sparrow David Thompson (born November 10, 1844, deceased December 12, 1894).

Ascension

Douglas Stewart had a cab waiting for the Aberdeens when they arrived in Ottawa early Thursday afternoon, December 13. He loaded the couple on board and told the driver to take them straight to the Thompson house on Somerset.

The Aberdeens had grown close to the Thompsons since they'd arrived in Canada fifteen months earlier. John Hamilton Gordon — Lord Aberdeen — trusted and valued Sir John's always measured advice and Ishbel Marjoribanks — Lady Aberdeen — delighted in having an intelligent, witty friend to navigate Ottawa's notoriously closed and catty social circles. The two families saw much of each other; the Aberdeens treated the Thompson children as nieces and nephews.

Despite their familiarity, the trip to see Annie Thompson wasn't entirely personal. Thompson's death had dissolved Canada's Fifth Ministry and Aberdeen had a constitutional responsibility to ensure that a first minister who could command the loyalty of a cabinet and the confidence of a majority in the House of Commons was in place to conduct Crown business. And, while not binding, tradition had it that the Governor General should at least consider any recommendations a prime minister might have made regarding succession. Thompson had said nothing to either Aberdeen or his colleagues on the topic, nor left anything in his personal papers (which Sir Charles Tupper, who'd taken charge of his things in London, confirmed to the Associated Press that morning). But maybe Sir John had said something to Annie. Aberdeen would leave it to Ishbel to find out. The Aberdeens were a team, domestically and professionally, a "modern arrangement" they'd established during Aberdeen's first viceregal posting as lord lieutenant of Ireland in 1886 and maintained since.

The youngest Thompson, thirteen-year-old Frankie, met the Aberdeens at the front door. She was, as always, a ray of sunshine, doing her best to prop up everyone's spirits. She ushered the Aberdeens into the living room, where Annie was sitting with John and Joe. The boys had arrived in from Toronto earlier that morning.

Black Day

Lord and Lady Aberdeen and family. Standing, left to right: Dudley Gordon, Lord Aberdeen, Haddo Gordon, and Archie Gordon. Seated: Marjorie Gordon and Lady Aberdeen.

Lord Aberdeen didn't stay long. He paid his respects to Annie, told the boys if he could ever "act in your father's place be sure to come to me," and then left for the office.

Lady Aberdeen judged Annie was "very brave and strong and quite natural and like herself — but at the same time utterly overwhelmed with the thought of being *alone*."

"Never to hear his voice again," Annie told Ishbel, "never to hear him come in at the door, never to hear him come up the stairs again — never, never. I am afraid of the nights and I am afraid of the days and I am afraid of the years and if it were not for the children I should long to creep away in some corner and die."

Ishbel waited a bit and then asked if Sir John had "ever expressed any opinion about his successor?" Did he ever mention Sir Charles Tupper, say?

There was a group of hard-core loyalists who'd long believed Sir Charles Tupper was the rightful heir to the Conservative throne. His credentials were impeccable — former premier of Nova Scotia, Father of Confederation, long-time Dominion cabinet minister, and currently the country's most important diplomat in London. He was also a passionate and tireless campaigner who'd helped Macdonald secure Conservative victories in the 1887 and 1891 general elections. Yet it was unclear how much support Tupper had beyond his diehard followers. He'd been out of cabinet, out of Parliament, and largely out of the country since 1887 and the lack of broad-based support had been a key factor preventing him from seeking the prime ministership when Macdonald died in 1891. And besides, Tupper had for years been telling anyone who'd listen that "under no consideration would I accept the Premiership of Canada, one of the chief reasons being that I am too old." He'd taken up the mantra again immediately after Thompson died.

Annie was indignant at the suggestion that Tupper might succeed her husband. "There is only one thing — if *he* were sent for, I should look upon it as an insult to my husband's memory — and to think that *he* should be in charge of my poor pet — that *he* should touch him and arrange things — *he* of all people!"

Lady Aberdeen wasn't fussed on Sir Charles either. He was as gruff, bombastic, and Conservative as she was refined, genteel, and Liberal. Ishbel assured Annie that "Never if he [Lord Aberdeen] could help it should Sir Charles be again in Canadian politics!"

Ishbel asked if Sir John had mentioned anyone else as possible successor. Annie said Sir John thought "Haggart was the man that would be best to keep the party together, even though John felt that there was really nobody ready to step into his shoes and lead."

But Lady Aberdeen had already crossed John Haggart off the list as well. Haggart was a long-serving member of the House of Commons and had been in cabinet since 1888. He had broad support within Ontario

Conservative ranks, served as head of the provincial caucus and held the province's election purse strings. Lady Aberdeen agreed that Haggart was probably "the strongest man," but she thought him "a Bohemian & also idle." Haggart had lived apart from his wife for nearly a quarter-century and was rumoured to have "a lecherous instinct for a plump lass of the typewriter variety." The 1892 parliamentary investigation into the McGreevy affair had revealed that when Haggart was postmaster general in Macdonald's Third Ministry he'd hired a Miss Craig as a temporary typist. Craig worked for two months, but the record of employment showed she was then absent for five. Despite the absence, Haggart continued to provide her with a paycheque, delivered weekly via personal messenger. Then yet another scandal confirmed that Haggart would never rise above the rank of cabinet minister. Just after Abbott appointed him minister of railways and canals in 1892, Haggart personally approved the construction of a new supply canal for the Rideau system — the Tay — which just happened to provide a new and enhanced supply to his flour mill operation at Perth as well.

A few minutes after leaving the Thompson house, Lord Aberdeen slipped into his second-floor office in the East Block. He was anxious to hear back from Colonial Secretary Lord Ripon, whom he'd cabled the previous evening for advice on "the present situation." He'd summarized that situation for Ripon like this:

> Bowell acting Premier is elderly and has not commanding influence although an estimable man, but an Orangeman.
>
> Minister of Finance Foster for an alternative is undoubtedly ablest. He is a Protestant but not bigoted. Sir John had high opinion of him.
>
> Doubtful which has most following or which would be preferred as leader by party in coming elections.

On public grounds I would deprecate either Sir C. Tupper's.

I go to Ottawa tomorrow morning. Please telegraph instructions.

Lady Aberdeen was less sanguine on Foster. She judged him "an able man, a good speaker & a good man, but he has no power over other men & showed no power for leading in House once before when Sir John was away. And then that clique against him and his wife...." A decade earlier, Foster had fallen in love with his landlady, Addie Chisholm. Chisholm's husband had deserted her years before, but she didn't have the means to get a divorce; the costs of sponsoring a private member's bill through the Senate were prohibitively high. So Foster, wealthy from a decade as a public speaker on the temperance circuit, moved Chisholm to Chicago for two years until she met state requirements to file for an uncontested divorce there. This allowed Foster to marry Chisholm, but many in Ottawa — including the still-influential Agnes Macdonald — judged the divorce illegal and Chisholm a bigamist. As progressives, the Aberdeens were sympathetic to the Fosters' plight and had, on Sir John and Annie Thompson's recommendation, invited the couple to the first viceregal engagement in Ottawa, where they made it clear to everyone that at least in their presence the Fosters would be welcomed and treated as equals. But as sympathetic as the Aberdeens were to Foster's personal situation, at least Lady Aberdeen was realistic enough to realize that Ottawa's conservative mores would prevent him from garnering the support he'd need to form a new ministry and hold the confidence of a still very conservative Parliament.

The longer the day went on, the more Mackenzie Bowell was looking like a comer. Despite the misgivings Aberdeen had communicated to Ripon, Bowell was Aberdeen's most experienced cabinet minister and longest-serving parliamentarian. He'd held the fort for the Conservatives while in the wilderness during the Mackenzie administration, even forcing seven Liberals — including the Liberal speaker and minister of militia — to resign in a conflict of interest scandal. Sir John A. rewarded Bowell for his dogged loyalty by naming him customs minister in 1878, a position he held until

Hon. Sir Mackenzie Bowell (Minister of Customs) in July 1888.

1892 when Thompson promoted him to government leader in the Senate and minister of the new super department of trade and commerce. Bowell also had foreign affairs experience. As acting militia and defence minister under Abbott, he'd negotiated a settlement with Great Britain for funding the Royal Navy dockyard at Esquimalt and in 1894 had organized the second Colonial Conference in Ottawa, with attendees from Australia, Cape Colony, Fiji, and Hawaii. And, unlike anyone else in cabinet, Bowell had actual experience in the big chair. He'd served as acting prime minister for both Abbott (three months in 1892) and Thompson (five months in 1893 and six weeks in 1894).

Make no mistake, though: there was nothing daring nor dashing about Mackenzie Bowell. No one ever mistook him for a brilliant orator nor his administrative skills for anything other than plodding and punctilious. But everyone liked Mack. He was warm and funny and exuded a genuineness that was rare in Ottawa's rarefied social circles. John Payne said Mack "exhibited an utter lack of guile." More importantly, most everyone respected him. In discussing Abbott's succession in 1892, Thompson had written that "Mr. Bowell has the respect of all of us and that any of us would follow him while we could agree with his policy."[1] Even Lady Aberdeen, who thought Bowell "rather fussy, & decidedly common place, and also an Orangeman," admitted that he was "a good & straight man and he has great ideas about drawing together of the colonies and the Empire, as was evidenced by all the trouble he took about getting up that Conference." And, unlike Haggart and Foster, Bowell came scandal-free.

Lady Aberdeen joined her husband in his East Block office around three thirty in the afternoon, just after Ripon's response to Aberdeen's request for assistance came in:

> This is not an occasion on which instructions can be given by Her Majesty's government. But my advice as a friend is to ask the acting Premier after consultation with his colleagues to come and advise you as to whom you should send for to form an administration. This is preferable to your making any independent selection.

Aberdeen took heed and wrote a note to Bowell asking him to "consult his colleagues" and then "come and talk over the present situation in a preliminary way." Arthur Gordon took the note down the hall to the Privy Council Chambers where Bowell was discussing Thompson's funeral arrangements with the eleven ministers now in town. Bowell scribbled a note back, saying he could not consult his colleagues "in the way he [Aberdeen] suggested" as three ministers — Auguste-Réal Angers, John Carling, and

Charlie Tupper — were not then in Ottawa. Nevertheless, Bowell said he'd be "very glad to come over for a talk, leaving His Excellency quite free to send for someone else afterwards." He then repeated something Foster had said the previous day, "Here we are, twelve of us, and every one of us as bad, or as good as the other — Jack as good as his master." The absence of any rivalry amongst the cabinet for the prime minister's job was a sentiment Thompson had also commented upon back in '92.

Bowell arrived in Aberdeen's office at four thirty and stayed for twenty minutes. Aberdeen offered his condolences — he knew Bowell and Thompson had worked closely for years — and asked about the funeral arrangements. Bowell said the ministers had agreed on a state funeral, with the body lying in state in the Senate, as per Macdonald's funeral. Aberdeen said the British government had offered to convey Thompson's remains home on a man-of-war, the *Blenheim*, an honour typically bestowed only upon members of the royal family. It also meant Thompson's remains would arrive in Halifax. Accordingly, Aberdeen said he thought it made more sense to hold the funeral in Halifax. Bowell agreed and said he'd let Lady Thompson know of the change in plans. He said he thought she'd be pleased.

The meeting confirmed Lord Aberdeen's thinking on "the present situation": there was, in fact, no one who could meaningfully replace Sir John Thompson and the best move was to appoint a caretaker prime minister who could handle day-to-day affairs until an early election could be called in the spring. The current Parliament still had eighteen months left in its term, but its currency had been sapped by the deaths of three prime ministers since June 1891.

Aberdeen wasn't the only one who thought an early election was a good idea. A group of senior Conservatives (including MP Sir Donald Smith, senator and Bank of Montreal president George Drummond, and Canadian Pacific president Sir William Van Horne) would tell Sir Charles Tupper in early January 1895 that "the present is the best time to go to the country, but that success is impossible at this time as the Government is now constituted." All — including Tupper — thought "defeat at the polls was the best thing that could happen" to the party. It would clear out the deadwood that Macdonald had collected over the years and allow a new generation of leaders — including Tupper's son, Charlie Hibbert — to come to the fore.

And so, despite Annie Thompson's advice regarding John Haggart, and Lord Ripon's advice not to make "any independent selection," the Aberdeens "came to the opinion that Mr. Bowell would under the circumstances suit best." The *Globe* concurred. John Willison said in an editorial that morning that Bowell was well-suited to the job of serving as "the assignee with this insolvent estate; his job to wind it up with as little disaster as possible, but not to engage in new enterprises."

There was just one nagging question: Could Bowell count on the support of Roman Catholics in cabinet and Parliament, given his long association with and involvement in the Orange Order? Aberdeen had Arthur Gordon see if Senator Frank Smith, a long-time minister without portfolio, was still in the building. Smith was a successful businessman, rising from an impoverished immigrant childhood to become one of the most successful retail merchants in the country. He was also Irish Catholic and had served for years as a key power broker in the Macdonald, Abbott, and Thompson cabinets. He was another parliamentarian whose opinion Aberdeen had come to value.

Gordon showed Smith into Aberdeen's office just after 6:00 p.m. Aberdeen asked Smith how Canadian Catholics would receive Bowell as prime minister given his Orange Lodge past. Smith said he'd known Bowell for years, "and although he has been a strong Orangeman and very earnest and outspoken in his opinion, as he has a perfect right to be, I have never known him to say an offensive word about Catholics, or to do anything which they could regard as offensive. I think I can also say Mr. Bowell has been so careful in the administration of his cabinet duties that he has never to my knowledge offended a single Catholic."

Smith's testimony sealed the deal: a caretaker administration under Mackenzie Bowell it would be.

After meeting with Smith, the Aberdeens rode over to Rideau Hall to inspect the renovations then underway and then had dinner back on board

Black Day

their private car at Union Station. At six thirty, Lord Aberdeen walked back to East Block and on the way sent Gordon to fetch Bowell from the Russell for another chat. It was 10:00 p.m. by the time the two sat down together in Aberdeen's office. The Governor General asked Bowell if he was prepared to assume the responsibility of forming a new ministry on the understanding that an election be called soon, perhaps April or May. Bowell said that at the first possible opportunity he'd consult with his colleagues about whether they'd serve under him and report back as quickly as possible. He cautioned that not all his colleagues were in the capital just then and it might take another week or so until a "full and complete consultation" could be done. Aberdeen said he understood and agreed to the timeline.

Bowell got back to the Russell at eleven and found Fred Cook and Solicitor General John Curran sitting with Frank Smith in the lobby, waiting for news. Bowell recounted the conversation he'd just had and encouraged Cook to get an announcement out to his publisher before the evening deadline. Cook thought it might be more appropriate if Bowell himself wrote the announcement. Bowell looked chuffed and took up the pen and paper offered to him:

> It was ten o'clock when Hon. Mr. Bowell was summoned by His Excellency to meet him in the Governor-General's office in the East Block, whither he at once proceeded and remained in consultation with His Excellency until eleven o'clock.
>
> The result of his interview, the newspapers are authorized to state, was that His Excellency informed Mr. Bowell that after fully considering all aspects of the situation, he had decided to ask him if he was prepared to undertake and assume the responsibility of the formation of cabinet.
>
> Hon. Mr. Bowell replied, in effect, that while fully realizing the difficulties and responsibilities of assuming so important a duty, he could not, appreciating the mark of confidence reposed in him by this request, decline the

responsibility of acceding to it, and that he would at the first possible opportunity consult with his colleagues and report to His Excellency at the earliest moment.

Pretty good copy for an old hack, Cook teased.

Sixth Ministry

Prime Minister–designate Mackenzie Bowell spent Friday, December 14, assessing just how much of the old wood in Thompson's Fifth Ministry could be used to build his new cabinet. He met with Foster first and offered him his old finance portfolio. He then met everyone else who was in town over the course of the day (only William Ives and Charlie Tupper were still away). By Friday evening, Fred Cook reported that nine of Thompson's fourteen cabinet ministers had agreed to stay on and join Bowell's government: the three French-speaking Catholic ministers from Quebec (Auguste-Réal Angers, Adolphe Caron, and Joseph-Aldric Ouimet), two Protestant ministers from Ontario (John Haggart and James Patterson), the Irish Catholic representative (Frank Smith, from Ontario), the two New Brunswickers (George Foster and John Costigan), and the West's sole representative (Thomas Daly). In addition, the two controllers, Nathaniel Clarke Wallace at customs and John Wood at inland revenue, and the solicitor general, John Curran, agreed to stay on as part of Bowell's ministry as well.[2]

Bowell encountered surprisingly little politics in building his cabinet. What politics there were occurred on Saturday, December 15. Prince Edward Island senator Samuel Prowse was lobbying hard to get Bowell to name an Islander to cabinet. (There had not been one since James Colledge Pope died.) As Prowse told the *Globe*'s Ottawa correspondent, Arnott Magurn, on Friday, "When PEI was admitted into the union, it was understood by the negotiating parties and promised by Sir Charles Tupper, that the Island should have representation in the Government. Conservatives of PEI are a unit in their choice of a representative in the person of Hon. Donald Ferguson." John Haggart was also pressuring Bowell to have his protegé, the newly elected member for Haldimand, Dr. Walter Montague, appointed to cabinet. Bowell acceded on both counts and agreed to make Ferguson and Montague ministers without portfolio.

At some point over the weekend, William Ives agreed to continue in his role as Quebec's English-speaking representative in cabinet and Arthur Dickey, the capable and well-respected Amherst lawyer, agreed to fill Thompson's Nova Scotia vacancy in a promotion from the Conservative backbenches.

By Sunday evening, the only remaining piece of the personnel puzzle was Charlie Hibbert Tupper. He was on his way back to Ottawa from the West Coast where he'd been consulting with sealers and salmon canners about a proposed settlement of outstanding Bering Sea claims.[3] The British high commissioner's thirty-nine-year-old son was a rising star in Conservative ranks. He was a Harvard law grad and had practised with Sir John Thompson's firm in Halifax. In 1882, at the age of twenty-six, he was elected to the House of Commons (Pictou) where he proved himself a strong and capable debater. But he also proved to be a little too much like his father — mercurial, aloof, "bumptious," as Macdonald complained to Thompson. Thompson, though, liked Charlie and assured Macdonald "he is of good metal, and is the best of his name." On that recommendation, Macdonald named Tupper minister of marine and fisheries in 1888, the country's youngest cabinet minister to that point.

Tupper arrived back in Ottawa late Monday morning, December 17. James Patterson met him at the station and drove him to Bowell's office in the East Block. There the two talked for an hour, during which time Bowell offered him the justice portfolio. Tupper said he'd think about it over lunch and sometime that afternoon said he'd be honoured to accept.

With Tupper in at justice, the last work on assembling Canada's Sixth Ministry came down to reshuffling some portfolios. Bowell moved John Costigan from secretary of state to fill Tupper's spot at marine and fisheries and Arthur Dickey got secretary of state. Bowell traded his trade and commerce portfolio with William Ives to become president of the Privy Council. Trade and commerce was a good fit for a prominent businessman like Ives and the presidency allowed Bowell, as he told Fred Cook, to "devote all my time to the duties of the Premiership." By Monday evening, work on Canada's Sixth Ministry was complete:

MINISTERS

Prime Minister & President of the Privy Council:
    Hon. Mackenzie Bowell (Senator)
Minister of Agriculture: Hon. Mr. Auguste-Réal Angers (Senator)
Minister of Finance/Receiver General of Canada:
    Hon. Mr. George Foster
Minister of Interior/Superintendent of Indian Affairs:
    Hon. Mr. Thomas Daly
Minister of Justice/Attorney General of Canada:
    Sir Charles Hibbert Tupper
Minister of Marine and Fisheries: Hon. Mr. John Costigan
Minister of Militia and Defence: Hon. Mr. James Patterson
Postmaster General: Sir Adolphe-Philippe Caron
Minister of Public Works: Hon. Mr. Joseph-Aldric Ouimet
Minister of Railways and Canals: Hon. Mr. John Haggart
Secretary of State/Registrar General of Canada:
    Hon. Mr. Arthur Dickey
Minister of Trade and Commerce: Hon. Mr. William Ives

MINISTERS WITHOUT PORTFOLIO

Hon. Mr. Donald Ferguson (Senator)
Dr. Walter Montague
Sir Frank Smith (Senator)

OFFICES NOT OF THE CABINET

Controller of Customs: Hon. Mr. Nathaniel Clarke Wallace
Controller of Inland Revenue: Hon. Mr. John Wood
Solicitor General: Hon. Mr. John Curran

Black Day

Old Party, Old Policy

On Thursday, December 18, a "severe cold" confined Bowell to his bed at the Russell. (In fact, Bowell had returned from Australia the year before with a cough he hadn't been able to shake. He told anyone who asked he was fine, "couldn't be better.") In typical fashion, though, Bowell ignored doctor's orders, roused himself, and joined the five ministers who needed to be sworn into office by the Governor General on the 4:30 p.m. train to Montreal.

A good-sized crowd was waiting for Canada's fifth prime minister when the train pulled into Bonaventure Station that evening. Bowell, Costigan, Dickey, Ives, and Tupper debarked the old campaign car, the *Cumberland*, and proceeded to glad-hand and chat for twenty minutes. (Montague, "deathly ill," stayed on board with his doctor to "avoid any unnecessary excitement.") Bowell then announced that he and his ministers would "tromp it" north to the Windsor Hotel as they'd been sitting all afternoon. Bowell set off at a fast clip, leaving the newest — and much younger — members of his cabinet behind.

After dinner, Fred Cook asked Bowell how he felt about the promotion.

"I will never forget the many encouraging words that have been addressed to me from all parts of the confederation, and especially from the good people of the province of Quebec," Bowell replied.

Cook asked about his government's program.

"The old party will carry out the old policy and follow the lines laid down by Sir John Thompson. I have every confidence the country will support the Conservative Party in the future just as it has done in the past." Bowell was coughing noticeably — the cold night air had obviously played old Harry with his lungs.

The next morning, a few minutes before eleven, Bowell, his five ministers, and Clerk of the Privy Council John McGee (D'Arcy's brother) arrived at the Aberdeens' Sherbrooke residence and were shown into the study where the

Governor General was waiting. McGee gave Montague and Dickey a copy of their privy councillor oaths, which Aberdeen administered (the others were members already). McGee then distributed copies of the departmental oaths. Bowell as premier and president of the Privy Council went first, followed by Costigan at marine and fisheries, Tupper at justice, Ives at trade and commerce, Dickey as secretary of state, and Montague as minister without portfolio. When the oaths were finished, Costigan fulfilled tradition and returned the Great Seal of Canada to Aberdeen, telling him, "I hereby return the Great Seal, which has been in my keeping since I was sworn as Secretary of State." Aberdeen then gave the seal to Dickey, the new secretary. Aberdeen congratulated his new advisers while McGee collected the requisite signatures. Within an hour, the ceremony was complete, and Canada's fifth prime minister and Sixth Ministry were officially installed.

3

Halifax

Knight Commander

Mackenzie Bowell's first official duty as prime minister was, along with his cabinet, to represent the Dominion government at Sir John Thompson's state funeral in Halifax on Thursday, January 3, 1895. Bowell was to accompany the Aberdeens on the official mourning train that departed Ottawa on Friday, December 28, but his doctor intervened that morning. He "enjoined strict bedrest," and forbade the prime minister from speaking with anyone "until his throat gets better."

Bowell defied his doctor's orders again and left Ottawa on Saturday with Frank Smith, Thomas Daly, William Ives, and Fred Cook, arriving in Halifax early Sunday morning. The group drove Bowell to his old friend MP Thomas Kenny's house, where he'd been invited to stay. Smith urged Bowell to keep to his room for the day and save himself for the busy schedule to come. Bowell ignored him as well. After checking in at Kenny's, Bowell made the rounds, calling first on the Aberdeens, who were staying with Nova Scotia Lieutenant Governor Daly at Government House, then Archbishop O'Brien, who would be presiding over Thompson's service.

Back at Kenny's for dinner, Lord Aberdeen sent over a note he'd just received from Queen Victoria. It announced the appointment of "Hon. Mackenzie Bowell to a Knight Commander of the Most Distinguished Order of St. Michael and St. George." Kenny, Smith, Daly, and Ives stood up from the dinner table and congratulated Bowell. Smith offered a toast, wishing their new chieftain "many years of life in which to wear your new honour."

News of Bowell's knighthood spread quickly. Before dinner was finished, a gaggle of reporters arrived on Kenny's doorstep looking for a quote. Kenny invited them into the study where Bowell held court for the better part of an hour.

"During the short time that I have been Premier I have been accused of nearly everything," Bowell said. "But I am glad to know that I have never shrunk from any of my duties or principles in either my public or private life. My policy has always been 'equal rights for all.'"

"I have never asked favours of anyone, and if I have risen to any position of honour it is due to my integrity and perseverance. Whatever I have received I have received without solicitation, and it will be a great satisfaction for me to know that I will hand down to my children a name untarnished and a name that has fulfilled duty to its country. And that is why I accept this honour as it is entirely unsolicited, and is, therefore, particularly prized."

One of the reporters asked Bowell why he thought the Queen bestowed the honour on him. Bowell said the "great distinction" was for "long and useful public service" and on that ground he accepted it. "It is my earnest hope that the Canadian people find me worthy not only of the honour which the Queen has bestowed upon me but of their continued esteem and confidence."

Before the evening was out, Bowell premiered a soon-to-be-familiar ditty:

> When I was a lad I served my term
> As junior imp in a printing firm;
> I washed the windows, swept the floor,
> And daubed the ink on the office door.
> I did it all so thoroughly
> That now I am Premier and KCMG.

Halifax

Fred Cook thought Bowell was "in much better health" that evening, although the cough was still persistent.

Home

The sun rose just before eight the next morning. The wet snow was shifting to pelting rain and Halifax Harbour was lost in a thick, grey fog. Despite the weather, ten thousand Haligonians lined the waterfront to welcome home the remains of their beloved prime minister, Sir John Thompson. Every possible viewing spot was taken — on the adjacent wharves, the roofs of the low buildings, any place that promised a view.

The fog obscured the progress of the *Blenheim* through the harbour. The only recognition of the ship's headway was the signal flag at the citadel announcing it had made McNabs Island. A few minutes later the minute guns from the island forts signalled steady progress.

Arrival of HMS *Blenheim* with the body of Sir John Thompson, prime minister of Canada, at Ordnance Wharf, Halifax.

For half an hour the *Blenheim* idled forward unseen, until 11:46 when another minute gun announced it had come to anchor off Gun Wharf. On cue, the tug *Argus* shoved off from Queen's Wharf, bringing John and Joe Thompson out to the *Blenheim* to accompany their father's body on its final passage home. From Ordnance Wharf, the steamer *Lily* cast off with Reverend Murphy, the rector at St. Mary's Cathedral, and the Dominion representatives — John Curran, Thomas Daly, William Ives, Frank Smith, and Charlie Tupper. Bowell's doctor had forbidden him from coming down to the harbour for the reception. "The Premier is in very good health," Dr. Reid told Fred Cook, "but an affection of the throat, which has remained since he undertook the voyage to Australia, produces severe coughing on slight provocation from the atmosphere."

At noon, the *Blenheim* dropped anchor opposite Ordnance Yard and both the *Argus* and *Lily* were run up alongside. Captain Poe — a Canadian — invited the passengers aboard.

Senator William Sanford was standing on the foredeck — tired, wet, sad — ready to greet the visitors. Sanford shook hands with John and Joe and offered a few words of condolence. As he greeted the others — "Isn't it awful," he said to Smith as he came aboard — Reverend Murphy whisked the Thompson boys into the ship's makeshift mortuary for a private prayer service with their father. The others made way for the captain's cabin to give the boys some privacy.

The Union Jack draped Thompson's plain mahogany coffin in the centre of the mortuary. Ten burly, bearded bluejackets stood on duty around the perimeter. Murphy knelt beside the coffin with the Thompson boys and led them in a short prayer. When they finished, the other visitors came in to pay their respects.

Preparations began at one fifty to transfer Thompson's body from the *Blenheim* to the *Lily* for transport to the mainland. Poe signalled the ship's bugler to call the crew to quarters and forty Royal Marine Light Infantry paraded on deck and took up stations. The bluejackets emerged from the companionway with Thompson's coffin on their shoulders, the rain plastering the flag fast to the coffin. John and Joe followed behind, then Sanford, the five ministers, and finally Murphy. Two petty officers brought up the rear, carrying the laurel wreaths presented by the Queen and Bowell.

The bluejackets carried the coffin to a portside davit, placed it on an empty trestle, and pulled a rope covered with black cloth securely around it. Captain Poe himself made sure the tackle was made fast.

"Sound silence," Poe called when the coffin was ready, every officer and sailor snapping to. For a moment, the only sound was waves splashing against the *Blenheim's* massive steel bulwarks and the rain pelting down.

"Commence the salute," Poe ordered. A roar emitted from a two-inch starboard Hotchkiss to begin a fifteen-minute gun salute. When the last echo came back through the fog from the surrounding hills, the band struck up the "Dead March" from *Saul*. The bluejackets raised the casket clear of the deck, swung the davit slowly overboard, and lowered Thompson's remains onto the bow of the *Lily*. The Marine Guard on board there presented and reversed arms to receive the casket. Once settled, the coffin was covered with a tarpaulin and the mourning party made their way down the gangplank.

The *Lily* peeled off the *Blenheim* at two fifteen and set course for Ordnance Wharf. Two hundred dignitaries and soldiers were gathered on the carpet there, the Aberdeens front and centre. Behind them was the King's Own Regiment honour guard and its two bands. When the *Lily* emerged from the fog and approached the wharf, the Aberdeens stepped toward the empty gun carriage to officially receive Thompson's coffin.

Sanford and the Thompson boys stepped off the *Lily* first, followed by the bluejackets with Thompson's coffin on their shoulders. The sailors placed the casket gently on the gun carriage, saluted, and marched back to the gangway.

The rain prompted the funeral procession to form up quickly — first the bands, then fifty of the King's Own honour guard, then the gun carriage pulled by four black chargers, and then the other fifty of the honour guard.

The route from the wharf to the provincial legislature where Thompson's body would lie in state until the funeral Thursday morning wasn't long — just four blocks. The bands struck up "Dead March" again and the procession moved out of Ordnance Yard and up Water Street. Despite the near-deluge, the route was lined twelve-deep, the roofs of buildings lining the route packed. A double line of soldiers had to link arms to keep the passage clear.

Farewell

There were seven hundred seats available in St. Mary's Cathedral for Thompson's funeral on the morning of Thursday, January 3. Most of these went to dignitaries, but a hundred or so were made available to the public via raffle. These lucky few began queuing up in the dark that morning. The crisp morning air was a mixed blessing; while it was cold, the two inches of sleet and muck from the day before were at least mostly frozen.

Annie and the children arrived at nine thirty, entered through a side entrance, and were ushered to their seats — two pews at the front of the nave ensconced behind a set of deep purple curtains. Fifteen minutes later, the Aberdeens arrived through the front entrance. The simple elegance of the place was impressive. Over eleven thousand yards of black, purple, and white drapery had been used to transform the interior. The walls of the nave were draped in black cashmere, the windows covered in the same, as were the ten pairs of Corinthian pillars, each sixty-five feet high. From the top of the pillars, a canopy of black cashmere hung; two more canopies hung on the aisles on the outside edges of the pews. To offset the darkness, 210 incandescent lamps were strung throughout the nave — on the tops of the pillars and in clusters along the walls. The sanctuary was lit by hundreds of candles and tens of gaslights. The lighting was complemented by silk stars arranged in the dark recesses of the canopies; these caught and reflected the lights, as did the large silver crosses set over windows and on the pillars.

Once the Aberdeens were settled, the diocesan procession entered from the side chapel entrance. First came the acolytes in purple and black soutanes and then a sea of royal purple vestments on fifty diocesan priests and a handful of bishops from as far away as Newfoundland and Ottawa. Last to enter were Bishop John Cameron of Antigonish, one of Sir John's oldest and most trusted friends, and Archbishop Cornelius O'Brien. O'Brien's long silk train was attended to by four pages in red-and-white soutanes.

In front of the altar sat the casket. It was Queen Victoria's idea for the inscription:

> The Right Hon. Sir. John S.D. Thompson,
> P.C., K.C., M.G., M.P., Q.C.,
> Premier and Minister of Justice of Canada
> Died at Windsor Castle, December 12th, 1894.
> Aged 50 years,
> R.I.P.

On top was a simple gold-and-white funeral pall, a gift from the Aberdeens. Lady Aberdeen had overseen its construction — white Irish poplin with a large gold cross down the middle, with gold fringes around the end. The Queen's wreath was placed on the head of the casket, the Aberdeens' wreath of maple leaves and heather at the foot. On either side were pyramids of floral arrangements from home and abroad.

The cathedral was full by 10:05 a.m. — and deathly quiet. All eyes turned to Cameron when he rose in his black-and-gold vestment and approached the pulpit to begin the requiem mass. The sixty-eight-year-old was clearly struggling with the loss of his close friend. He'd told Lady Aberdeen the day before he hadn't been able to sleep or eat much over the past few days and feared he'd break down in the middle of the service.

Cameron nodded to Professor Compton to lead the choir in the *Miserere Mei*. The eighty-five members had volunteered to come together from across the diocese for the occasion. After the *Kyrie*, they sang the *Dies Irae*. To help the Protestant members of the congregation, Lord Aberdeen himself had translated the words and had them printed on the program.

When the *Libera* was finished, Cameron took his seat next to Archbishop O'Brien. The cathedral fell silent again as he made his way to the pulpit. O'Brien looked out at the congregation and pulled a set of notes from his sleeve.

Before the remains of the honoured dead are borne hence to their last resting place, it is meet some words should be spoken in this sacred edifice to tell of life and hope amidst the sadness and gloom that encompasses us round about.

When a nation mourns, we may be sure that the loss is a national one. Few indeed will deny that by the death of the Right Honourable Sir John Thompson our great mother Canada has suffered an almost irremediable loss. The reason of this is found in the qualities that were based and rooted in the character of the man as he appeared in the eyes of his fellow-citizens in the discharge of the duties of his high public station.

He had held various trusts during his earthly career — in the City Council, in the Provincial Legislature, on the Bench, in the Department of Justice and in the Dominion Parliament. At each successive stage of his upward course, he acquitted himself in a manner satisfactory to the public and gave a guarantee that to whatever further heights of national importance he might attain, he would be found equal to their responsibilities.

How did the late Premier rise to the lofty eminence from which he was stricken down by the hand of death? It was not by the aid of the outward accidents of wealth and birth, much less was it by an unworthy pandering to the passions and prejudices of the people, or by the employment of cunning arts and devices by which a corrupt public man sometimes treads his way successfully to ambitious distinction. No! It was industry, sobriety, and a conscientious attention to the details of each duty were the pinions which bore him onward in a career which can only be rightly characterized as phenomenal.

Can the word "great" be legitimately applied to Sir John Thompson? What elements go to compose that special manifestation of a faculty or faculties which we call great?

As a lawyer, Sir John Thompson was never found unable to meet the legal points, which unexpectedly arise in the conduct of a case. As a judge, his summing up of cases was noted for its method and impartiality; his decisions were ever clear and satisfactory. As a speaker on the floor of the House of Commons, Thompson may not have had the tricks of voice and gesture which, in a ruder age, and even now among the less cultured, are supposed to constitute oratory. His speeches nevertheless were masterpieces of clear, logical reasoning. As an envoy of Canada, whether at Washington or Paris or London, he impressed all with whom he came in contact as a man of superior abilities and possessed of a miraculous grasp of the intricacies of every question discussed. In view of all this varied and continuous success, both at home and abroad, we are but expressing a legitimate conclusion and not the exaggeration of funeral eulogy by claiming for him the appellation of "great."

If England mourned and all Canada wept at the sudden falling of his night, there are those whose agony is too sacred to be unveiled. The faithful wife and loving children and sorrowing relatives must bear not only their full share of the public bereavement, but also a bitter personal loss. Our prayer is that his grieving family will find consolation in reflecting on his well-spent life and simple Christian conversation. He has left to them an inheritance more precious than gold, a spotless reputation, an untarnished name, and the memory of noble qualities nobly employed. Though soon to be borne from their sight, their hearts shall not be bereft of hope, for the God whom he loved and served will whisper in their souls — "Thy husband, thy father, thy brother, shall arise."

In this sure hope, we commit to the earth his mortal remains, and as we pray for the speedy entrance of his soul into the eternal joys of heaven, let us not forget to pray for his family, that they may be comforted, sustained, and for our country, that it may be the fruitful mother of many such sons as the late Right Honourable Sir John Thompson.

O'Brien returned to his seat and the choir stood and sang the English-language hymn, "Now the Labourer's Task is O'er," in recognition of the Protestants in the house. The choir finished a couple of minutes after eleven and O'Brien stepped to the front of the sanctuary. After a moment of silence, the archbishop spoke the absolution, sprinkled the coffin with holy water, and incensed it. He stood aside while members of the King's Regiment filed along both sides of the coffin, picked it up, and carried it from the church. The official pallbearers fell in behind the casket in pairs — George Foster and Charlie Tupper, Frank Smith and John Costigan, John Haggart and Joseph-Aldric Ouimet, James Patterson and William Ives. Bowell wasn't among them; the doctor had confined him to his bed at Kenny's.

Outside, the day was crisp and still and the sun shone clear in the bright blue sky. South along Barrington, from Spring Garden Road where the

State funeral procession for Sir John Thompson, prime minister of Canada, photographed on Barrington Street, Halifax.

cathedral was located, the massive funeral procession formed up with military precision. At the centre was the funeral car, a specially constructed carriage that was beautiful but ungainly at fourteen feet long, seven wide, and seventeen high. The coffin was placed on a catafalque two and a half feet off the main platform. The second storey was another two and a half feet higher, supported by four Corinthian columns. These were draped with various floral arrangements. The roof on the second storey of the carriage curved upward, ordained with a silver cross and crown and four two-foot plumes. Six large Clydesdales were hitched to the wagon, each covered in a heavy black pall with a silver letter *T* on each side. An undertaker's assistant stood ready to lead each horse.

In front and behind the funeral car the official procession sprawled. Annie Thompson and her family were lost in the sea of viceregal representatives, military bands, honour guards, and civic officials. Crowds stood six-deep along most of the mile-long route, closer to twenty-deep at the cemetery. All the roofs were packed again, some of the more adventurous onlookers assuming perches in trees and on telegraph poles. Soldiers from the King's Regiment linked arms along the entire course to ensure the way was clear.

It took the procession an hour to reach Holy Cross Cemetery. Another band of the King's Regiment met the procession at the cemetery gates and struck up Chopin's "Holy Funeral March" as it led Thompson's coffin to its final resting place twenty yards in. Four rows of King's Regiment men with bayonets fixed held the public back at the gate.

The funeral detail removed the casket from the carriage and marched it to a platform erected over the open grave. There, O'Brien delivered a short graveside service and, when he finished, the coffin was lowered. Three volleys of shots rang out through the crisp, cool air. Granite slabs were then placed into position, followed by the floral arrangements. When the ceremony was finished, the honour guard moved into position to guard the vault for the remainder of the day. Annie and the children watched the proceedings from inside the caretaker's little cottage a few yards away.

4
Ides

Brophy

Prime Minister Mackenzie Bowell had overdone it in Halifax. When he got back to Ottawa on January 8, his doctor again ordered bedrest and "strictly prohibited interviews" with anyone for ten days in order to "allow irritation of the throat to subside." Rumours of Bowell's illness were rife and dire, to the point that Queen Victoria herself cabled Lord Aberdeen asking if he was all right. Bowell scribbled a note to Aberdeen that he should "thank her Majesty for the interest evinced in his health" and tell her "he was better and not considered to be at all seriously ill."

Bowell's illness postponed cabinet business for most of January, including an important meeting set for January 9 where "the whole political situation was to have been thrashed out, and the question of the date of dissolution decided." By the time Bowell was well enough to attend cabinet at the end of the month, the question of dissolution had been sidelined by the Judicial Committee of the Privy Council's final ruling on the Manitoba schools question.

The case had begun over Manitoba premier Thomas Greenway's 1890 *Public Schools Act*. It abolished Manitoba's separate school system that had been in place since the province entered Confederation in 1870 and had included both Catholic and Protestant schools, with a separate administration for each. The 1890 Act replaced that system with a single non-denominational one. The Manitoba government argued that the numbers no longer warranted a divided system: in 1870, there had been roughly the same number of French-speaking Roman Catholics as English-speaking Protestants in the province; but by the late 1880s, Roman Catholics made up just 13 percent of the provincial population, and French speakers were down to 7 percent. The legislation — accompanied by a companion piece making English the sole official language in the province — was also popular, playing to anti-French and anti-Catholic sentiment on the rise not only in Manitoba but across the country since the Northwest Rebellion in 1885 and the *Jesuit Estates Act* in 1888.

Manitoba's Roman Catholic minority, led by Saint-Boniface archbishop Alexandre Taché, was quick to denounce the *Public Schools Act* as a violation of their constitutional right to denominational schooling. Section 22 of the *Manitoba Act, 1870*, gave the province authority to make laws "in relation to education" as long as those laws did not "prejudicially affect any right or privilege with respect to Denominational Schools." In the event these rights or privileges were impaired, section 22 provided a right of appeal to the Dominion and gave the Dominion the power to enact remedial legislation. Taché wouldn't wait that long and demanded that Ottawa disallow the legislation as soon as it was passed, in March 1890. Prime Minister Macdonald declined, judging the best place to settle the question to be in the courts. As then-minister of justice John Thompson put it, if the legislation were *ultra vires*, it did not need to be disallowed. If it were *intra vires*, it should not be disallowed. And if the case of the minority failed in the courts, then it would be time for the Governor General in Council to consider the appeal contained in the petitions that had been presented.

By the end of April 1890, the Dominion government and Catholic organizers had enlisted the help of Winnipeg Roman Catholic ratepayer John Barrett in launching a test case against the *Public Schools Act* with local lawyer John Ewart as counsel. At trial, Ewart argued that Barrett's constitutional right to denominational schooling had been prejudicially affected, because under the Act "each Protestant will have to pay less than if he were assessed for Protestant schools alone, and each Roman Catholic will have to pay more than if he were assessed for Roman Catholic schools alone." This was because the Catholic Church (as Taché put it in his affidavit) "insisted upon its children receiving their education in schools conducted under the supervision of the church" and the *Public Schools Act* made no provision for Catholics to opt out of the public school levy.

Barrett's case was dismissed, the trial judge ruling that his rights weren't affected by the 1890 legislation as it did not compel anyone to send their child to public school nor did it prevent anyone — Catholic or Protestant — from establishing, maintaining, and conducting their own schools.

Barrett's appeal reached the Supreme Court of Canada in October 1891. That court held that Roman Catholics' constitutional right to denominational schooling had been prejudicially affected "when they are taxed to support schools of the benefit of which, by their religious belief and the rules and principles of their church, they cannot conscientiously avail themselves, and at the same time by compelling them to find means to support schools to which they can conscientiously send their children, or in the event of their not being able to find sufficient means to do both to be compelled to allow their children to go without either religious or secular instruction." On this basis, the Supreme Court overturned the two lower courts and ruled that the *Public Schools Act* was *ultra vires* section 22 of the *Manitoba Act*.

The Greenway government appealed *Barrett* to the Judicial Committee of the Privy Council (JCPC) in the summer of 1893. The JCPC overturned the Supreme Court, arguing that while denominational schools may have been in existence when the *Manitoba Act* was passed in 1870, Roman Catholics technically had no legal rights or privileges to denominational schooling at that time and thus no rights or privileges were protected in section 22 of the Act. The only way the 1890 legislation could have prejudicially affected Roman Catholic rights or privileges would be if it had compelled Roman Catholic children to attend the public school system. But it didn't, so their rights weren't prejudicially affected. Said the JCPC, "It is not the law that is in fault. It is owing to religious convictions that everyone must respect, and to the teachings of their Church, that Roman Catholics and members of the

Church of England find themselves unable to partake of advantages which the law offers to all alike."

The JCPC ruling marked the end of the line for *Barrett*, but not for the Manitoba schools issue. Back in August 1890, Manitoba's Catholic clergy and four thousand laity had petitioned the Dominion government for remediation under section 22 of the *Manitoba Act*; a second appeal organized by Archbishop Taché had been lodged in September of 1892; and a third, signed by all but one of Canada's Roman Catholic bishops and archbishops, had been submitted in November 1892. Thompson, who'd just been sworn in as prime minister, had struck a cabinet committee to hear the appeals. These had been presented by John Ewart on November 27.

In January 1893, Thompson suspended those hearings and announced that the Dominion would refer the matter to the Supreme Court before proceeding any further. Specifically, Thompson was looking for the court to clarify three things: Had the JCPC's ruling in *Barrett* "disposed of or concluded" the issue? Were the grounds for an appeal well founded (i.e., did section 22 of the *Manitoba Act* confer a right to denominational schooling)? And did the Dominion have the power to remediate through legislation?

It took a year for the Supreme Court to make a decision. In February 1894, it ruled in *Brophy* that *Barrett* meant no denominational rights or privileges had been prejudicially affected by the *Public Schools Act*. And as an appeal to the Dominion cabinet could only be made if such rights had been prejudicially affected, the Court said there were no grounds for such an appeal. Besides, said the Court, "every legislative enactment is subject to repeal by the same body which enacts it, every statute may be said to contain an implied provision that it may be revoked by the authority which has passed it."

In its turn, *Brophy* was appealed to the JCPC, and hearings on that began in the same week of December 1894 that Thompson died at Windsor Palace. On January 29, 1895, the landmark decision was released. The JCPC overturned the Supreme Court, ruling that denominational school rights did exist in 1870 and were protected under section 22 of the *Manitoba Act*. As a result, the Roman Catholic minority did have a right to appeal to the

Dominion and the Dominion did have the authority to legislate remediation. With that, in historian W.L. Morton's words, the JCPC passed the poisoned chalice to Prime Minister Mackenzie Bowell and Canada's Sixth Ministry.

He's All Right

Wilfrid Laurier was the first Dominion leader to address *Brophy* after the JCPC ruling, in a speech at Toronto's Massey Hall on February 5, 1894. Despite temperatures of minus fifteen, people lined up 'round the block hoping to squeeze in to see the widely popular opposition leader. Police had to link arms in front of the entrances to prevent the crowds from getting into the already packed venue.

Laurier arrived at the Victoria Street entrance at seven thirty and slowly made his way inside. The crowd was rowdy and raucous; the balcony was packed with students from the University of Toronto, and every seat on the main floor was full. Students who couldn't find a seat stood crowded in the aisles; a couple of dozen sat perched on the edge of the stage, their feet dangling in front of the first row. On stage was a who's who of Canadian Liberal Party elite — Oliver Mowat, Arthur Hardy, George Ross, Richard Cartwright, William Mulock, et cetera.

Laurier made it onto the stage and took a seat at just after eight.

"What's the matter with L-A-U-R-I-E-R?" bawled the students in the east half of the balcony; "He's all right!" came the roar from the west.

Laurier stepped to the podium at centre stage. On his way, he took a minute to pin one of the red badges everyone was wearing to his lapel, going slow enough to make sure everyone saw. The place went mad.

"Mr. Chairman, ladies and gentlemen — I can assure you that Laurier feels all right when he stands before such a meeting as this." He was magnificent, a man coming into his own. Six foot six, slim, with grey wavy hair brushed back over that famous high brow. One hand on his hip holding back his stock-in-trade frock coat, the other on the podium. He scanned the audience and nodded to several people.

"Speaking this evening in the great city of Toronto before one of the largest audiences that it was ever my privilege to address, I might perhaps put the question: Is this Toronto?"

The students took up the challenge with abandon: "Hear, hear!" they chanted, "Hear, hear!"

"It is Toronto, and let me, ladies and gentlemen, at once acknowledge your presence here as a token of good fellowship, extended by fellow men to another fellow man coming from another province." And on it went. Laurier commanded the stage for the next hour, excoriating Bowell and his administration for their position on tariff reform, their national policy, and their dithering on whether to dissolve Parliament.

Laurier came to the schools issue at the end of the speech. "Legislation has been passed in Manitoba, which deprives the Catholics of separate schools; and they have appealed to the Government. And until the Government has spoken upon it I have nothing to say, I stand upon that ground. The *Bleu* papers call upon me every day to speak upon the question of Manitoba and to solve it for the Government. Well, I have no objection. The appeal, however, is before the Government. Let them give an answer to it, and then we will judge that answer. I do not want to make any political capital out of that."[4]

Two days after Laurier's speech, on February 7, the Young Conservative Association of Ontario held their annual meeting at their new offices on Melinda Street, downtown Toronto. Featured on the bill were Prime Minister Mackenzie Bowell, ministers Charlie Tupper and James Patterson, and the controllers Nathaniel Clarke Wallace and John Wood. By 7:00 p.m., the room had reached its capacity of four hundred. At eight twenty, Association president William Newsome took to the rostrum, apologized for the tight quarters, and regretted not booking a larger room for the occasion. "If Laurier can fill Massey Hall, the Conservative party would have no difficulty in filling all the rest of the available space in the city of Toronto."

Ides

Bowell opened the proceedings, his first formal speech as prime minister.

> Mr. Chairman, in accepting the invitation to be present here tonight I made a special provision — a proviso, rather — that I should not be asked to attempt delivery of a speech upon the political issues of the day. I fear that until my throat gets a little better — and I hope it may be sufficiently recovered by the time you hold a mass meeting at Massey Hall — it will not enable me to discuss intelligently and with that physical force necessary to address a large audience. My friend, Sir Charles Hibbert Tupper, will attend to that part of the business.

The audience clapped respectfully.

"The last time I appeared on the platform in this city was in company with my late chief, Sir John Thompson. He introduced me as one of the youths — the youngest member of his cabinet." The young men who made up the audience warmed a little, a few laughed.

> Well, I have the pleasure tonight, young as I am and as youthful as I appear, of introducing to you one of the oldest members of my cabinet, the Honourable Sir Charles Tupper, and I am quite sure that after you have listened to him for an hour, or an hour and a half — and if your patience be not exhausted, for double that length of time — you will form an opinion, when an old man like him, having the physical ability that he has, is able to address you for so long a period, what you might expect from a youth like myself were I to attempt the task.

Clearly in his element, Bowell had won the room over. Everyone was laughing and clapping.

> Now, I do not propose to say anymore. I think I have spoken fully my five minutes, maybe a little longer. I simply

felt desirous of appearing before you, occupying the important position that I do today so that I might look upon the faces of those who are ere long to take the places of those who are now controlling and ruling the destinies of Canada. I have no fear of the future of Canada. The destiny of this country is in the hands of those whom I see before me here tonight.

Mr. Chairman and gentlemen, when you think on the progress of this country during the last fifty years, I think you have no cause for regretting that you belong to the Conservative party and that you are following in the footsteps of that great leader of Conservatism — the late Sir John A. Macdonald.

Bowell waved to the crowd, nodded to Newsome, and returned to his seat on the platform. The applause was warm and steady. But it was nothing like the ovation young Charlie Tupper received when he was introduced next. The boys rose to their feet, cheered, applauded loudly, and broke into successive rounds of "For He's a Jolly Good Fellow." Tupper let them continue, basking in the adulation.

Newsome eventually called for order and asked Tupper to get under way.

"I need not ask, as that silver-tongued orator had to ask, whether this is Toronto," Tupper began. "The cordiality of your welcome, to my delight, reminds me that it is. In no part of Canada have I ever received a warmer or more cordial greeting than in this city."

Bowell was bang-on in his assessment of Tupper: the younger minister exceeded his hour-long time slot by forty-five minutes. As Newsome motioned for him to wind it up, Tupper came round to the Manitoba schools question. He said the government would not shrink from its constitutional obligation to "sink the politician in the judge" and fulfill the "judicial duty" to hear the Roman Catholic appeal. And then, "we must come before the electorate, not only to account for the discharge of the judicial function but for political functions as well."

"It would be well," Tupper told the crowd,

if Mr. Laurier would follow the principles that he lays down — to endeavour to keep this question out of the political arena. As soon as the decision of the Privy Council is on this side of the Atlantic the Government will proceed to give this question its consideration, and when that consideration is given, the Government knows it must assume the political responsibility and must be tried at the bar of public opinion. We are not flinching from our duty. We will maintain a dignified silence until the time to speak has come, and when the time has come I believe you will find the Conservative leaders as true to the traditions of the Conservative Party as they were ready to stand by the constitution and what it teaches, and willing to respectfully abide by the verdict of the people.

It took Newsome physically walking up to the dais to get Tupper to finally stop. "The next speech will not be so long," Newsome promised. As Nathaniel Clarke Wallace stepped forward, the chairman added, "In the near future we hope Sir Charles Hibbert Tupper will return and have an opportunity of finishing his speech."

Preliminary Canter

Cabinet met on the afternoon of Friday, February 16, from two until six, to discuss two questions: Should it continue the hearings from the Roman Catholic minority on the Manitoba schools question that Thompson had initiated in December 1893? And should the current Parliament be dissolved, and an election called?

There was quick consensus on the first question. With *Brophy*, it was clear that the Dominion cabinet *could* hear the appeal. And Charlie Tupper had made it clear in Toronto — with Bowell on the same platform — that cabinet *should* hear the appeal. Joseph-Aldric Ouimet reiterated his support for that position in Montreal a week later, telling *La Minerve*, "We have bound ourselves to settle the question by the constitution, and we shall settle it so as to protect the acquired rights and privileges without injuring the rights and privileges of any province. I see no difficulty in this, for the declarations are the same as those already made by the Cabinet through the late Sir John Thompson and is fully ratified by the Cabinet of his successor, Sir Mackenzie Bowell."

It was dark when cabinet let out at six. Bowell told reporters huddled outside the main East Block entrance: "The Government has decided that a hearing shall be given to counsel for the Roman Catholic minority of Manitoba in regard to the application to the Federal power for remedial legislation in connection with the operation of the Manitoba school law." "And what about dissolution?" one of the reporters asked. "Until the hearing has taken place no announcement respecting the calling of a session or the dissolution of Parliament will be known," Bowell replied.

Bowell was dodging — dissolution was a far more fractious issue. Tupper was the only cabinet minister who favoured a snap election. As he'd argued in Toronto in February, cabinet should hear the Roman Catholic appeal, pronounce in favour of remedial legislation, and then "go at once to the country for authority to act." He said the Dominion government was bound by the constitution to "consult the people upon whatever conclusion we reach, as this Parliament was not seized with this grave question, and there has been a redistribution with the creation of a new electorate."

Everyone else around the cabinet table opposed heading to the polls at that moment. The three French-speaking Roman Catholic ministers from Quebec (Angers, Caron, and Ouimet) agreed that the Dominion government had a constitutional duty to "enforce the respect of every right, however modest it might be." But they also believed the Dominion had a moral obligation to act immediately to remediate the situation, i.e., within the life of the existing Parliament. As Ouimet and Angers made clear, if the government went to the polls without having made any effort to remediate Roman Catholic rights in Manitoba, Conservative candidates could expect a trouncing at the polls. Senior church officials were also clear that their support of Conservative candidates was dependent on remedial action being taken before an election was called.

The Ontario ministers — Haggart, Montague, Patterson, and Smith — favoured pushing the election off as well, but for different reasons. They felt the party simply didn't have the money to fight a divisive election campaign at that moment. If Montague's recent campaign in the southwestern Ontario riding of Haldimand were any indication, they'd need a massive war chest to fight a national campaign on the schools issue. More time, not less, was what the party's coffers needed, regardless of how turbulent another parliamentary session might be for the government.

Despite the agreement Bowell had worked out with Aberdeen in December, the prime minister now wanted to delay dissolution as well. Bowell believed compromise and negotiation with Greenway's government were the best way to avoid messy, divisive action by the Dominion government. To this end, Bowell was still encouraging Manitoba Lieutenant Governor John Schultz to try and convince Premier Greenway that compromise on the schools issue was ultimately in the province's best interest: If the Dominion government were forced to act, no provincial government would ever be able to alter the legislation and a separate school system would be "fastened upon [the province] forever" even as it "becomes more Protestant than at present." Despite a lack of evidence, Schultz told Bowell at the beginning of April that he thought Greenway was amenable to negotiations. At best, that was wishful thinking. Greenway and his government had shown no sign of wavering over the previous five years.[5]

Lord Aberdeen appreciated the complexity of the Manitoba schools question but nevertheless tried to hold Bowell to their December agreement for early dissolution and election. After the February 16 cabinet meeting, Aberdeen pushed Bowell for a definitive position on when Parliament would be dissolved. Bowell said he'd have an answer within forty-eight hours. Aberdeen asked that he write out "a few lines indicating the main points of any decision that may be arrived at regarding the question of a Dissolution. This would facilitate any subsequent conversation we have upon the subject." Bowell responded:

> I concur unreservedly in the view expressed by Your Excellency that the fullest information, as to the reasons

which induced me to suggest to my Colleagues the advisability of a dissolution, should be laid before you, and receive your approval, before any information is given to the Press, or to any person outside of the Cabinet ...

I notice that you intimate that a "statement mentioning the proposed time for a dissolution, and the main grounds upon which it would be based" should be given. In this I also concur, but I am not in a position to indicate the time of dissolution, for the reason that no time was fixed.

Bowell came back to Aberdeen five days later and said the timing of dissolution was dependent on the finalization of the voters' lists. He said that as of February 1, the Queen's Printer had received official voters' lists from only 102 of the 215 ridings across the country. And of these, only 50 had been printed. At three lists per day, it would take until at least the end of March for all to be printed. After that, the lists needed to be sent back to the ridings for revising officers to verify. The earliest point at which dissolution could occur was thus late April, maybe May. Aberdeen agreed to revisit the conversation once the Roman Catholic appeal wrapped up in March and the voters' lists were complete.

Appeal

On Monday, March 4, at 11:00 a.m., the historic appeal of the Manitoba schools question to the Dominion cabinet resumed. To accommodate all the supporters and reporters, Bowell moved the hearing from the Privy Council chambers to the Railway Committee Room in Centre Block.

While most had heard the name John Ewart, very few people outside Winnipeg had seen him. Not so with his opposing counsel, D'Alton McCarthy. Under John A. Macdonald's tutelage, he'd gained prominence as the Conservative Party's lead elections lawyer in the 1870s. He parlayed that success into founding the prestigious law firm McCarthy, Hoskin, Plumb and Creelman in 1879, one year after his election to the House of

Commons. While Ewart was starting his practice in Winnipeg, McCarthy was becoming one of the country's — and Macdonald's — pre-eminent constitutional authorities, arguing key cases on dominion-provincial rights before the Supreme Court of Canada and the Judicial Committee of the Privy Council. Once considered a possible successor to the Old Man, McCarthy drifted from the Conservative Party as he became increasingly critical of what he called "French Canadian nationalist aggression." The *Jesuits Estates Act* in 1888 pushed McCarthy even further. He founded the Equal Rights Association to better advocate for an English-only policy for Canada and an end to religious education across the country. It was McCarthy's speech to a large, rowdy crowd in Portage la Prairie in August 1889 that was, in part, the inspiration behind the Greenway government's *Public Schools Act* of 1890.

Bowell and his ministers sat along one side of the long, rectangular table, which ran the length of the committee room, McCarthy and Ewart on the other. Everyone else crowded around the perimeter, the lucky ones seated, the others standing.

Bowell checked the time and told Ewart, "We are ready to hear your argument."

Ewart spoke for three hours, focusing first on the state of separate schooling in Manitoba in 1870 and the history of negotiations that led to the separate school protections set out in section 7 of the *Manitoba Act*. After lunch, Ewart walked through the draft legislation that he proposed be passed to provide relief to his clients. Modelled on Ontario's *Separate Schools Act*, his remedial bill proposed to restore Manitoba's separate Catholic school board, which had existed before 1890; exempt Roman Catholics from taxation in support of Protestant or public schools; give Catholics the power to organize a school system; and entitle them to their share of public monies raised for education purposes.

The hearing resumed Tuesday morning. Trade and commerce minister William Ives asked Ewart if his proposed remedial legislation was designed to amend the 1890 legislation or replace it. Ewart said, technically, neither. Following the 1895 Judicial Committee in *Brophy*, Ewart said what he proposed to be created was a Roman Catholic board within the framework of the Department of Education system set up by the 1890 legislation.

The solicitor general, John Curran, asked if the proposed legislation went beyond the rights and privileges in place since 1870. Ewart told him, "We ask only for that which we had before and must be careful not even by concessions to change in any material respect the position which we formerly occupied. If we did, any statute that the Dominion might pass might be *ultra vires*."

After lunch, McCarthy dragged his heels with procedural wrangling and didn't begin the substance of his address until Wednesday morning at eleven. McCarthy used a scattergun approach that hit at least nine main points over the next day and a half. These ranged from refusing to recognize the federal cabinet's authority to hear the appeal, to presenting an alternative history of Manitoba's entry into Confederation that drew into question whether separate schools were even asked for in the Métis Bill of Rights, to the argument that "at all events, there are very few Catholics in Manitoba, and the injustice therefore cannot be very great."

McCarthy wound up just before lunch on Thursday, March 7, by singling out a comment Ewart had made in his closing remarks. Ewart had suggested McCarthy was a member of the Protestant Protective Association and in that capacity had launched a campaign of open hostility to the Roman Catholics. "There is not a word of truth in that," McCarthy defended. "I am not and never have been a member of the order of which the President of the Council was, and may be still, a distinguished ornament."

"I hope so," Bowell replied, "but you were not complimentary in a speech you made up west, to which I will reply on the stump."

McCarthy got his hackles up. "I will be quite willing to meet you on the stump. I never said anything against the order of which my father was a member, as I have too much respect for his memory. I acknowledge the right of the Roman Catholics in their religion. The statement I object to was a slander, and I am sorry my learned friend had not the manliness to make the charge in a more straightforward manner."

Everyone was tired and punchy, and Bowell adjourned the meeting at that point.

Ides

Micawbers

Cabinet met on Sunday, March 17, to decide what to do about remediation. Going into the meeting, ten of Bowell's fifteen cabinet ministers were either on record as supporting remediation or could be expected to do so.

Bowell believed the Dominion government had a constitutional responsibility to protect minority rights. As he'd tell the Senate in July 1895, "I say here frankly — so there is no misunderstanding — that *per se* I am not in favour of separate schools. I believe Manitoba came into this Dominion with the distinct and positive promise, incorporated in the constitution of the province, that they should have the right of separate schools retained to them forever in the same manner that they are enjoyed by the provinces of Ontario and Quebec; and as such, no matter what my individual opinion may be, as a public man I consider myself bound — and I will take my party with me as far as I can — to carry out to the fullest possible extent the promises that were made to the minority at confederation."[6]

Tupper and the five Roman Catholics in cabinet (Angers, Caron, Costigan, Ouimet, and Smith) also believed the Dominion government had a moral and constitutional responsibility to protect minority education rights in Manitoba. William Ives was expected to support remediation as his Sherbrooke riding in Quebec's Eastern Townships was split between French and English voters and the Liberal nominated to run against him was a strong remediation advocate. He'd have no choice but to support remediation if he wanted to be re-elected.

Arthur Dickey (recently elected in Cumberland, Tupper Sr.'s old riding) was expected to vote whichever way the Tuppers told him to — and Tupper Sr. was as supportive of remediation as Jr. was. And the other new member of cabinet, Ferguson, was expected to vote whichever way Bowell told him to.

The five ministers who opposed remedial action — Haggart, Patterson, and Montague (Ontario), Daly (Manitoba), and Foster (New Brunswick) — did so primarily on pragmatic grounds. They agreed that protecting the rights of Manitoba's Roman Catholic minority was the right thing to do but believed any remediation effort by the Dominion government would spell certain defeat of the government in the coming election. The risk was particularly acute in Ontario, where several key ridings were subject to Orange votes and anti-French and anti-Catholic sentiments.

While consensus going into the March 17 cabinet meeting seemed to favour remediation, it was unclear exactly what form remediation should take. To make a definitive statement on the matter, the Quebec ministers wanted Parliament to pass remedial legislation before going to the polls. Others, like Bowell, preferred a softer approach that would see cabinet issue a remediation order compelling Manitoba to pass the required legislation and not the Dominion. The compromise that emerged Tuesday afternoon had three parts. First, cabinet would "declare and decide that for the due execution of the provisions of section 22 of *The Manitoba Act* the system of education embodied in the aforesaid two Acts be supplemented by a Provincial Act (or Acts) which would restore to the Roman Catholic minority the rights and privileges set out in paragraphs a, b and c." Second, "refusal or neglect on the part of the Legislature of Manitoba to enact remedial legislation which to your Excellency-in-Council seems requisite will confer upon Parliament authority to pass such a law." Third, Parliament would dissolve upon issuance of the compelling order to give Parliament a clear mandate to pass remedial legislation if required after an election.

Angers waited until Wednesday morning to voice his opposition to the deal. He met Bowell in his East Block office and told him that unless remedial legislation was passed in the coming session, i.e., *before* an election, he'd resign from cabinet, form a new political party, and take his Quebec colleagues — and support from Quebec's clergy — with him.[7] Backed into a corner, Bowell promised Angers that he'd ask Parliament to pass remedial legislation in the coming session if Manitoba failed to act. The promise was enough to keep Angers in the fold — at least for now.

Daly, Foster, Haggart, and Montague came to see Bowell next. They repeated their opposition to an early election on the grounds that it would result in the government's certain defeat, particularly in Conservative ridings in Ontario. Their preference was to let the session play out while party coffers built up. Bowell said he'd already come to that conclusion and drafted an order that Aberdeen could sign the next day authorizing the start of

Ides

a new session on April 18. It was enough to keep the five ministers in the fold — at least for now.

At some point on Wednesday, Bowell realized it was easier to hang Tupper out to dry than lose his ministers from both Quebec and Ontario.

On Thursday afternoon, March 21, cabinet gathered in the Privy Council chambers in the East Block. At three, John Payne came in to let Bowell know that Governor General Lord Aberdeen had arrived and was waiting in his office. Bowell went down the hall and escorted Aberdeen back into the chamber. Bowell was chuffed: it was a rare occurrence these days for the Queen's representative to personally attend a meeting of the Privy Council.

Aberdeen took the prime minister's spot at the round council table, farthest from the door. Bowell stood to his right and presented Aberdeen with the order in council directing the government of Manitoba to pass legislation restoring the rights and privileges of the Roman Catholic minority. After signing, Aberdeen was presented with a second order summoning Parliament back for a session on April 18. The first order didn't surprise anyone. Tupper, however, looked ready to blow when the second was read aloud.

When the ceremony ended, Bowell and his ministers made for the door. Most — including Bowell — were headed to Quebec, where two important by-elections were coming up in April. The government considered these important bellwethers of public sentiment, the first to be held in the aftermath of the JCPC decision, the appeal, and the remedial announcement. The Conservatives could not afford to lose either.

Tupper was staying in Ottawa on business. When he got back to his office, he began writing the first in a series of letters to Bowell. In Thursday's, Tupper asked Bowell what had happened between Tuesday's cabinet meeting and the signing ceremony that day. "When you last discussed the subject in my presence very strong views were expressed. This was the state of affairs until Tuesday. What followed?" Tupper wondered whether "two or three" cabinet ministers threatening to resign had anything to do with Bowell's change of heart. "You committed my English-speaking colleagues including the dissentients behind my back. [It was an] extraordinary change of front on the part of colleagues to whom I refer coupled with their silence when you brought the Minutes forward convinced me all had been arranged in my absence." Tupper concluded by throwing one of his infamous resignation tantrums:[8]

> Your ground for the sudden change of opinion, viz: the fear of defeat — is to my mind no warrant for the change of policy. I cannot be a party to a course dictated by dread of the people. I have from the first conscientiously regarded this MB School question as imposing great responsibility. I consider our course should be above all, both honest and bold. Our judicial duty has been well-done. Our political action ought to be equally fearless. I hope we are all agreed to initiate and carry if possible remedial legislation if MB fails to act.
>
> We can, however, do nothing effectively or properly without a direct mandate from the people. We have entered a course; I believe that we should not go one step further without consulting our constituents ...

Bowell wrote back on Friday and admitted Tuesday's cabinet meeting had ended with an expectation of an early election, but maintained it was his prerogative and his alone to determine when an election should be called. He also denied having consulted with "the English-speaking members" behind Tupper's back and urged Tupper "to withdraw his resignation in the interests of the Party's unity and future." Bowell defended his decision on the grounds that debate in Parliament "would be the best means of correcting false views which had been presented to the electors by designing agitators, whose only hope of success in public life lies in arousing the prejudices and passion of a large number of honest and well-meaning people." He closed by pointing out that an appeal to the people "while the political heather was ablaze throughout the country, would be a piece of political folly, inexcusable in any public man," and would result in "the defeat of the very object which you express so decided a desire to attain."

Tupper responded on Sunday, telling Bowell "the beginning of the blaze is a more auspicious period than the middle … you cannot, I fear, keep Parliament together long enough to see the end of this fire." Bowell's chosen course, he said, was ultimately "fatal to remedial legislation, and to our party's success with honour." At some point that day, Tupper also wrote his father and called his colleagues a pack of "political micawbers. I do not believe my colleagues as a whole want or seek remedial legislation."

As with Tupper's previous resignations, this one was kept under wraps as family and colleagues worked to persuade him to rescind it. In two telegrams, Tupper *père* urged Charlie to remain in cabinet. He agreed dissolution was the only chance for success but was anxious Charlie not be held responsible for embarrassing the party and causing its defeat at the polls. Thomas Daly wrote Tupper and upbraided him for resigning over a "minor difference" and possibly "wrecking the party." Charlie shot back:

> I am certain ultimate blame will rest on my colleagues for wrecking the party. You may hold on till the end of your term, but your fate then is certain defeat. The ship could have been saved by pluck, or by carrying out the course upon which most of the Commons representatives on the Cabinet were set. You speak of my best friends. I have none, so far as I know in the Cabinet. One man alone could have retained me in the Government when I protested against an old man's folly and tyranny. Not a man stood by me.

Despite efforts to keep Tupper's resignation secret, it wasn't long before rumours were flying. By Monday, March 25, reporters from the *Ottawa Citizen*, the *Toronto World*, and the *Globe* were running down leads that, by Tuesday, were looking authoritative enough to run. The Aberdeens stepped in at that point and invited Tupper to dinner Tuesday evening. Tupper was still fuming — "v. wroth," Lady Aberdeen told her diary. The couple tried appealing to the good of the party and the good of the country but couldn't get Tupper to budge and were forced to call in reinforcements from Montreal — Sir Donald Smith and Senator George Drummond. These *éminences grises* arrived Wednesday afternoon and met with Tupper at the Russell that evening.

Echoing advice Tupper Sr. had given his son two months earlier, Smith and Drummond told Charlie to keep his eye on the long game. If he stayed his course and resigned, he'd take a drubbing. His friends would claim he didn't have the courage to ask a Parliament in which his party had a clear majority to render justice to a fragile minority. His enemies would point and say the only thing he was interested in was his own ambition.

If he had any political ambitions at all, the smart move would be to turn up as leader while in opposition. The Conservatives were certain to go down to Laurier and the Liberals in the next election, but if Charlie stayed to fight for remediation in another session, he'd go down surrounded by Quebec supporters. Not to mention the election would clear out all the deadwood that'd built up, leaving the ranks thinned and healthy.

Besides, with the debt the size it was and the economic forecasts the way they were looking, think about the financial mess Laurier would inherit — particularly with no previous experience in office. A Liberal government would last, at most, one term. Think about the last great Liberal experiment under Alexander Mackenzie.

Around nine, the conversation was going well enough to ask Bowell to sit in. The prime minister told Tupper a negotiated settlement with Manitoba was close at hand; Manitoba Lieutenant Governor John Schultz said Greenway was amenable to compromise and Hugh John Macdonald had cabled to say Archbishop Langevin (Taché's successor at Saint-Boniface) was open to talking as well. Tupper was interested, but not yet convinced. Bowell then promised that the new legislative session would be short, that the only business would be remediation, and then they'd go to the polls — in April, say, or May at the latest. He said he'd even pledge remedial legislation if Manitoba failed to act, right in the text of the Throne speech itself.

Whatever it was — his father's entreaties, the advice from Smith and Drummond, or Bowell's promises — Tupper caved. Again. Drummond sent a note to Aberdeen before he went to bed, "The Premier and Tupper have just left (11:00 p.m.) and have adjusted all differences and I consider the incident ended."

If Tupper was cowed by the experience he didn't let on. A couple of days later, the *Globe*'s Arnott Magurn asked Tupper if the rumours of his resignation were true. Tupper denied having done so, or "even talking of resigning over the matter. Obviously, the story was the work of a correspondent who had little or no regard for the truth. I have never concealed my opinion that before taking final action on this important matter the Government should appeal to the people. But I now have strong hope the Manitoba government will act, for if it does there would be no need for federal interference." And then, for good measure, Tupper added, "If the correspondents who circulated the report that because I was not at home, or in my office, or at the club house, I, therefore, was in hiding; if the correspondents had looked at the cabinet meetings they would have found me there. The Ottawa press men are a disgrace to the profession."

Word Inviolate

The perfume of hyacinths and Easter lilies was heavy in the Commons when Speaker Peter White took his chair on the afternoon of April 18, 1895. The chamber was full, everyone waiting to be summoned to the Senate to hear the Speech from the Throne. It had been nine months since the commoners had last been together — and the first sitting since Thompson died — and everyone was shaking hands, getting reacquainted, happy to be back together once again. On the opposition side, Laurier was resplendent in a crisp, new frock coat, a red rose in the buttonhole. He moved slowly up and down the aisles, extending the gracious cordiality that was his trademark. The mood on the government side was more sombre. On Thompson's desk, a massive floral arrangement had been placed bearing the words, "His Memory Green."

On the stroke of three, the flag in front of the Governor General's office in East Block was run up, a signal to the artillery on Nepean Point to open its twenty-one gun salute. As the shots died out, the helmets of the Princess

Louise Dragoon Guards came bobbing onto the parliamentary grounds from Wellington Street ahead of the Governor General's carriage. Aberdeen alighted in front of the main doors with help from uniformed footmen as a band played "God Save the Queen."

Mackenzie Bowell, William Ives, and Auguste-Réal Angers stood as the reception party beside the Governor General's throne at the front of the Senate chamber. Once Aberdeen was seated, Speaker John Jones Ross bade the Gentleman Usher of the Black Rod, René Kimber, to command the attendance of the members of the House of Commons. Kimber bowed, backed out of the chamber, and proceeded across the lobby to the locked doors of the Commons, upon which he knocked three times. Inside, the sergeant-at-arms announced, "A messenger from His Excellency." The Speaker asked that Kimber be admitted. The doors were unlocked, and Kimber strode to the middle of the floor, bowed, and announced stentoriously, "Mr. Speaker, his Excellency the Governor General desires the immediate attendance of your honourable House in the Senate Chamber." Kimber then backed up, bowed and scraped, turned around, and waited for the commoners to queue up behind him for the short walk back to the Senate.

When the commoners were seated in the upper chamber, Aberdeen began.

> Honourable Gentlemen of the Senate; Gentlemen of the House of Commons: It is with much satisfaction that I again have recourse to your advice and assistance in the administration of the affairs of the Dominion.
>
> By the sudden and lamented death of the late Right Honourable Sir John Thompson Canada has sustained a grievous loss. The deep and heartfelt sympathy expressed by her Most Gracious Majesty the Queen, and the manifestations of sorrow with which the distressing intelligence was received throughout the empire, as well as tokens of esteem and respect everywhere paid to the memory of the deceased statesman, have been gratefully appreciated by the people of Canada.

> In conformity with a recent judgment of the Lords of the Judicial Committee of the Privy Council, to the effect that the dissident minority of the people of Manitoba have a constitutional right of appeal to the Governor-General in Council against certain acts passed by the Legislature of the Province of Manitoba in relation to the subject of education, I have heard in Council the appeal, and my decision thereon has been communicated to the Legislature of the said Province. The papers on the subject will be laid before you.

At that point, Aberdeen shifted to French and the din from conversation amongst the English-speaking commoners rose. Perturbed, Aberdeen stopped reading, and warned, "If this noise is not stopped, I shall not read another word!" The pronouncement sparked Kimber to glower and bark, "Silence! Silence! Silence!" The din subsided enough for Aberdeen to continue. He finished in English: "Honourable Gentlemen of the Senate; Gentlemen of the House of Commons: It is with much satisfaction that I again have recourse to your advice and assistance in the administration of the affairs of the Dominion."

The Senate debate on the Throne Speech began on Monday, April 22. After introductory remarks by Clarence Primrose (Pictou) and Joseph Arsenault (P.E.I.), Senate opposition leader Richard Scott (Ottawa) offered Bowell his "congratulations and the congratulations of those who sympathize with me politically on the recognition of his services which has been extended to him by our sovereign." While Scott said he couldn't go so far as to hope Bowell's reign would be long, he did credit Bowell with being "actuated by high and conscientious motives and that he will act in all cases in what he believes from his standpoint to be the best interests of the people of Canada."

Bowell began his maiden speech as prime minister by thanking Scott for his kind remarks.

No member of this chamber feels the high responsibility devolving upon him more deeply than I do. When I consider for a moment the illustrious gentlemen who have been prime ministers of this country since confederation, I must say that I feel my utter inability to occupy the position and to perform the duties attaching thereto in the manner in which they have been discharged by my predecessors. I can say that whatever my defects may be in the important position which I now hold, I shall continue in the future as I have endeavoured in the past, to do my duty to my country as far as in me lies, firmly convinced when I adopt a course of action that is right, and that is conducive to the advancement of the best interests of the Dominion.

On the matter of the Manitoba schools question, Bowell said it was with "the greatest reluctance that any government should interfere with the rights and privileges given to a province under the constitution which governs it. And although I am not an advocate, nor am I in favour *per se* of separate schools, I hold that the word of the sovereign, when pledged, whether it is in accord with my particular sentiments or not, should be held inviolate in the governing of the country." Bowell recalled the debate on the *Manitoba Act* in 1870,

> when the resolutions were introduced, admitting Manitoba into the confederation, it was believed at that time that we were granting the same rights and privileges to the Roman Catholics of Manitoba that had been granted to the minority in Quebec and the minority in Ontario in relation to schools. It was for that reason, believing that we were making that concession to the Roman Catholics to that province, that I recorded my vote as I then did. And I take the same position then that I take today and the same position that I maintained in 1863 when I was defeated in my own county, that if the question was whether we should establish

separate schools in this country or not, I should vote against it. But separate schools having been established, I would not be a party to depriving the minority of rights that they had acquired under the constitution which governed them.

Despite his commitment to protecting the constitutional rights of Roman Catholics in Manitoba, Bowell made it clear he preferred that

the people of Manitoba may see their way clear to settle this question among themselves and to relieve the Parliament of Canada from the serious obligation which will devolve upon them otherwise. It is a very serious matter for the Government of the Dominion to undertake to deal with a question that affects solely any one section of the country. If the people of Manitoba are patriots they will keep this question out of the arena of Dominion politics, but if they desire to continue to fling fire brands among the electorate of this country (who I am sure are desirous of living in peace and harmony) if they reject all overtures and act upon the suggestions of those who are leading the Opposition throughout the country, I can only say that when the time comes, if it should come, for action by this government, the people of Canada will find that the present administration is quite prepared to assume the responsibility which may fall upon them, no matter what the results may be.

5
Blazing Heather

First Spike

Eighteen ninety-five was an auspicious year for William Mackenzie and Donald Mann. Up to that point, the two men had built successful businesses supplying material and construction services to railways across Canada and around the world. But then, in the spring of 1895, the future railway barons hatched a plan to build Canada's second national railroad, the Canadian Northern. It was an ambitious plan that required support from both the Manitoba and Dominion governments and private markets. It also offered Prime Minister Mackenzie Bowell and his Sixth Ministry a way out of the Manitoba schools quandary.

Mackenzie and Mann had come into their own as contractors with the Canadian Pacific Railway (CPR) and other, smaller lines across western Canada in the 1880s. They also maintained a keen interest in the original northern transcontinental route the CPR abandoned in 1882 in favour of the southern road, which ran closer to the U.S. border. The northern route ran northwest from Winnipeg through the so-called fertile belt of the central prairies and then on through the Rockies to the Pacific via the Yellowhead Pass.

Mann was the first to stake a claim in that route. In 1884, Winnipeg-based promoter Hugh Sutherland hired Mann and his then-partner Herbert Holt to construct his Winnipeg and Hudson Bay Railway (WHB). The WHB promised to give western grain producers access to foreign markets more directly and cheaply via a line that ran from Winnipeg, north along the western shores of lakes Winnipeg and Winnipegosis, and then on to Hudson Bay along the Saskatchewan River. Mann and Holt finished the first forty miles of the WHB in the fall of 1886, but Sutherland didn't have the cash to pay them so assigned them shares in the WHB instead. In 1887, Mann and Holt joined forces with William Mackenzie and James Ross to take on more railway contracts across Canada and the United States. The new company assumed Mann and Holt's original contract to build the WHB and their shares in Sutherland's company.

The global recession of the early 1890s ended the railway boom of the previous decade. Private financing dried up as grain prices dropped to historic lows and immigration slowed to a trickle. In the deflated market, Mann picked up cheap options on another proposed railway — the Lake Manitoba Railway & Canal Company (LMR) — which had running rights near and along the start of the northern route. The original LMR charter lapsed in 1893 because the promoters couldn't meet their financing or construction obligations. Mackenzie and Mann purchased the lapsed charter in early 1895.

The Manitoba government also had an interest in the northern route that owed, in part, to a small but vocal population that had settled in the Dauphine region west of Lake Winnipeg on the promise of proximity to a national railway. When the CPR changed plans in 1882, the settlers were irate and took it out on the Manitoba government to get a railway built. With no money in the provincial coffers, all Premier Greenway could do in 1891 was commit to paying a cash bonus of $1.5 million to any company that built a line through the Dauphine region and on to Hudson Bay by 1896.

Unable to secure private financing at the start of the recession, Hugh Sutherland turned to the Dominion government for assistance. In 1890, Prime Minister Macdonald agreed to pay Sutherland a subsidy worth $80,000 to carry mail and provide other transportation services but as part of the deal required Sutherland to come to terms with his creditors. A Manitoba Court of Queen's Bench had just ruled that Sutherland owed Ross, Mann, Holt, and Mackenzie $270,000 for work completed back in 1886. Sutherland agreed to bring Ross et al. on board as contractors (at the original 1886 rate of $11,000 per mile for the 210-mile distance, or $2.31 million) and creditors of the outstanding debt.

Parliament approved the WHB transport subsidy in 1892. On its own, the subsidy didn't provide the capital needed for construction. Its value stood as a government-backed annuity that could pay the interest on $2 million worth of bonds. But this still wasn't enough to cover construction costs (pegged at $2.31 million) or the debt owed to Ross et al. Sutherland was convinced other revenue streams would open up once the line was running, such as the Manitoba bonus, the sale of land the company would assume title to as the line was constructed, municipal bonuses, and operating revenues. While this made sense to Sutherland, the problem was convincing private lenders to assume the risk. London markets were still not interested in prairie railroads when Sutherland travelled there in search of assistance in 1893. And neither were Ross and Holt; they dropped out of the partnership late that year.

Sutherland wouldn't be put off. In the fall of 1894, he came up with yet another plan to try to convince Thomas Daly, member of Parliament for Selkirk, a long-time Bay line supporter and recently appointed as minister of the interior by Prime Minister Thompson, to lobby the Dominion cabinet for a loan of $2.5 million. Discussion of the loan was put off when Thompson died in December.

It was then, just after the *Brophy* decision was released in January 1895, that William Mackenzie and Donald Mann launched an audacious plan to get their Northern Railway project off the ground. The plan involved 1) having Parliament pass legislation to revive the Lake Manitoba Railway (LMR) charter and its attendant running rights; 2) getting the Dominion cabinet to approve Sutherland's $2.5 million loan request; 3) getting the Dominion cabinet to transfer the guarantees for the $2.5 million loan and the $80,000 subsidy from Sutherland's WHB to the revived LMR; 4) using the Dominion guarantees to leverage financial assistance from the Manitoba government; and 5) using the Dominion and Manitoba guarantees as collateral for whatever remaining funding was needed from private lenders to begin construction of Canada's second transcontinental railway.

Mackenzie and Mann felt confident they could secure Manitoba's support because the Greenway Liberals were under intense pressure to build new railways. Only forty miles of track had been laid in the province since the 1892 election and no one had started on a new Bay line to claim the $1.5 million bonus Greenway had promised in 1891. The schools issue had provided a welcome distraction from the lack of progress, but a viable plan to build new tracks — particularly in the Dauphine region — was going to be essential to re-election in 1896.

As for Dominion support, providing generous financial support for a railway through a politically important region might just be the ticket for getting Greenway and Sifton to compromise on the schools question. Nothing else had worked so far. And, who knew? If the Conservatives played their cards right, they might even be able to siphon some boodle off the loan into party coffers, as Adolphe Caron had masterfully done so many times before. As the Old Chieftain used to say, there wasn't a political problem that couldn't be solved if a railway ran through it.

On March 5, the Dominion cabinet took the first step in executing Mackenzie and Mann's plan and issued an Order-in-Council committed to putting the $2.5 million WGN loan request before Parliament in the coming session and reserving from public sale and settlement the lands to be earned by the company under its land grant. A week after Parliament resumed on April 18, notice was given in the Commons to introduce a bill reviving the LMR charter and amendments to make Gladstone the new starting point and change the line's terminus to "not more than one hundred miles" to the northwest in the "Lake Dauphine neighbourhood."9

And then all work on the Northern Railway file was put on hold. On his own initiative, Lord Aberdeen invited Premier Greenway and Attorney General Sifton to meet with him in Ottawa to see if a solution to the schools crisis could be sorted out in private between the three of them. But those meetings, at the end of May, failed. Greenway and Sifton wouldn't negotiate without a specific proposal from the Dominion and refused to meet with Bowell or any of his ministers. When Aberdeen apprised Bowell, Caron, Costigan, Haggart, Foster, and Daly of the discussions, Bowell "got angry and said that was too strong, that this conduct proved Greenway et al.'s bad faith. 'We've let them know,' he said, 'our way of looking — does he accept the order-in-council? If so, then to what extent? — if not, let them say so.'" And they did. On Monday, June 17, Clifford Sifton told the Manitoba legislature that "we cannot accept the responsibility of carrying into effect the terms of the remedial order." He explained that the Catholic system was abolished in the first place because it was "inefficient," its "conduct, management, and regulation defective." The Dominion had obviously failed to avail itself of "full and accurate information" about how the system worked because the March remedial order did not provide any guarantees to improve the system. As such, the remediation order, if acted upon, would do nothing more than leave "a large section of the population with no better means of education than was thus supplied" and in the "state of illiteracy" in which they grew up. Sifton did offer an olive branch, of sorts. He said it was "not yet too late to make a full and deliberate investigation of the whole subject," which his government would "cheerfully assist in." The result, Sifton was convinced, would "furnish a substantial basis of fact upon which conclusions could be formed with a reasonable degree of certainty."

Ablaze

It took a few weeks for Dominion politicians to figure out what the Manitoba statement meant and how they should respond. Quebec's Conservative caucus set up shop in Senate Speaker John Jones Ross's chambers to consider three options: introduce remedial legislation now and defend it at the polls at the end of the current session, introduce remedial legislation now and promise a vote on it at a future session, or promise to introduce legislation and a vote at some future session. Angers and Ouimet and about half the sixty-member caucus favoured immediate action. Caron and a small minority were leaning toward the longer timetable. Regardless of their position, the three ministers pledged to stand *en bloc* with their comrades and resign their cabinet positions if the government did not accede to the wishes of caucus, whatever they might be.

Meanwhile, down the hall in Committee Room 16, Ontario's fifty-one Conservatives were debating their response. On Wednesday, July 3, thirty-nine of them signed a pledge circulated by George Taylor, the Conservative whip, to refuse support of any further remediation efforts.

The two sides collided in cabinet the next day. The question was whether to proceed with remedial legislation in the current session or push it off to a future one in the hopes Manitoba would agree to some form of compromise. To begin the meeting, Bowell had Tupper present an overview of the remedial bill John Ewart had recommended back in March as the basis for what might be submitted to Parliament, i.e., legislation to re-establish the separate school system that had been in place prior to 1890. When the meeting broke at 3:00 p.m., it looked like a slim majority favoured introducing a modified version of Ewart's bill into Parliament before the current session prorogued on July 20. Eight of the fifteen ministers were in favour of this option: the five Roman Catholics (Angers, Caron, Costigan, Ouimet, and Smith), Bowell, Tupper, and Daly.

The effort to derail the pro-remediation momentum began Friday morning before cabinet met when Nathaniel Clarke Wallace, the customs controller and sitting Grand Master of the Grand Orange Lodge of British America, threatened to resign if Bowell went ahead with remedial legislation — and to take Orange votes with him. Bowell got his hackles up and told Clarke Wallace that, thank goodness, the life of the government "didn't hang upon his constancy."

The exchange gave Haggart an opening at cabinet later Friday morning. The railway minister said he was "appalled" when Tupper had read the draft remediation bill on Thursday: the French ministers celebrated and not one word of dissent was offered. Haggart said if Bowell proceeded on this path not only would he follow Clarke Wallace out the door, but he'd take the thirty-nine Ontario Conservatives who'd pledged to oppose remedial legislation with him. See how Bowell and his government would fare without them.

The Quebec ministers cried foul, asking what business the party's whip had in fomenting discord in caucus.

Ouimet ignored the ruckus and appealed to Bowell. He reminded the prime minister of the promises he'd made to introduce remedial legislation during the current session if Manitoba did not act on its own. Bowell said he remained steadfast in his commitment to remedying the Roman Catholics' grievances and pointed to the fact that a majority of cabinet had agreed to Ewart's draft remedial bill as proof of the government's resolve on the issue. He also made the point that amicable settlement was still the best possible outcome and Manitoba's reply to the remedial order had to be read as leaving that door open. He said the Dominion government could not risk any action that could be interpreted by the Manitoba government as precluding a negotiated settlement.

By this point, Angers had had enough. He said Manitoba's response gave no reasonable hope for the kind of compromise or settlement Bowell hoped for. Sifton and Greenway, he said, opposed separate schools in principle and in practice. And besides, the wording of the declaration itself was very clear: the Manitoba government had distinctly refused — again — to restore the schools. How much more "clarity" did one need? As for Bowell's commitment to redress minority rights, Angers said he was afraid the same anti-remediation pressure currently preventing the bill from being introduced would only intensify. He told Bowell that he, Bowell, had the power and the strength to push forward and do the right thing, right now, but that power and strength could — and would — vanish tomorrow. For all of this, Angers said he couldn't remain as a member of the cabinet and would tender his resignation immediately.

In the moment, it looked like Caron and Ouimet would follow Angers out the door. But Caron didn't have the independent means or media access Angers had to fight a long and divisive election; Caron's political survival was much more reliant upon party finances and whatever other resources he could leverage as a cabinet minister. As a result, he favoured letting the clock run on a bit, and introducing remedial legislation in a future session. To this end, Caron proposed a compromise to give both Bowell the time he needed to seek compromise with Manitoba and Angers some certainty about the government's resolve on the issue. What if everyone around the table, he suggested, gave a written-and-signed pledge that they would support remedial legislation in a January session?

Haggart had now had enough and put his foot down. He told Caron that he and his French friends had no reason to complain — they were getting everything they wanted. They were simply acting like "spoiled children."

And that did it. Ouimet and Caron demanded that Bowell force Haggart to retract his statement — and failing that, they'd accept nothing less than his resignation. Angers didn't care; Haggart had just proven his point.

The meeting then broke up. Off the record, Caron told the *Globe*'s Arnott Magurn that cabinet had agreed that remedial legislation would not be introduced in the current session and the government would pledge to hold another session during which remedial legislation would be introduced. After that, Ouimet was spied walking over to Centre Block at one thirty, alone, with "a very serious air." Haggart was seen at the Railway Committee "looking as if he had scored a point." All Bowell would say in the Senate was, "On Monday I expect to be in a position to state what course the Government intends to pursue on the question."

Cabinet reconvened Saturday morning to approve the wording of a statement explaining the Dominion position on the Manitoba schools issue that Bowell intended to read in Parliament on Monday. Before the meeting started, Ouimet reminded Bowell of his promise to introduce remedial legislation in the current term and if he didn't, he'd follow Angers out the door. Haggart and Montague countered with similar threats, claiming Ontario votes would follow *them* if *they* left. Bowell reminded them all that it was his prerogative and his alone to request dissolution of Parliament and they'd all do well to remember it. He then had Foster read out the short statement outlining the hope the Dominion had for an amicable settlement with Manitoba — and if one couldn't be found the government's commitment to introduce and pass remedial legislation in a January session.

The political heather was ablaze once again. On Sunday, July 7, Bowell telegraphed Lord Aberdeen at his home in Montreal to ask that he return to Ottawa "with as little delay as possible" owing to "reports of growing differences" in the cabinet. Bowell met the Aberdeens at the Russell Monday morning (Rideau Hall was still under renovation) and told them Angers, Caron, and Ouimet had threatened to resign if remedial legislation were not passed in the current session. While he had Angers's resignation in hand, Bowell hoped to "win over" the other two before they physically handed theirs in.

Growing Differences

George Foster entered the House of Commons Monday afternoon, just before three. The galleries in the chamber were packed with Ottawans curious to see the drama first-hand. Lady Aberdeen had taken up her regular seat on the floor of the chamber to the right of Speaker Peter White. Conspicuous by their absence were Caron and Ouimet, and most of their Conservative colleagues from Quebec. The vacant seats added fuel to the drama.

After opening prayers and routine proceedings, the Speaker called on the Leader of the Opposition. Laurier rose and buttoned his coat.

"I suppose the honourable gentleman leading the House will now make to the House the statement he promised on Friday last?" Laurier asked.

Foster rose from his seat, adjusted his wire-rimmed glasses, and removed two typewritten pages from his inner pocket. He unfolded them slowly and then read in a clear voice into the anxious silence.

> Mr. Speaker, I desire to state that the government has had under its consideration the reply of the Manitoba legislature to the remedial order of the 21st March 1895 and, after careful deliberation, has arrived at the following conclusion:
>
> Though there may be differences of opinion as to the exact meaning of the reply in question, the government believes that it may be interpreted as holding out some hope of an amicable settlement of the Manitoba school question on the basis of possible action by the Manitoba government and legislature; and the Dominion government is most

unwilling to take any action which can be interpreted as forestalling or precluding such a desirable consummation.

The government has also considered the difficulties to be met with in preparing and perfecting legislation on so important and intricate a question during the last hours of the session. The government has, therefore, decided not to ask Parliament to deal with remedial legislation during the present session. A communication will be sent immediately to the Manitoba government on the subject, with a view to ascertaining whether that government is disposed to make a settlement of the question, which will be reasonably satisfactory to the minority of that province, without making it necessary to call into requisition the powers of the Dominion Parliament.

A session of the present Parliament will be called together to meet not later than the first Thursday of January next. If by that time the Manitoba government fails to make a satisfactory arrangement to remedy the grievance of the minority, the Dominion government will be prepared at the next session of Parliament to be called as above stated to introduce and press to a conclusion such legislation as will afford an adequate measure of relief to the said minority, based on the lines of the judgment of the Privy Council and the remedial order of the 21st March 1895.

Foster nodded to the speaker, folded the statement, put it back in his pocket, and took his seat. As he did, members on both sides of the House sprang from their desks and scurried out into the lobby. The whips were just able to hold back a bare quorum to debate the business of the day, a motion to make unsold islands in the St. Lawrence into a Dominion park.

The lobby was packed. Parliamentarians, civilians, and reporters waited noisily for any further news on the resignations. Quebec Conservatives huddled in one corner, denounced Foster's statement, and waited to hear if their ministers would resign. The member from Chicoutimi, Louis de

Gonzague Belley, told the *Globe*'s Arnott Magurn that "the decision of the Government as read in the House today does not suit us because it does not recognize the refusal of the Manitoba Legislature to render justice to the minority. In addition, the Quebec Ministers have no confidence in the other Ministers. There are several ministers, especially from Ontario, who the Quebec Ministers believe are not sincere in promising another session and the remedial bill."

On the other side of the lobby, Ontario Conservatives pressed George Taylor for information about just how serious the government's commitment was to introduce and pass remedial legislation in a future session. In the middle — literally — stood English-speaking Catholic Conservatives Costigan, Curran, Smith, and Kenny.

The Liberals spied an opportunity and dispatched their whip, Philippe-Auguste Choquette, over to his Conservative confreres. To member after member Choquette expressed sympathy with the Manitoba minority and promised that his Liberal Party would champion the cause of remedial legislation. Perhaps if they'd just vote with the Liberals, they could show their dissatisfaction. Seeing Choquette's campaign, the Conservatives counter-dispatched Joseph Girouard, chair of the Privileges and Elections Committee, to douse the fires and advise moderation and calm. Fairly quickly the Quebec Conservatives were telling Choquette to mind his own business.

Around 5:00 p.m., Ouimet and Caron made their way into the lobby and were mobbed. The volume rose, everyone talking at once. But the two *causes célèbres* didn't stay long. On their way out the door, Ouimet told a reporter from the *Montreal Gazette* that "unless the Government brings a written pledge signed by every member agreeing to remedial legislation next session I will take my seat as an independent member, and move a want of confidence motion. My colleagues and myself are not schoolboys. The pledge, too, must be of the most emphatic character. I go so far as to demand a complete system of Catholic Separate Schools."

One reporter asked where Angers was. Ouimet said they'd seen him at his East Block office packing up his things.

Pressure

By Monday, July 8, it was clear Angers wasn't coming back. Bowell had promised the Roman Catholic minority remediation, and nothing had come of the promise. And Angers simply didn't trust Haggart, Montague, Clarke Wallace, and the other anti-remedialists. As he would state in the Senate later in the week, Bowell's promise was reliant upon a "procedure which may deprive the leader of this Government of moving it before Parliament."

The work to entice Caron and Ouimet back into the fold started Monday evening with an appeal to the English-speaking Roman Catholics. Their ministry representatives — Costigan, Smith, and Curran — had originally sided with the Quebec ministers to have remedial legislation introduced in the current session. But at a meeting in Thomas Kenny's (Halifax) office during the Monday dinner break, Bowell and Foster convinced the group that, given the stakes, a five-month delay wasn't unreasonable. Later in the week, in the Senate, Frank Smith explained why they changed their minds: "This question has been before the country five years, and I ask any reasonable man, clergyman or layman if a further delay of five months is an unreasonable request for the government to make for the purpose of giving time to settle this vexed question amicably, rather than impose the power of the Dominion Parliament upon the province of Manitoba." Smith and the English Catholics were clear, though, that if the government "shrunk from doing what is right and proper" they'd be the first to "declare war on them and say they are unworthy of administering the affairs of the country."

In the Commons on Tuesday, Laurier decided to test just how deep Conservative dissent had extended into caucus. He asked Foster if there were any truth to the rumours regarding the "resignation of certain members of the Administration." The finance minister said he didn't have any authority to speak on the matter as the ministers were in the employ of the Governor General and the Governor General had not authorized him to speak. All he *could* say was that "no resignation has as yet been received by His Excellency."

Laurier pushed on. "Official or not," it was obvious they were in the midst of a "grave ministerial crisis." Caron's and Ouimet's seats in the Commons were vacant for a second day, as was Angers's in the Senate. And with no representation from Quebec, Laurier said the government was in an untenable position before Parliament as "under our system of government, we have it as an unwritten law" that all provinces need to be represented in cabinet. Without that representation, the government "has no right to ask Parliament to vote a single penny." Laurier said the present state of affairs bound him to move for adjournment to give the government "an opportunity of either making up the vacancies that exist or advise His Excellency of the condition of things which does exist" — namely, though Aberdeen might not yet have the resignations in hand, "three of his Ministers are not here to discharge the business which His Excellency has entrusted to them."

As with Choquette's entreaties to disaffected Conservatives the day before, there were no Conservative takers on Laurier's motion. It was defeated straight down party lines, 111 to 72. And not one of the twenty-six Quebec Conservatives in the House broke ranks to censure Bowell or his Sixth Ministry.

By this point in the week, the pressure was on Caron and Ouimet to make up their minds about whether to stay or go. The support the English Catholics had originally given for remedial legislation in the current session had evaporated by Monday evening. And by Tuesday evening it was clear the Quebec caucus could not be trusted to put their votes where their mouths were. Ouimet felt the pressure the most. He'd sided with Angers privately in cabinet and publicly in the media. But at the end of the day, Ouimet was as beholden to Conservative Party resources for re-election as Caron was. At least Caron had seen the political value of waiting to introduce remedial legislation in a later session. What both men needed was *something* that would allow them to climb down with a modicum of grace.

Bowell asked Caron and Ouimet to get together with him late Wednesday morning at the Russell. Meeting in the parlour that adjoined his and Aberdeen's suites, Bowell reiterated his commitment to bring down remedial legislation before dissolution but stressed his preference for amicable settlement. He pointed to Tupper's draft of the legislation itself as proof of moving that agenda forward.

Around one, the Governor General stuck his head in. Aberdeen said it wasn't his place to intrude but he wanted to encourage Caron and Ouimet to do what they felt best to right whatever wrong they felt had been done to the Roman Catholic minority. Holding off their resignations, though, would at least give them the right to lay claim to any collective victory, should one come about. Aberdeen asked Caron and Ouimet to let Bowell know of their decision either way by noon the next day.

Foster joined Bowell, Caron, and Ouimet in the prime minister's East Block office at six Wednesday evening to continue the negotiations. Caron floated the idea of putting out a supplementary statement that would define more specifically what the Dominion would accept from Manitoba as a "satisfactory arrangement to remedy the grievance of the minority." Ouimet said that wouldn't go far enough to address the real issue. He again proposed that every minister sign a written pledge agreeing to remedial legislation in the next session. Foster told them neither idea would fly, as Haggart and the others had come as far as they were going to with Monday's statement. He said Caron and Ouimet had to be realistic and they had to be honest. If they really believed a settlement with Manitoba could be negotiated and wanted to share in that success then just 'fess up to needing time to think, and time to canvass their colleagues in Quebec and across the country, to make sure their decision to support the government was the right one — right for them, right for their constituents, and right for upholding Roman Catholic rights. There was no shame in taking time to make the right decision about such an important matter. And besides, nothing prevented either of them from resigning in January if they still felt the need to.

Whatever it took, Bowell's meeting with Foster, Caron, and Ouimet broke at ten, and Caron and Ouimet agreed to meet again the next morning to settle on wording for a statement explaining how it was that they were still in cabinet.

On his way out of East Block that night, Fred Cook asked Bowell about the status of the resignations. "A positive announcement on the position of the Government will be made tomorrow in both Houses of Parliament," the prime minister said.

Bats

The parliamentary galleries were packed again on Thursday, July 11. Caron was standing in the aisle as Speaker White finished prayers. He then walked over to take his seat on the government benches. The two New Brunswick Liberals, Colter and Gillmore, welcomed the postmaster general with ostentatious bows, replete with hand flourish, as if they were greeting some dignitary in a high court of the *ancien régime*. Pretty quickly everyone on the opposition side was doing the same. Caron nodded stiffly, adjusted his monocle, and took his seat. Ouimet got the same treatment when he emerged from the Speaker's vestibule a minute later.

"And the cats came back!" Liberal James Lister shouted.

"Bats!" George Foster shouted back, his best at witty repartee.

Laurier spoke first. "I see that everything is serene once more in the atmosphere of the Cabinet." The opposition leader waited for the cheers and laughter to die down. "Perhaps the honourable gentlemen will be able to give us information as to the non-existing crisis which was supposed to exist."

"I am glad my honourable friend shows such skill in reading political weather predictions, if I may so denominate them," Foster replied. He didn't have to wait for the ranks to quiet down; no one was laughing.

> I have but a few remarks in reply to the questions which my honourable friend has put.
>
> Some differences arose between members of the Cabinet with reference to the question of remedial legislation and the statement which I made the other day to the House. These differences arose chiefly on two lines. Some of our colleagues were of the opinion that it was useless to prolong negotiations with the Manitoba Government with a view to the settlement by that government of the question.

The other difference arose consequently from that. They believed that remedial legislation should be introduced at once, starting from the premise that there was nothing to be hoped for from the action of the Manitoba Government and legislature itself.

I regret to say that one of our colleagues finds it impossible to accede to the view of the majority of the Government. He still holds very firmly and strongly to his view that remedial legislation should be undertaken and pressed to a conclusion at once; and as he finds it impossible to accede to the view of the majority in that respect, his resignation has not only been sent in but accepted, and he is now no longer a member of this Government, I regret to say.

With reference to our other two colleagues, I must say they showed a disposition to canvass and discuss and look thoroughly into the grounds of difference between their own views and the views of the majority of their colleagues and in the end found these differences to be rather a misunderstanding as to details than a real divergence of opinion as regards the principles that were involved.

My friends have come to the conclusion that in the statement which was made on Monday last by me, the remedial legislation was actually and positively promised, and that there is no intention at all of going one single jot outside that statement, and that our intention is to carry out in perfect good faith the statement of the Government on Monday last.

Having come to this conclusion, my two honourable friends believe it to be their duty which they owe to their party, to their country, and to the cause which they themselves have deeply at heart, to work in harmony with their former and present colleagues and that we should carry out the policy of the Government in this way.

Caron followed Foster. He looked as miserable and tired as he must have felt.

> Mr. Speaker, I have very little to add to what has just been said. The question, as I view it, is one of the gravest that Parliament has been called upon to consider since confederation. Believing, as I do, that minorities must be protected under the constitution, and being anxious for the settlement of the school question — after repeated interviews, and, to my mind satisfactory assurances, from the Premier and from my colleagues, I consider that refusing to help the government in carrying out remedial legislation upon the lines of the Privy Council judgment I would be sacrificing the interests of the minority and jeopardizing the settlement of the question. This induces me to continue to act with the Government to secure, as I believe, remedial legislation in accordance with the pledges given by the Premier and by the leader of the House.

"Next! Next!" the opposition chanted and laughed.

Ouimet half-rose. "I do not think I need to add much to what has been said by my colleagues."

"Yes, you do!" the opposition shouted. Ouimet sighed and stood up.

> I must say that if I am at this moment occupying the seat which I formerly held it is solely due to my sense of the duty which I owe to my country, to my party, and especially to the cause, the success of which I have so much at heart. If I am here, it is because I have become convinced, after the repeated assurances which my colleagues have given us and the warm sympathies which have been shown us by all of our friends, that, in delaying the settlement of this question we are rendering the more sure, its settlement in a definite manner and in a manner perfectly satisfactory to

the country and to all those who desire to see justice done, who love peace and who are devoted to the well-being of their compatriots.

Ouimet stopped here, mid-tack, and waited until the speaker could get the assembly back under control. It gave Ouimet a chance to try a different tack.

Mr. Speaker, I am above the accusations which will be levelled against me in the Province of Quebec and elsewhere. I am prepared to endure those attacks in the hope that we will have our reply in six months, in the session which will be held on the 3rd of January next. And if in the course of those six months I should be covered with opprobrium and insult instead of being covered with flowers and greeted as a hero, I will console myself with the hope that this question will then be settled, and that I will then have not only the consolation but the happiness of being able to say to my compatriots: that, today, by yielding somewhat in regards to my personal dignity, I have done so in the interests of my country and of those I represent in this House.

Ouimet sat down and Laurier rose again. "Once upon a time, Mr. Speaker, not very long ago, in a country which I need not name, there was a rumour prevalent that the cat came back to the cream." Laurier waited again for the laughter to subside.

Feline nature will assert itself, and today we have a small family of kittens coming back to the Premier. Only a few days ago they started upon what they represented to be a crusade for a holy cause, but after three days experience in the cold, far from the kitchen, exposed to the inclemency of the season, they have come back to the cream.

Even the staidest Conservative in the chamber chuckled. The man had presence, you had to give him that.

Laurier then moved another motion to adjourn which the House debated for the next three hours. At some point, Tupper challenged Laurier and the Liberals to spell out finally and definitively where exactly they stood on the schools issue. He had as much success as Laurier's motion: for the second day in a row, the government ranks held.

Meanwhile, across the lobby in the Senate, opposition leader Richard Scott asked Bowell about the resignations. The prime minister said he could indeed confirm that three Quebec members had dissented from the cabinet decision outlined by Foster on Monday and considered "in the interests of the Dominion, and in the interests of those whom they represented and in the interests of the minority of the province of Manitoba, it was the bounden duty of the government of Canada to proceed at once, during the present session, with remedial legislation." While he regretted that Angers "still holds that opinion," he was glad that "after mature deliberation and in a firm belief in the honesty of their colleagues, two of them have consented to remain in the Government on the assurance that should Manitoba refuse to grant legislation, restoring to the minority of Manitoba the rights of which they were deprived by the Act of 1890, the present government would risk its position, each individual his own political reputation, and introduce remedial legislation." Bowell did caution that "without having exhausted every possible means to obtain from Manitoba redress for the grievance of the minority in that province" he looked "with much apprehension to the effect of a policy which would force on an almost independent province, so far as local matters are concerned, a law which would have to be carried out in all its details by the Dominion Government or by the Dominion Parliament. The difficulties which present themselves, to my mind, in attempting to force upon an unwilling people any kind of legislation will render whatever relief we may grant useless to those whom it is the intention of Parliament to aid if they possibly can."

Then it was Angers's turn. He said he could not agree with the cabinet position that there were grounds for amicable settlement with Manitoba. He walked his colleagues line by line through the Manitoba statement and concluded that it was "impossible to find here a hope of an amicable settlement." As for the commitment to introduce remedial legislation if Manitoba failed to act by January, Angers said it was hollow. Bowell had already committed his government to act back in April and that commitment had yet to be acted upon. "Was it necessary to get another declaration of the same kind? In my opinion, the first one was good, but the second one is not so good. The second one is embarrassed with a procedure that may deprive the leader of this Government of moving it before Parliament. That noble voice that we heard at the beginning of the session granting this release when the time would come, and it has come, to the minority, has been suppressed."

"What exactly has been suppressed?" Bowell asked.

"Your promise has been suppressed by an influence which acted like a damper. I fear that the opposition made to the execution of the remedial order is stronger and greater than your intention. The honourable leader has in his hand the present; no man perhaps in Canada could more effectively have given remedial legislation to the minority than himself this session but having the present in his hand he has not the future. In my opinion remedial legislation, by the inaction of the government, has been so imperilled that the minority may never have it, and consequently, I cannot accept the responsibility of such a risk."

Milkmaids

While Mackenzie Bowell and at least some members of Canada's Sixth Ministry clung to faint hope for a negotiated settlement with the Manitoba government on the schools question, the opportunity had passed for Parliament to authorize the $2.5 million loan for the Hudson Bay Railway by July 20, the date set for prorogation. In the first place, the government didn't have the money to loan. For 1895–96, the deficit was set to hit $4.5 million (up from $1.2 million the previous year) and the debt an all-time high of $250 million — all on an operating budget of $38 million (up from $24 million the year before). The prospect of adding $2.5 million for another railway scheme was simply too much, especially for finance minister George Foster.[10] Second, early in the session, Laurier had placed the government on notice that his Liberals would fight tooth and nail any effort to pass "one of the most flagrant constitutional outrages that ever was perpetrated by any Government of any country." Laurier explained that "a statute was passed only a few years ago, granting aid to that company towards the construction of the Hudson Bay Railway, under certain terms which, up to the present time, have not been carried out; and, in the face of the letter and spirit of the statute, the Government take upon themselves to pass an Order in Council altogether at variance with the terms agreed to by Parliament, and promising an expenditure of not less than $2,500,000 for the same purpose."

Liberal George Dawson said there were "additional temptations lurking" in the proposed subsidy: "We must not forget that there are milkmaids in Cabinet. Expert, confessedly expert in the art of extracting, by gentle pressure, a golden stream from railway bonuses. The milking of bonuses is an accomplishment which the Postmaster General [Caron] is passing around. Do not put temptations in his way. $2,500,000 — fancy what golden vistas open up before his enraptured gaze. What possibility it suggests, just on the eve of an election. $2,500,000 — would 10 percent be too much to expect as the result of his expert manipulation? What a magnificent election fund that would make."

Third, by mid-July, it was unclear just how much political capital Bowell and his cabinet had left, especially for getting a major, controversial piece of legislation through Parliament. Caucus was fractured, cabinet was divided, and the opposition was united behind their increasingly popular leader. Even if Parliament approved the loan, it was unclear how much latitude Manitoba had to compromise, given its public refusal to re-establish a separate school system. Given the circumstances, it wasn't surprising that George Foster, on July 18, confirmed the government's decision not to proceed with the loan, telling Laurier such a "superannuation bill" might be taken up in the next session "when there is more time to discuss it."

For those still clinging to faint hope for a negotiated settlement of the schools question, the only bits of leverage to use on Greenway that were still left in Mackenzie and Mann's Canadian northern plan were reviving the Lake Manitoba Railway charter and transferring the $80,000 Dominion subsidy from Sutherland's Winnipeg Great Northern to it. It was worth a shot and wouldn't cost much, financially or politically.

On Friday, July 19, George Foster moved third reading of the Lake Manitoba Railway Bill (it had languished in committee hearings since May) and then John Haggart gave notice he'd introduce the *Winnipeg & Great Northern Railway Act* the next day. Haggart's bill came up for debate when the business of supply was finished late next morning. Laurier said he "hoped some explanation" would be given. Centre Block was already hot and stuffy, and the skeletal crew left to finish the session's business were keen to catch the evening trains out of town to start the summer break.

Haggart explained that the bill would change the starting point of the W&GNR line from Winnipeg to "Gladstone or Portage la Prairie," from whence it could extend "northerly to the Saskatchewan." The change was necessary as another line from Winnipeg west would duplicate the existing Canadian Pacific or the Northern Pacific lines, something that would be "manifestly undesirable." The bill would also make the payment schedule for the existing federal transport subsidy more flexible by allowing the company "to earn $40,000 a year upon the completion of half the road from Gladstone or Portage to the Saskatchewan River, rather than $80,000 upon completion of the full road as was originally intended." Finally, in the event the W&GNR was unable to comply with these terms, the bill proposed to give cabinet the authority to transfer the subsidy "to a company authorized to construct a line of railway from Portage la Prairie or Gladstone to Lake Dauphin or thereabouts."

The Commons broke for lunch at one thirty and resumed at three, with a note from Speaker White saying the Governor General intended to proceed to the Senate at five thirty to prorogue Parliament. To speed things along, Foster tried to move second reading of the W&GNR bill, but Liberal David Mills rose on a point of procedure. He argued the bill was essentially a private bill — "an amendment to an Act of incorporation of the company" — and could not proceed as a public bill. Justice minister Charlie Tupper said the bill involved "the re-arrangement of a parliamentary grant" and could not "be carried out except by legislation introduced by the Government on resolution." Speaker White ruled for Mills after consulting with the clerk: "This portion of the Act should be introduced as a private bill," but as regards the subsidy, "no doubt that is a public matter and that part of the Bill has been properly introduced."

Foster and Haggart agreed to rescind the offending section and moved that the House reconstitute for committee review. Laurier asked how they could proceed "now that such an important part of the bill has been withdrawn?"

Haggart had to lay his cards on the table. "In the event of the company not performing the work, we may ask to have the power to give that part of the subsidy to another railway which may have power to build from Gladstone, or some other point, in the direction of the Saskatchewan."

"What railway is that?" Laurier asked.

"There is a railway company whose charter was passed today or yesterday," Haggart explained.

Foster jumped in. "Mr. Speaker, I think we might go into committee on this bill."

Committee review finished at four fifteen, with third reading completed by four thirty. As he registered the vote, White sent a messenger to the Senate telling Speaker Ross the W&GNR bill would be on its way over momentarily.

Bowell was on tenterhooks by this point in the day. In less than an hour, Aberdeen was scheduled to arrive and prorogue Parliament and neither the LMR nor W&GNR bills had cleared the Commons. When Bowell saw the House messenger enter the chamber with news the W&GNR bill was on its way over, he sprang to his feet and moved first reading.

Richard Scott (the opposition leader) was incredulous. "I think it is scarcely fair that we are called upon to consider a bill of this important character without possession of the bill itself. There is only in this Chamber now a single copy of this bill, and the bill has been changed materially since it was introduced this morning. It has been changed so often that it is quite impossible to understand its provisions and I do not think it is fair for us to take up a measure of this character without having an opportunity of reading it. I tried to get it. I went half a dozen times to the distribution office to ask if they had a copy of it. They said they had not. I said, 'I believe there are copies of it in existence because I was told a certain gentleman had a copy of it.' Then I made them telephone the printing office, and they said 'no, it had not been printed there.' Which I thought very extraordinary and concluded it must have been printed elsewhere."

"It does not matter where it was printed," Bowell said sharply.

"Except that I would have got a copy of it!" Scott snapped. "In all my experience in Parliament, I never knew of an instance of this kind, where a bill of such importance was held back until the very last day and brought on at the eleventh hour to be run through the Senate when it is very well known that the people outside are very much excited over this matter. A very large public opinion is that it is not proper legislation at all; that the only object in building it is to earn the government subsidy. There could not be any other reason for it."

Bowell tried to stop Scott there. "If the honourable gentleman would not consider it an impertinence on my part to interrupt him — I do not desire to be impertinent — I would remind him that he is talking now on matters not contained in the bill at all."

"I beg pardon, I am," Scott replied.

"No," Bowell pointed out, his frustration rising, "you are discussing a question of changing the route and giving the company an opportunity of building it. That has all been eliminated by the Speaker in the Commons on account of it being considered part of a private bill."

"I will read the bill if you will let me have it," Scott enjoined.

"Yes, and then you will save yourself all the trouble of talking." Bowell's patience was shot: the assistant adjutant-general and the quarter-master general had just taken up position at the front doors of the chamber, ready to escort Aberdeen into the chamber to begin the prorogation ceremony.

Scott was also aware of the time — and Bowell's position — and continued the filibuster. "No member of Parliament can point to a case in which the government have dared to so insult the representatives of the people as to submit such a measure at the eleventh hour. Is the Senate to be asked to pass a bill of this nature, coming up forty-five minutes before His Excellency is expected to appear to prorogue the House, and to pass it without recording a vote, without having a copy of the bill before us, without understanding the amendments made to it elsewhere, without being in a position to look at the amendments or to modify the great evil that is likely to ensue?"

The speaker prompted Scott to get back on track.

"All right. The foundation of the bill goes back to last November when the correspondence that ought to have been on the table this morning would have shown that the government had been preparing to assist the contractors. And we know, as a matter of fact, that on the fifth of March last, the government proposed to hand over from the exchequer of this country $2,500,000 as a loan to a company that had no assets."

Bowell rose on a point of order. "I call the attention of the Speaker to the fact that the honourable gentleman is discussing everything but the provisions in this bill."

Scott turned to Bowell. "Is it not a fact that the government were going to lend this company $2,500,000, and because public opinion was so pronounced, they did not dare to do it? At the time they proposed to give $2,500,000 they intended to have a general election. Some people are wicked enough to say — of course, I would not join in that — that the government had an interest in it — that they were to share the spoil with the promoters."

Bowell was indignant. "I call the honourable gentleman to order! He ought not to have the audacity and impudence to accuse the government of taking part in a swindle!"

The usually unflappable Frank Smith got his dander up at this point. "The government is not made of that material that the honourable gentleman insinuates, he had better take care!" Smith threatened, wagging his finger at Scott for good measure.

The debate continued, Scott arguing against provisions of the bill that Bowell assured had been excised in the Commons. Eventually, Lawrence Power (Liberal, Nova Scotia) jumped in.

"Mr. Speaker, the country has had some experience of this railway company. The Government of Manitoba advanced this company, in the way of subsidy, something like $240,000 and this company, who must have got a very considerable sum of money out of the bonds which they disposed of, got nearly a quarter a million from the Manitoba government, for which they have given nothing in return …"

As Power launched in, Bowell walked over to the Speaker's dais, where Caron, Daly, Haggart, Foster, Ouimet, and Tupper had come to watch the proceedings. Daly told Bowell the Governor General's bodyguard had just reached the front doors and the Dragoons had been dispatched to fetch Aberdeen. Bowell was fretting and pacing back and forth behind the dais. Foster told him he had to cancel the prorogation ceremony if he wanted the bill passed. Bowell paced some more and then told Foster to send a messenger to Aberdeen telling him the ceremony would be put off until Monday. Bowell returned to his seat as Power was finishing.

"… the disposition of this money is a very mysterious matter indeed. No one appears to be able to tell what has come of the immense sum which these people received. They did not use the money for the purpose of paying the men who did the work on the road, or the men who supplied the material. What did they do with it?"

Bowell asked the Speaker if he would permit a short statement.

"Mr. Speaker, we have decided, on the part of the government, more particularly after insinuations of the character that were thrown out with reference to the members of the government being interested in this scheme, to advise His Excellency not to prorogue Parliament until this bill is either defeated or carried."

Scott held up his hands. "The honourable First Minister is wrong when he says that I insinuated that the government had any interest in this bill. What I said was that at the time the order in council was passed, there were rumours outside that this bill was being passed to enable friends of the government to make contributions to elections, but I said I did not believe them. I simply quoted a newspaper report. I did not endorse it. I never for one moment insinuated, in the slightest degree, that the government had any interest in the scheme."

The house broke for dinner at that point and everyone, despite the heat, took a breath and cooled off. When the session resumed, Bowell rose on a point of privilege.

> I desire, after reflection, to apologize, and I do it most sincerely, to the members of the Senate as well as to His Honour the Speaker, for the little ebullition of temper exhibited by myself today. I have no objections whatever to any public man attacking my political career, whether it be right or wrong. I occupy a public position, and am subject to that, and have no right to find fault; but when anyone makes an assertion which I think is a reflection upon my personal character and my reputation for straightforward honesty, whether in my public or my private life, I must confess that I cannot refrain from resenting it in language which, perhaps, is heated and out of harmony with the dignity of this House. On reflection, I deem it my duty to yourself, Mr. Speaker, and to my fellow Senators to make this explanation and to apologize for having used language which, under the circumstances, would have been unjustifiable.

"I am sorry if any language of mine led the Premier into the position for which he now expresses regret," Scott replied. "I can bear testimony to his suavity of manner and courtesy, and I have known him a great many years. I did not think of reflecting on him or the government. Perhaps I should not have mentioned the rumour. I am sorry if I offended anybody. Had I known that the statement would have created any ill-feeling I should not have referred to it. The Premier can feel assured that I had not the slightest intention of reflecting on him personally or on the members of the government."

After Bowell and Scott made up, the debate continued until the session adjourned at 10:00 p.m. It resumed on Monday, when the W&GNR bill, along with the LMR, were passed just before the Governor General entered the chamber for an abbreviated prorogation ceremony. "In bringing this Session of Parliament to a conclusion," Aberdeen said, "I have to congratulate you on the industry and zeal which have marked your labours. The reply of the Provincial Legislature of Manitoba to the Remedial Order issued by my Government on the twenty-first of March last was considered of such a character as to justify postponement of further action until next Session."

Aberdeen moved on to sign the bills passed that session, including the LMR and W&GNR legislation, and then Speaker Ross closed the proceedings. "It is His Excellency the Governor General's will and pleasure that this Parliament be prorogued until Monday, January 6, 1896."

6

Friendly Negotiations

Tour

Without a railroad, Prime Minister Mackenzie Bowell and Canada's Sixth Ministry had no leverage to get Greenway and Clifton to the bargaining table on the Manitoba schools question. And so, once again, a Dominion prime minister was reduced to high hopes and moral suasion, a position Bowell admitted in a memo penned to the Greenway government on July 27. As Thompson had in the one he had sent the year before, Bowell reminded Manitoba that the Dominion had "complete jurisdiction in the premises," but said it should feel no obligation to "follow the exact lines" of the March remedial order. Bowell's preference was to "ascertain by friendly negotiations what amendments to the Acts respecting education in public schools in the direction of the main wishes of the minority may be expected from the Manitoba Legislature." The prime minister "hoped that a middle course will commend itself to the local authorities, so that Federal action may become unnecessary."

Bowell took on responsibility for conducting the "friendly negotiations" himself as part of a tour of western Canadian reserves and residential schools he'd already planned to take that summer with Thomas Daly, the interior minister in charge of Indian affairs; Hayter Reed, Daly's deputy at Indian affairs; John Payne (Bowell's private secretary); and John Carleton (Bowell's messenger). This group left Ottawa on Friday, July 27, with the Aberdeens, who were setting out on their own cross-country tour that summer.

First stop was Winnipeg on Sunday, July 29, where the Aberdeens met with Premier Greenway and Provincial Secretary John Cameron. Aberdeen asked if anything had changed on the schools question since they'd met in Ottawa back in May. Greenway told him "the whole province is set against any concession." Lady Aberdeen said the conversation went downhill from there. She commented to her diary that "even the suggestion of exempting RCs from the School Tax was scouted as impossible." Meeting up later in the evening, Aberdeen told Bowell he wasn't hopeful about a compromise on the schools question. Bowell admitted that he too had "but little hope."

With "friendly negotiations" off the table for the moment, Bowell carried on to Regina the next morning with the Aberdeens. There, the Governor General was set to open the first Northwest Territorial Exhibition. The entourage was met at the fairgrounds Tuesday afternoon by a "splendid corps" of Northwest Mounted Police and troupes of Cree and Blackfoot. Bowell spoke briefly after Aberdeen, telling the crowd he'd made many visits to the Northwest[11] but had "never seen brighter prospects for a bountiful harvest nor more encouraging evidences of substantial progress." He closed with a common stump speech refrain of his: "I only hope that my own experience as an immigrant from England and the son of a lowly carpenter might encourage you in the belief that the highest position in the land is within your reach."

Pacific Coast

Bowell and his party left the Aberdeens at Regina on August 1 and arrived in Vancouver on the third. There, they boarded the Dominion steamer *Quadra* for a twelve-day tour of eleven west coast Indigenous communities and four residential schools: Cape Mudge (We Wai Kai First Nation) on the southern tip of Quadra Island (August 5); Alert Bay (Kwakwaka'wakw First Nation)

Friendly Negotiations

on Cormorant Island and St. Michael's Residential School (August 6); Fort Rupert (Kwakwaka'wakw First Nation) on the northern end of Vancouver Island (August 7); Port Essington at the mouth of the Skeena River (August 8); the village of Metlakatla (Tsimshian First Nation) and the Metlakatla Residential School (August 9); Port Simpson (Tsimshian First Nation) and the Crosby Home for Girls and Crosby Boys' Home[12] (August 10, morning); the village of Gingolx at the mouth of the Nass River (August 10, afternoon); Low Inlet (Tsimshian First Nation, August 11); the village of Nawitti, Hope Island, and Nanaimo (August 12–14); and Kuper Island (Penelakut First Nation) and the Kuper Island Residential School[13] (August 15).

The residential school visits typically included presentations by Indigenous students. At Kuper Island, one student referred to as "James" presented Bowell with a letter to demonstrate his penmanship and composition. He assured Bowell: "We will answer to the views of the Indian department, try to improve ourselves now, and later on spread the advantages of a Christian education amongst our parents and friends at home." Bowell congratulated "James" on the letter and told the class, "There is no position in the land to which with education the Indians may not aspire."

The *Quadra* arrived back in Victoria on August 16 and five days later the group departed for Calgary, stopping for a night at Coldstream Ranch, the Aberdeen's summer retreat near Vernon. Bowell said it was "beautiful valley land" that would one day "be a great fruit country."

PM on the Prairies

Bowell's first stop in Calgary was William Roper Hull's 4,250-acre ranch just south of Midnapore to see the recently installed irrigation system. It was said to be a marvel of modern engineering, with over five miles of ditch work, one of which cut eighteen feet into the ground. The height of the oat crop aided by the irrigation — over six feet — impressed everyone. At some point, Bowell took a short walk into the field until "he could not be seen from the outside." He was gone long enough for Payne and the others to become "afraid they had lost him."

At a private dinner hosted by Calgary Conservatives that evening, Bowell told a local reporter that he thought the kind of non-partisan "round table conference" idea then being advocated by former British prime minister William Gladstone to resolve the Home Rule situation might be useful in resolving the Manitoba schools issue. Asked about the idea when the story reached Winnipeg on August 28, Premier Greenway said he had no objection to talking with Bowell about such a plan. "There can be no possible objection to hearing what Mr. Bowell has to say on the subject. If he wants to talk it over we shall be glad to hear of his intentions." Greenway made it clear, though, that the only way Manitoba would consider a proposal from Bowell or his government would be as a formal proposition laid before the Manitoba legislature.

On Sunday morning, August 26, Bowell left Calgary for Edmonton. Two-thirds of the way there, the train stopped at Ermineskin Reserve, where a large crowd of Cree people had gathered to welcome the prime minister. A local Chief greeted Bowell. He held his right hand skyward, pressed it to his

On the car *Ottawa*, bound for Edmonton. Left to right: two unknown individuals, Thomas Daly, Margaret Daly, Mackenzie Bowell, unknown, Hayter Reed.

heart, and then to the ground. The interpreter said it meant the "Almighty witnessed his devotion to country, to the Government, and to the man before him." The local Indian agent then proceeded to give the group a wagon tour of the reserve, followed the entire way by "a great band of horsemen who rode with dash and reckless daring."

Early on August 27, Bowell and company travelled north to St. Albert, where Father Hippolyte Leduc had organized a reception at the industrial school. Over one hundred and fifty students "thronged the hall" and delivered several speeches and recitations. Bowell told those assembled that when Daly had told him about a trip he'd made to the Northwest a year before, he (Bowell) was "slow to believe all." When Daly proceeded to ask for additional moneys for his Department of Indian Affairs and the industrial and boarding schools, Bowell said he thought Daly was "overzealous, was extravagant, and in short was wasting the public money." He said, "But now when I see your beautiful Industrial school, men and women devoting their lives to the purpose of civilizing, Christianizing and educating the wild men of this country from the hunter and the fisherman into a state equal to our own, as self-reliant, self-supporting, and law abiding citizens of Canada, then I feel that I would be willing to expend twice or thrice the sums now spent in such a great cause."

The group reached NWMP "G" Division headquarters at Fort Saskatchewan (22 miles northeast of Edmonton) on August 28, where it was set to begin the next leg of the journey — an eight-day, 350-mile overland journey to Battleford via buckboard and democrat. Meeting them at Fort Saskatchewan for this part of the journey were Amédée-Emmanuel Forget (Indian commissioner for Manitoba, Keewatin, and the NWT), NWMP Commissioner Lawrence Herchmer, NWMP Comptroller Frederick White, and Joseph Nelson, engineer-promoter for the then-proposed Hudson's Bay and Pacific Railway. After lunch at the home of "G" Division Commanding Officer Inspector Arthur Griesbach, the tour got underway, Griesbach leading the group himself.

On the open prairie, Payne said the prime minister's party averaged about fifty miles a day. Most days began with striking camp between 5:30 and 6:00 a.m. and then, after a quick cup of beef tea, "running off ten or

The Hon. Mackenzie Bowell (fourth from left) at Fort Saskatchewan, August 28, 1895. Left to right on the porch: future Lieutenant Governor Amédée-Emmanuel Forget, Hudson's Bay Railway promoter Joseph Nelson, Mackenzie Bowell, Arthur Griesbach, Emma Griesbach, future brigadier general William Griesbach, Thomas Mayne Daly. Below: Edith Griesbach and Hayter Reed.

fifteen miles before breakfast." "Nothing finer," Payne said, "than rolling along over the smooth roads by moonlight early in the morning." In the evening, the Mounties pitched camp and "within twenty minutes of time the horses were unhitched, picketed for the night, tents pitched and the meal underway." Soon after, the call of "dinner" drew the hungry travellers to the eating tent. *Après* dinner was usually spent around the campfire "for a half hour's smoke and chat." By nine, everyone was bedded down for the night. Payne said Bowell was "always one of the first up and one of the last to bed. He enjoyed the trip very much and became decidedly brown from exposure."

The wagon train reached Saddle Lake Reserve (80 miles north-north-east of Fort Saskatchewan) on August 29. That evening around the campfire, local Cree Chief Pakan told Bowell and his party the story of his role in preventing the outbreak of an Indian war during the Northwest Rebellion. When he

Friendly Negotiations

The Mann family, Onion Lake. Standing, left to right: George Mann, six unknown individuals, Joseph Nelson. Seated, middle row, left to right: unknown Mann child, Mackenzie Bowell, unknown Mann child, Thomas Daly, Sara Mann. Seated, front row: unknown Mann children.

finished, Bowell thanked Pakan for his actions, shook his hand, and presented Pakan with a gift of tobacco. Stories from the Rebellion continued the next day at Frog Lake, the site of the infamous massacre, and again at Onion Lake on September 1, where Bowell and company spent a couple of days with Indian Agent George Mann and his family. At dinner the first night, Mrs. Mann regaled the group by describing her family's "thrilling experience" of being held hostage for two and a half months by Wandering Spirit and his group of Cree warriors following the massacre at Frog Lake.

On Wednesday the fourth, Bowell and company reached Battleford, where they were the guests of honour at a ball hosted by the local Conservative association. It was there that Bowell met Geraldine Moodie, the prairies' first female professional photographer. He must have been impressed because he granted Moodie a commission to photograph Northwest Rebellion sites on the spot.

Believed to be Prime Minister Sir Mackenzie Bowell in discussion with two other individuals at either Onion Lake or Battleford during his tour of the districts between Edmonton, Battleford, and Prince Albert.

On Thursday morning (September 5), the group inspected the Battleford Industrial School where the old printer's devil was delighted to find some of the 135 students there "setting up and distributing some type and displaying a thorough knowledge of all the details of a printing office." As a gift, the "print shop boys" presented Bowell with copies of Canada's national anthem that they had printed in Cree. After a day in Prince Albert, the group spent Sunday touring more Rebellion sites around Duck Lake and Batoche where "some of the old warriors were spoken to and one of them took the trouble to explain all about the Batoche encounter." One of these was Joe McKay, who claimed to have fired the first shot in the Rebellion while under the command of Major Leif Crozier at Duck Lake.

After a stop in Prince Albert on September 7 — "the first occasion on which the prime minister of the Dominion has visited our country," declared the *Prince Albert Times* — Bowell and his companions inspected Duck Lake Residential School[14] on September 9 and were back in Regina on

Friendly Negotiations

"Gentleman" Joe McKay telling the Bowell party about firing the first shot at the Battle of Duck Lake, 1885.

the tenth for an official state dinner hosted by Lieutenant Governor Charles Mackintosh. En route back to Winnipeg on the eleventh, Bowell and Daly stopped to address Brandon city council. Bowell said his visit to the reserves and schools was "a revelation," and he could "return to Ottawa entertaining a very different impression of the Indians and their requirements, and their importance from that which he had previously had."

Exclusive

After stops at the Moosomin and Elkhorn (Washakada) residential schools, Bowell's train reached Portage la Prairie on Thursday morning, September 12, where two local reporters (James Lawlor from the *Daily Nor'Wester* and R.J. Burd from the *Winnipeg Daily Tribune*) joined Bowell for an exclusive interview:

"How are the Indians progressing?" Burd asked.

"I wish that you could see them," Bowell said. "The rapid progress which the Indian is making has to be seen to be believed. They have some good crops of grain at most points, but their great advance has been in cattle raising. At Onion Lake reserve the Indians have over 1,300 head of cattle, at Red Deer 700 head and so on at the other reserves. Stock raising is one of the industries in which the Indian excels and in this way we hope to soon have all bands on a firm basis of self-support."

"What civilizing influences are at work among them?"

"There are the missionaries of the various denominations and the Indian Industrial schools. These schools are conducted by the churches assisted by the government. There is Bishop Ridley at Metlakatla, and other Church of England missionaries, then Rev. Mr. Crosby at Fort Simpson and other Methodist missionaries. Then the Presbyterians, Roman Catholics, and others have excellent missions."[15]

"How did you find the Industrial schools?"

"The Industrial schools are a marvel. The children are very apt. The schools are well kept, clean and the discipline and teaching are excellent."

"Is English spoken at all?"

"Yes, English is spoken more or less at each mission, and in the schools, both boarding and day schools, English is the only language used."

"What are the principal industries in which the Indians are engaged?"

"Fishing, hunting and working in the seasons for the people lower down the coast. There are only a few horses in that northern region, and practically as yet no agriculture. They are great canoe-men, and their dug-out canoes, 40 and 50 feet long, are very creditable specimens of naval architecture."

"In your trip by buggy from Edmonton to Prince Albert how did you lodge at night?"

"Camped out every night for ten nights."

"And how did you enjoy it?"

"Delightful. It could not have been better. We drove between 50 and 60 miles per day and camped at night. We had only one bad night on the whole trip."

Friendly Negotiations

"You saw a great deal of the mounted police on this trip. How did you find the service?"

"They are as fine a body of men as are to be found anywhere and what they have done to maintain peace and order and to establish law on a firm basis is incalculable."

"What do you think, then, of the future of all this northern country?"

"It is past thinking. I have been more than ever assured of the greatness into which the whole Northwest is rapidly developing. This country has a grand future before it."

Last Stop: Winnipeg

Bowell's train pulled into Winnipeg late Thursday morning, September 12, and was set to leave for Ottawa on Saturday after tours of the Saint Paul's, Saint Boniface, and Rupert's Land industrial schools. No "friendly negotiations" with the Manitoba government were scheduled (Greenway had made that clear on September 8) and none took place. Bowell, however, did bump into Greenway at the Manitoba Hotel Friday evening. The premier, along with Provincial Secretary John Cameron, had dropped by to say hello to newly installed Lieutenant Governor James Patterson. While there, Bowell also popped in to say hello. R.J. Burd reported that "the two premiers shook hands and engaged in general conversation for a short time [but] the school question was not broached." Shortly after, "all withdrew without a word having been said on this subject." Next morning at Union Station, James Lawlor asked Bowell if he'd spoken with Greenway about the schools issue while in town. "No," the prime minister said as he boarded the train, "not a word."

Backlogged

After seven weeks away, a mountain of paperwork was waiting for Bowell when he got back to Ottawa, including a batch of unfilled vacancies. The most important of these were Angers's spot in cabinet; three seats in the House of Commons; sixteen seats in the Senate; one seat on the Supreme Court; six deputy minister appointments; customs collectors in Montreal, Sherbrooke, and Winnipeg; and a post office inspector in Montreal. Three more Commons seats opened in early October. John Curran's Montreal Centre riding opened when Bowell appointed him to the Quebec Superior Court in fulfillment of promises made by Macdonald and Thompson. Cardwell, the Ontario riding, became vacant when Bowell appointed Robert White as Montreal customs collector. And Jacques Cartier became vacant when cabinet appointed Désiré Girouard to the Supreme Court.

Of all the vacancies, Angers's cabinet spot was the most critical and the most difficult to fill. After resigning in July, Angers had issued a mandament against anyone who would accept the position without Parliament's first passing remedial legislation regarding the Manitoba schools question. Bowell first tried to lure Joseph-Adolphe Chapleau, the Lieutenant Governor of Quebec, back to Ottawa. Chapleau had left the Dominion cabinet in 1892 after falling out with Prime Minister Thompson over the latter's decision to send the Manitoba schools decision to the courts rather than legislating the restoration of denominational school rights. After three years, Chapleau was reluctant to return to a cabinet — and an issue — that had barely changed. He told Caron and Ouimet the only way he'd return to Ottawa was if Bowell retired and Ontario Protestants like Haggart, Montague, and Clarke Wallace pledged fealty to passing remedial legislation immediately that fall. Bowell couldn't meet Chapleau's terms and moved on to other candidates by the end of October.

By November, Bowell's inability to fill the vacancies in general — Angers's in particular — became a lightning rod for frustration around the cabinet table. In a November 1 letter to Sir Charles Tupper, Arthur Dickey (by now militia and defence minister) wrote that the task of governing the country was "too heavy" for Bowell. "He does his best and is not afraid of work but in every direction, public affairs show the want of a firm hand at the helm." Dickey judged that the issue of succession was also now in jeopardy, with "the prime minister's personal feelings" preventing star candidates like Chapleau, Quebec Provincial Secretary Pelletier, Sir John A.'s

Friendly Negotiations

son Hugh John, and former Ontario Conservative leader and current chief justice William Meredith from running in the coming election. "Gradually but surely the public is losing confidence in the government … If we were to go now to the country, we would I believe be hopelessly beaten, not by reason of our opponents' strength but of our own weaknesses."

Frustration boiled over at a November 4 cabinet meeting; the first full cabinet meeting convened since the beginning of October. William Ives, minister of trade and commerce, lit into Bowell about appointing Curran, a Catholic, to the Quebec Superior Court. He said Montreal owed its commercial welfare to the province's English-speaking Protestant minority and any spot on a Montreal bench should have been filled by an English-speaking Protestant lawyer. Only such a lawyer, by virtue of his training and commercial practice, would have the competence to hear commercial cases brought before him. Ives warned Bowell that the appointment of an Irish Roman Catholic would be seen not only as an unjust infringement of the minority's rights but would seriously prejudice the government's interests in Montreal and other parts of the province. As evidence, Ives held up a petition signed by English-speaking Protestant business leaders demanding an English-speaking Protestant appointment.

Bowell defended himself by asking Ives why the English-speaking Protestant minority, which he spoke so highly of, hadn't bothered to put a name forward for the appointment. The French-speaking bar had forwarded a long list of names of highly qualified lawyers for the position. Given the circumstances, Bowell thought it better to at least have an English-speaking judge on the bench, wouldn't Ives agree? And given the promises two prime ministers had made to the solicitor general, Curran was a qualified candidate. Ives told Bowell the government shouldn't try and redeem old promises at the expense of Quebec's English-speaking Protestant minority. If it helped, Bowell said, he'd pledge there and then to fill both the solicitor general and Montreal customs collector positions with English-speaking Protestants to ensure the minority's interests were fairly represented. Ives didn't think that was a fair price to offset the loss of a judgeship. Bowell told him the positions were important and both had been previously held by Irish Roman Catholics. And so, yes, he did judge it a fair price.

While on the topic of appointments, Ouimet said he was miffed with Bowell's choice of Robert White — an English-speaking Protestant from Ontario — for Montreal customs collector. As the party official responsible for Montreal, Ouimet said it was his responsibility and his alone to dispense patronage in his district.

Ives then took a shot at Ouimet. He told him the less he had to do with Montreal the better. English speakers would have nothing to do with him and Ouimet would do well to stop meddling in Montreal affairs — especially the upcoming by-election in Montreal Centre. Ives then stomped out of the room and didn't return.

To this point, Haggart had kept to himself. But after Ives stormed out, Haggart asked Bowell if he still intended to call Parliament back in January as no official announcement had yet been made. Bowell said January 2 was the date and an announcement would be made shortly. Haggart asked if Bowell intended to introduce remedial legislation during the session. Bowell said it was his constitutional duty to see the policy through just as the Governor General had publicly committed to do in the Throne Speech. Haggart said if Bowell proceeded down that road he'd resign — and take Dickey, Montague, Clarke Wallace, and Wood with him. Bowell shot back, "If you do, I will call in Mr. Laurier."

The threats, on both sides, were hollow. A ministry could not be brought down because one minister — or a group — withdrew their confidence in a prime minister. Only Parliament had that prerogative. And the Crown might ask for an outgoing prime minister's advice on succession, but the Crown had no constitutional duty to abide by it.

Reckoning

It took Bowell two more weeks to get the ball rolling on the Commons vacancies. On November 17, cabinet confirmed the dates for the Ontario North and Cardwell by-elections (December 12 and 24, respectively). The Quebec races were proving more difficult. Everyone assumed Jacques Cartier was the most promising riding to showcase Conservative Party strength and electoral support for Manitoba schools remedial legislation, but Ouimet couldn't lure any candidates there and was having similar trouble in Montreal Centre. Bowell replaced Ouimet with Caron as chief wire-puller, but it took another two weeks, and pressure from the archbishops, to get the party's preferred candidates to throw their hats in the rings. December 27 was finally settled on for the Montreal Centre contest and December 30 for Jacques Cartier.

During this time, Bowell continued to struggle with finding a replacement for Angers. On November 25, he offered the spot to Louis-Philippe Pelletier, provincial secretary to Conservative Quebec premier Louis-Olivier Taillon. But to no avail; Pelletier told Bowell his long-term plans were to remain in Quebec. Angers's mandament was still proving effective.

On the Manitoba schools file, Bowell tried to gain some traction by naming Senator Thomas-Alfred Bernier (Saint-Boniface), MP Alphonse La Rivière (Provencher), and lawyer John Ewart to an ad hoc committee to advise on negotiations with Manitoba generally and the content of remedial legislation specifically. Despite being based on Ewart's March recommendations, the draft bill was still far from ready to submit to Parliament. Charlie Tupper warned Ewart on November 11 that cabinet troubles and the tight timeline before Parliament met in January would mean that the Roman Catholic minority would have to "carefully consider any compromise before insisting on the full enactment from us as all may then be lost." Tupper advised Archbishop Langevin at Saint-Boniface similarly, telling him he had to keep focused on "the essential elements of equality and justice" and pursuing anything other than compromise would mean "defeat in Parliament and afterwards in the country leav[ing] the minority without any redress, and our constitution dishonoured and ignored."

And then, on November 18, Greenway sent his long-awaited compromise proposal to Ottawa. The premier said his government would make every effort to ensure the provincial public school system was completely non-sectarian by removing "any tinge of Protestantism that may have worked into the system." In addition, priests would be allowed into the schools after 3:00 p.m. to "give any religious teachings to the children that they see fit." Ewart judged the offer a non-starter. Langevin agreed.

On December 2, the archbishop said Greenway's proposal would leave the Roman Catholic minority "entirely to the good will of our Protestant friends of the majority." As such, "we cannot even entertain the idea of adopting such a poor scheme."[16]

The impasse had repercussions. A few weeks later, Clarke Wallace asked Bowell if he intended to pursue remedial legislation now that Manitoba had once again refused to abide by the March remedial order. Bowell said it was his duty to do so and if Clarke Wallace remained in the ministry, he had a responsibility to support the policy as well. Clarke Wallace said he couldn't in all good conscience do that and Bowell told him the only honourable course left to him was to resign. And so, on Thursday, December 12, Clarke Wallace resigned: "It had been my hope that the Provincial Government of Manitoba would deal with this question in a way to remove it from the arena of Federal politics, to which it does not at all belong. But that hope being disappointed, no other course consistent with my opinions and what I conceive to be my duty was open to me."

For Bowell, things continued downhill from there. On the day Clarke Wallace resigned, results came in from the Ontario North by-election: the Conservative candidate there won handily, but he refused to pledge his support to the government's remedial policy. News reached Ottawa a few days later that British Columbia's six Conservatives were set to bolt on the government's remedial policy as well. In a panic, Bowell wired Lieutenant Governor (and long-time cabinet colleague) Edward Dewdney, asking him to "Kindly ascertain from Prior" — the nominal head of the B.C. caucus — "if he will accept a controllership with a seat in the cabinet. This would give British Columbia [its first] voice in the council." But Prior wouldn't be easily bought. He told a Conservative Party gathering that British Colombia was "thoroughly entitled to a seat in the cabinet" and would not accept a mere controllership. "If Sir Mackenzie Bowell made a mistake, and does not mean a seat in the cabinet, I shall tell him that he can't get E.G. Prior to represent British Columbia in that way." Dewdney wired Prior's reaction back to Ottawa and then on the seventeenth Bowell wired Prior, "Governor Dewdney wires me there is a misunderstanding as to your status in the Government. You are Controller of Inland Revenue, Privy Councillor, and a member of Cabinet, and have just as much voice in affairs of the Dominion as I have. I would have offered you nothing less."

Prior's appointment quelled the caucus revolt, but it was a messy fix. The controllers were cabinet-appointed undersecretaries reporting to the minister of trade and commerce. Neither the prime minister nor the Governor General could alter the terms of appointment or the reporting relationship without amending the governing legislation. More significantly, inviting the controllers to sit at the cabinet table was functionally untenable: the controllers would have the same vote as the individuals who appointed them, one of whom would be their boss. An editorial in the *Globe* put it like this: "A controller cannot be a cabinet minister, because there are not two classes of cabinet ministers, one inferior to the other, liable to be dismissed from office by the other, and in receipt of less salary than the other."

Bowell's troubles continued up to and through the holidays. On December 21, the Greenway government issued its formal response to the Dominion's July 27 order, declaring that "so far as the Government of Manitoba is concerned, the proposal to establish a system of Separate Schools, in any form, is positively and definitely rejected." After this, Greenway had the legislature dissolved and writs dropped for a snap election on January 15 that would focus on "the menacing attitude assumed by the Dominion Government with reference to the educational legislation of the province."

Trouble continued with cabinet's inability to deal with *Shortis*, an important criminal case. In March 1895, Valentine Shortis had shot and killed two men, and seriously injured a third, during a robbery in Valleyfield, Quebec. At trial in October, Shortis's lawyers pleaded insanity. In November, the jury rendered a guilty verdict and sentenced Shortis to be hanged on January 3, 1896. Valentine's mother, Francis, initiated a request for royal clemency, a power the Governor General has to commute a death sentence on the advice of cabinet. Lady Aberdeen had already suggested her husband would be sympathetic to such a plea. Just after the verdict was delivered in November, Francis met with Charlie Tupper to formally lodge the clemency request. Lady Aberdeen followed up with Tupper on December 3, pleading with him to "recommend that the sentence be commuted to life imprisonment." Tupper took the issue to cabinet on December 24. The justice minister argued the law should stand in this case as politicians had no right to interfere in the normal course of justice, particularly in important cases like murder. Caron and Ouimet agreed, saying a decision to commute the verdict would hurt the already too-close-to-call upcoming election contest. Besides, if the Dominion couldn't find a way to commute Riel's sentence on the grounds of insanity, it had no business doing so on a lesser case like Shortis's.

On cases like these in the past, cabinet had typically sided with the justice minister's recommendation. But late on December 24, the results from Cardwell came in: the Conservative candidate had lost to William Stubbs, a member of McCarthy's Equal Rights Association and a strong opponent of remedial legislation. With the Montreal-Centre by-election on December 27 shaping up to be a cliff-hanger, the Cardwell results spooked cabinet, and for the next two days it stood hung on *Shortis*. By the time the news of a Conservative loss in Montreal Centre came in on the twenty-seventh, cabinet was still stuck.

Cabinet met again on Tuesday, December 31, to finalize the text of the Throne Speech and to try again to settle *Shortis*. It succeeded on the former but failed on the latter. At the end of the meeting, Haggart asked Bowell if he'd been able to find a replacement for Angers. Bowell assured Haggart a replacement was close at hand. Haggart asked who, given that Senator Masson had just turned Bowell down on the grounds of poor health. Bowell said he, Ouimet, and Caron were in fact meeting with Senator Alphonse Desjardins at his house that very evening. Haggart reminded Bowell of his commitment to have in place a "strong and complete government" before Parliament resumed.

Desjardins returned to Montreal that evening. He wired Bowell the next day to say that he couldn't accept the offer.

Session Open

On Thursday afternoon, January 2, Governor General Aberdeen arrived on Parliament Hill to open the Sixth Session of Canada's Seventh Parliament. Lady Aberdeen was seated next to her husband at the front of the Senate

Friendly Negotiations

chamber, resplendent in a royal-blue velvet dress replete with a court train and a skirt of gold-embroidered white silk. Her headdress was made of white feathers, from which a court veil fell. The *pièce de résistance* was a stunning diamond necklace. With the Aberdeens on the floor of the chamber were Mackenzie Bowell, Frank Smith, and Adolphe Caron in their Windsor formals. The galleries were packed, as was the floor of the Senate, where a couple of dozen women — mostly legislators' wives — were seated amid other dignitaries in formal evening dress.

It took almost twenty minutes for the chamber to settle down. When it did, Senate Speaker John Ross told René Kimber, the Gentleman Usher of the Black Rod, that it was "his Excellency's pleasure" that the members of the Commons "attend him immediately in this House." Kimber gathered up his mace, walked to the main doors, bowed, and proceeded across the lobby to the Commons to lead the members there, piper-like, back to the Senate behind Commons Speaker Peter White. There followed the usual scramble for seats. Eventually Speaker White took up his position behind the bar, the signal for the Governor General to begin his address.

Aberdeen opened his ornate folder and read in a steady, strong voice.

> Honourable Gentlemen of the Senate; Gentlemen of the House of Commons. In accordance with the announcement made during the last Session, Parliament has been summoned somewhat in advance of the usual period.
>
> I congratulate you upon the evidence of increased activity in the various branches of commerce and industry. Several such indications have come under my personal observation during a tour made recently in the North-west Territories and British Columbia. A special feature consisted in the opportunities obtained for visiting a number of the Indian Reservations and also the Indian Industrial Schools. On the former, I was received with hearty demonstrations of loyalty and good-will, while in connection with the latter the proofs of proficiency and intelligence on the part of the children were highly encouraging.

Gentlemen, immediately after the prorogation of Parliament, my Government communicated through the Lieutenant Governor of Manitoba, with the Government of that Province, in order to ascertain upon what lines the local authorities of Manitoba would be prepared to promote amendments to the acts respecting education in schools in that Province, and whether any arrangement was possible with the Manitoba Government which would render action by the Federal Parliament in this connection unnecessary. I regret to say that the advisers of the Lieutenant Governor have declined to entertain favourably these suggestions, thereby rendering it necessary for my Government in pursuance of its declared policy, to introduce legislation in regard to this subject. The papers will be laid before you this session.

Honourable Gentlemen of the Senate; Gentlemen of the House of Commons: I commend these subjects and others which may come before you to your earnest consideration, relying upon your wisdom and prudence under the Divine guidance to discharge with dignity and effect the high trust committed to your care.

I do declare this sixth session of Canada's Seventh Parliament to be open.

7

Coup

Cometh the Hour, Cometh the Ram

Arthur Dickey didn't just complain about Mackenzie Bowell in his November 1 letter to Sir Charles Tupper in London. He implored the high commissioner to "come out as first minister," refresh the Conservative ranks, and "form a powerful government that would sweep the country" with popular policies like preferential tariffs and a fast Atlantic steamship service.

It wasn't the first time Tupper had been asked to help the party out. In the 1887 general election, Prime Minister John Macdonald had recalled Tupper from his post in London to bolster the party's efforts in Nova Scotia against William Fielding and his resurgent secessionism. Tupper delivered fourteen of that province's twenty-one seats for the Tories. In the 1891 election, Macdonald deployed Tupper again, this time having him travel 3,722 miles across most of eastern Canada to help the Conservatives secure a fourth-straight electoral victory.

And Dickey wasn't the first Conservative to have asked Tupper to help since Bowell became prime minister in December 1894. Even in early January 1895, four senior party officials, including Tupper's long-time colleague and friend, Sir Donald Smith, pleaded with him in London to take over leadership of the party, telling him it was the only way the government could be saved from certain electoral defeat under Bowell. At the end of January, Charlie, the high commissioner's son, followed up via telegram: "Everyone outside of our weak Cabinet demands you as leader, and in our Cabinet the best men want you as well ... The country yearns for you, and you could not be in Canada a month before the party would rally to your standard in grand style. You need not go into hard campaigning. A speech in Halifax, St John, Montreal, and Toronto could be your contribution. The young men would do the rest ... we want a leader bold and ready. Think this over, and if you consider it favourably wire me fully." Another Tupper booster, customs controller John Wood, wrote Sir Charles during the March crisis, saying that he had "grave misgivings as to the way things were going" and "more than ever does the party now want you." And then a week after Dickey's November letter, Charlie wrote his father again, "It seems a downright shame to follow tamely an old man to the slaughter when if we were up and doing with a real leader we could march on to victory ... I verily believe if you could visit Canada on some excuse the party would run up and form under you."

Sir Charles, in fact, came up with two excuses — the fast Atlantic steamship service and the Pacific cable projects he'd been working to gain imperial government support for. (The fast steamship service proposed to cut trans-Atlantic crossing times from seven days to five, using state-of-the-art vessels. Sanford Fleming's Pacific cable project proposed to build a direct telegraph connection between Australia and Great Britain using the CPR's cross-continent telegraph line.) On November 14, Tupper wired Bowell to tell him British prime minister Chamberlain had agreed to provide an annual mail subsidy worth $75,000 to the fast steamship service and that the imperial government was "on the verge" of announcing support for the Pacific cable as well. "Shall I come out to consult you about these two matters?" Tupper asked Bowell. "Think could render you material assistance." Bowell cabled back on December 2, 1895: "Regarding fast line, come out to consult. Get all information possible."

News of Tupper's homecoming spread quickly. On December 5, Arnott Magurn asked Bowell if Tupper's return was related to a coming election.

Coup

Bowell told Magurn, "He is not coming with reference to the general elections, although he is a pretty good fighter."

Caballing

Back in Ottawa on December 16, Tupper's first order of business was to gauge in person the level of support he had for displacing Bowell. Within a day, Dickey, Haggart, Ives, Montague, Charlie Tupper, and Wood had pledged their fealty. So too did George Taylor, the government whip, who said the entire Ontario caucus was solidly behind him as well. Party leaders from Nova Scotia and New Brunswick assured Tupper their caucuses were similarly supportive.

Tupper's next task was to get George Foster on board. The finance minister had leadership aspirations of his own but was shrewd enough to see how far party fortunes had fallen since the 1891 election and how much Tupper could do to revive them. Tupper, on the other hand, was interested in being prime minister only long enough to secure his pet policies (i.e., the Atlantic fast steamship service, the Pacific cable, the Chignecto railway, etc.), win the election, and pass the reins on to his son. As he told Charlie a year earlier, "I would sacrifice the rest for which I long and go into the Senate as President of the Privy Council until these things were attained and you could succeed me." But Tupper also saw value in a healthy competition to produce a party leader and had faith Charlie could prove his mettle. It was thus easy for Tupper to commit to Foster that he'd resign as leader after winning the election and for Foster, in turn, to pledge his support in the interim.

The last thing Tupper had to accomplish would take more time and much more diplomacy: he had to get Bowell to resign and recommend to the Governor General that he — Tupper — succeed him. The party simply could not survive another fractious division and Tupper needed the currency of being a consensus-builder in the coming election. What Tupper and his cabalists needed was for Bowell to bend. And that is exactly what John Haggart and Walter Montague set out to achieve the day after Parliament opened on Thursday, January 2.

Haggart and Montague came to Bowell's East Block office Friday afternoon, January 3. Haggart said the time had come for Bowell to resign as he would not have Parliament's confidence on the remedial bill. After accounting for illnesses, absences, resignations, and by-election outcomes, Haggart said the government's majority in the Commons stood at forty-five. And whip George Taylor was reporting that forty Ontario Conservatives who'd signed his petition in July were still opposed to remediation. Ten had gone on the public record during the fall saying they'd vote against such a measure and the remaining thirty, pointing to the party's recent losses, were convinced they'd lose in the coming election if remediation were passed. That meant Parliament's confidence in Bowell now hung with the cabinet. Haggart said seven ministers were ready to side with the anti-remedialists to get Bowell to resign. Montague told Bowell it was time to think about the good of the party.

Bowell got his hackles up. He said he resented Haggart and Montague's trying to "put a pistol to his head" and told them it was his prerogative and his alone to decide if, when, and where to resign. Then he reached into his desk drawer and pulled out two handwritten letters. Before anything was done, Bowell said, Montague would have to explain the letters. Montague pleaded ignorance. Bowell read out the first one, which he said he'd received in December 1894. It charged Sir Adolphe Caron with having accepted a bribe worth $25,000 for a parliamentary charter for the Montreal Island Belt Line Railway. The second letter, which he'd received in November, made similar charges. Both were unsigned. Bowell said the letters had been examined by a renowned handwriting specialist in New York, who reported that there was no mistaking that Montague was the author. Bowell said it was an act of cowardice to impugn the reputation of a cabinet colleague like that. If Montague had any honour, Bowell said, he'd have come directly to him and made the charges in person: he'd have to bring the letters to the Governor General's attention and let him know that a serious charge had been made against an adviser to the Crown. Montague said he'd welcome the appeal and the opportunity to clear his good name.

When Haggart and Montague left, Bowell asked John Payne to fetch Adolphe Caron to his office. It is unclear whether Caron or Bowell or both of them together decided to leak the story to the press, but, either way, the *Ottawa Citizen* got a copy of the letters Friday evening in time to break the story in its Saturday morning edition.

Cabinet met again Friday afternoon to discuss *Shortis* in advance of Bowell's taking the matter to the Governor General that evening. Charlie Tupper said the Colonial Office confirmed that in the absence of cabinet advice the Governor General indeed had the authority to decide the matter according to his best judgment. No one spoke; Bowell could tell Aberdeen to decide as he wished. With *Shortis* settled, cabinet turned to the next agenda item, the status of the fast steamship service and Pacific cable initiatives. Foster asked for permission to invite the high commissioner into the chamber to provide the briefing. It was another shot across Bowell's bow.

Bowell visited Rideau Hall for a couple of hours Friday evening, mainly bringing Aberdeen up to date on *Shortis*. But then, during the meeting, a note for Aberdeen came in from Foster and Haggart saying they needed to see him "on matters most important." When Bowell left, the conspirators were invited up. They told Aberdeen that they and five of their colleagues — Tupper, Montague, Ives, Wood, and Dickey — no longer had confidence the prime minister could get the throne speech through Parliament. Aberdeen asked if there was anyone in which they did have confidence. Foster named Sir Charles Tupper. Aberdeen said he "could only accept the news of resignations through his prime minister."

Hackles

By breakfast Saturday morning, the "The War of Ministers" (the *Citizen*'s description of the Caron-Montague affair) was the talk of the town. The satisfaction Bowell felt reading the story, though, eventually gave way to the sober political reality described by Haggart and Montague the day before. Bowell called Charlie Tupper and Arthur Dickey to his office at ten thirty to discuss where things stood. Bowell told them he had always trusted them to speak their minds — even if he didn't like what he heard. Tupper said the time had come for Bowell to step down, for the good of the party. But he had to act quickly before the dissentients handed in their resignations. That would go a long way to preventing any further rupture in party ranks. Bowell said he'd think about it but wouldn't be pushed. After all, it was his prerogative and his alone to decide when and where to resign. Tupper said he didn't have much time; Haggart and the others were planning to meet later that morning in Foster's office.

At eleven thirty, Tupper and Bowell walked over to Centre Block to attend a meeting of the Railway Committee. Tupper asked Bowell if he'd made up his mind yet. Bowell told him he'd decided to resign and would issue a statement later in the day.

The Railway Committee hadn't met since July and the halls of Centre Block were packed with railroad managers, lawyers, bureaucrats, and lobbyists; they'd been waiting since eleven for the committee members to show up. By eleven forty-five, the chair, John Haggart, was still absent, so Bowell in his *ex officio* status got things under way. Daly sat beside him. Then, as the hearings began, Haggart showed up and took over.

Bowell couldn't stand it. He packed up his papers and stormed out. Daly rushed after him and pulled him aside down the corridor. Bowell asked him if he knew about the caballing. Daly said he did. Bowell said he wouldn't be threatened with a pistol to his head by the likes of John Haggart and Walter Montague and George Foster. Daly told him whatever he did he needed to do it with dignity and not on impulse. He needed to remember his long and distinguished record of service to the party and not to do anything that would call it into question.

As always, Daly was patient and waited for Bowell to cool off. Then he told Bowell even his supporters — Caron, Ouimet, Costigan, Smith, himself — thought it was time to reach out to Sir Charles and talk about what was best for the party. "Snib all personal feeling, be magnanimous for the party's sake, and do not leave undone anything which will or can be used against you hereafter," he wrote Bowell later in the day.

Bowell asked Daly to set up a meeting.

At 5:00 p.m., John Payne showed Sir Charles Tupper into Bowell's East Block office. The meeting started well enough. Tupper told Bowell he infinitely preferred retirement from public life to taking on leadership of the Conservative Party. Bowell said with all he'd been through lately he saw the value in that proposition. They also agreed the most important thing at that point was that the Conservative Party remain in control of public affairs. Tupper said he hoped to have the same cooperation from Bowell as he was prepared to give him. Bowell said it was the duty of every member of the party to do whatever might be necessary to advance its welfare. The two talked about next steps in various permutations and combinations, Tupper suggesting that Bowell assume a lieutenant governorship or even the high commissioner position. Bowell said his place was in the Senate. Besides, if they really wanted to show party unity, he needed to continue to serve in whatever version of the ministry would go forward. Then they weighed the pros and cons of Bowell stepping down and recommending Aberdeen call upon Tupper to form a Seventh Ministry or Bowell staying on and inviting Tupper to join the Sixth Ministry as, say, finance minister.

The good will ended at seven when George Foster's private secretary came in and laid a manila envelope on Bowell's desk. Bowell opened it and read aloud. It was a letter of resignation signed by Arthur Dickey, John Haggart, George Foster, William Ives, Walter Montague, Charlie Tupper, and John Wood. And that was it. There the meeting ended. Bowell wouldn't resign with a pistol to his head, especially one put there by the likes of Haggart, Foster, and Montague. *Et tu*, Tupper?

Reconstruction

Sunday morning, Bowell was still chuffed at having resisted the pressure to resign — including that from the old Ram of the Cumberland! After lunch, the prime minister met with Aberdeen and replayed the events of the previous forty-eight hours — the threats by Haggart and Montague, the meeting with Tupper, the resignations. Aberdeen said he admired Bowell's pluck and reminded him that his constitutional responsibility as first minister — and his own as Governor General — was to ensure a responsible ministry was always in place to conduct the Crown's business, a responsibility made all the more imperative by the fact that Parliament was now back in session. Bowell said he'd get right down to work reconstructing his ministry. He'd send Richard Weldon to Toronto that afternoon with a carte blanche offer to sign up Chief Justice William Meredith. And maybe get Lieutenant Governor George Kirkpatrick ... and Halifax MP Thomas Kenny ... and Sir Donald Smith ... and Oliver Howland. Then he'd be able to "snap his fingers at all the rest!"

Monday morning, January 6, Bowell heard from Weldon that Meredith still wasn't interested in coming to Ottawa. The news wasn't much better on the Maritime front. It looked like the Nova Scotia and New Brunswick caucuses were choosing to stand behind their dissident leaders. As he did back in 1894, Bowell went first to his old friends, Thomas Kenny and Nathaniel White. After they turned his offers down, Bowell had to ask Charles Cahan, leader of a provincial Conservative opposition and former editor of the *Halifax Herald*, if there were any other "prominent men" available in Nova Scotia. In New Brunswick, Bowell knew it was a long shot, but offered a cabinet seat to Dr. Richard Weldon. The popular law professor said his public pronouncements against federal interference on the schools question would prevent him from accepting. Besides, even if he did, the newspapers and the opposition would make too much hay for the appointment to demonstrate the kind of unity Bowell needed right then. Young Douglas Hazen also declined the offer.

After Meredith, Bowell tried to canvass other possible Ontario recruits. Former minister John Carling declined on the grounds that he didn't want to put the people of London through an unnecessary by-election. (He was also still miffed at Bowell for passing him over for a cabinet posting in December 1894). Peter White, the Commons speaker, told Bowell he could not ally himself to a reconstructed administration that did not include the dissentient ministers, who, he said, represented the strongest elements in the Conservative Party. Alexander McNeill, like Weldon, couldn't square his position on remedial legislation with Bowell's. The prime minister found some traction with Roderick McLennan, who said he'd be willing to support the ministry if Bowell was able to secure the re-appointment of all seven dissidents.

By mid-afternoon, it was clear Bowell would not be able to reconstruct his ministry. He scribbled a note to Aberdeen telling him he'd failed and would likely have to resign: "I see no change in the aspect of the situation and fear that there is no solution of the present problem than for me to resign. I shall however defer final action until Wednesday next."

Shortly after, what remained of cabinet decided on a temporary reshuffle of portfolios:

Mackenzie Bowell, Premier, President of the Privy Council, Acting Minister of Finance, acting Minister of Militia and Defence
Adolphe Caron, Postmaster General
John Costigan, Minister of Marine and Fisheries, acting Minister of Trade and Commerce, acting Controller of Inland Revenue
Thomas Daly, Minister of Interior, acting Minister of Justice, acting Attorney General, acting Secretary of State
Donald Ferguson, acting Minister of Agriculture
Frank Smith, acting Controller of Customs
Joseph-Aldric Ouimet, Minister of Public Works, acting Minister of Railways and Canals

On his way out of the East Block Monday evening, Arnott Magurn asked Bowell for his opinion on the day's events. Bowell told him, "You may say that it is the blackest piece of political treachery on record." Magurn then asked if his plans for reconstruction included any of the dissentients. Bowell said he would "take care that Haggart and Montague do not get back into any cabinet."

Traitors

Rumours of an attempted coup brought Ottawans out to Parliament in droves again on Tuesday, January 7. The halls and lobbies of Centre Block were packed an hour before proceedings began, the sergeant-at-arms forced to issue tickets to manage the crowds. When prayers were finished just after three, the crowds streamed into the galleries. Every seat in the Commons was filled. On the floor of the chamber, beside the Speaker, Lady Aberdeen sat beside Mackenzie Bowell, who'd been invited by White to attend.

When the House settled, Adolphe Caron rose. "Mr. Speaker, before the orders of the day are called, I have an important statement to make to the House. Since the opening of Parliament, seven members of the Cabinet have tendered their resignations to the prime minister, which were submitted to the Governor General and accepted by His Excellency. At the next meeting of the House, I hope to be in a position to state definitely what course the Government has taken, or intends to take, under these circumstances. Considering the gravity of the situation, I have to ask that when the House adjourns today — of course, I am aware that without notice I can only move for an adjournment from day to day — it stand adjourned for ten days or a fortnight, which would allow time to consider the gravity of the circumstances. I move that when the House adjourns today it stand adjourned until Tuesday, the twenty-first."

The opposition cheered as Laurier rose and buttoned his jacket.

"Mr. Speaker, I understand very well that the Government are in a very peculiar position, and they are entitled, and I am not disposed to refuse commiseration to them in any way." Laurier waited while his compatriots chanted "hear, hear."

> But we must have something like Parliamentary government in this country. Sir Adolphe Caron has told us that seven

> members of the Administration have resigned. Sir, the honourable gentleman should have told us what is the cause which has brought on those resignations. Not a word, not a syllable, not a scintilla of information has been given to the House upon this most important subject. We are told by the Ministerial press that the Conservative party is dissatisfied with the leadership of Sir Mackenzie Bowell. As to that, I have nothing to say. It is a purely family quarrel in which I would not at all venture to take any part. I have to say that Parliament would be trifled with if that were given as the cause why we should not proceed with the business of the House. Parliament has been called to determine a certain policy, but to me, it looks very much as if this were another of those expedients of which we have had too many already in order to enable the Government to not carry out the pledges which they gave to Parliament.

"Is the motion of Sir Adolphe Caron objected to?" asked White.

"Certainly. Notice must be given," said Laurier.

"Then I will give it as a notice of motion for tomorrow and move that the House do not adjourn," replied Caron.

The House then went silent as George Foster rose to speak. Only his colleagues from New Brunswick clapped softly.

> Before the House adjourns I rise to perform a duty which I conceive should be performed at once, and to say at the same time that I do not propose, as neither, I think, do my colleagues who are acting with me in this matter, to enter into any discussion of the subject. I will today simply make a statement for the information of the House and the country as to our position — I mean the position of those gentlemen who thought it their duty to retire from the Government and I shall briefly state the reasons why they retired.

Throughout Foster's short address the Conservatives sat silent while the Liberals cheered, laughed, hooted, and hear-heared.

> I may say in the first place that there is no disagreement between ourselves and the Premier upon any question of public policy, trade, or constitutional, with regard to which action has been already taken, or in respect to which an attitude has been assumed by the Government under the present Premier.
>
> I beg also to say that we retain our firm belief in the principles and policy of the Conservative Party, with which we are in entire accord, and of which in common with others, we have been and will remain the exponents in so far as our ability admits.
>
> Though with many misgivings we finally agreed to enter the Government under Sir Mackenzie Bowell in succession to Sir John Thompson, we have nevertheless unitedly and loyally striven to the best of our ability to make it strong and efficient, and it has been with growing regret that we have seen our efforts result in a measure of success less than that for which we had hoped and striven.
>
> We are of the opinion that the Conservative party ought to be represented by the strongest Government possible to be secured from its ranks, that the necessity, therefore, was never greater than under existing circumstances, and we believe that such a Government can be formed without delay.
>
> This we have repeatedly urged upon the Premier, with the result that we found ourselves face to face with Parliament, having a Government with its number incomplete and with no assurance that the present Premier could satisfactorily complete it.
>
> Under these circumstances, we thought it our duty to retire, and in this manner to pave the way, if possible, for the formation of a Government whose Premier could

command the confidence of all his colleagues, could satisfy the Conservative party that its strongest element was at its head, and impress the country that it had a Government which was united and had the power to govern.

We affirm with the utmost sincerity that the action we have taken has sprung from no feeling of personal dislike or of personal ambition, but has been solely dictated by our wish to sink all minor considerations in the presence of our great desire that the best interests of our party and country should be duly conserved.

Liberal Richard Cartwright responded.

I do not know which is the more extraordinary, the request made by the present leader of the House, or the statement to which we have just listened from the ex-leader of the House. It is three-and-thirty years since I first sat in the Parliament of the then two Canadas, and in all that time, although I have seen many crises, and assisted in some, I can recall nothing in the faintest degree parallel with the present condition of things … It does appear that these honourable gentlemen have offered a direct insult to the representative of the Sovereign, and a direct insult to the House. It appears to me no matter what their grounds or their reasons may be, that for a Cabinet to place a speech in the mouth of his Excellency, and then, before the ink on the document is dry, to put a pistol to the head of their colleague, the Premier of the country — to place him in the utterly humiliating and degrading position in which they have tried to place him — it is, I am happy to say, utterly unparalleled in the history of any British community.

Then, over and above all this, the matter is complicated by another consideration. It appears to me that these gentlemen's honour demands now a full statement of the reasons, or what truth there is or is not, in the statement that one honourable minister, or ex-minister, has been caught in the act of slandering anonymously the reputation of an able and honourable colleague. I offer no opinion on the subject other than this: should it again become necessary, in the discharge of patriotic duty, for any gentleman in a similar position to address an anonymous correspondence to his Excellency, the communication should, for the sake of decency and for the sake of preventing future scandals, be typewritten and the typewriter be broken up immediately, so that there may be no possibility of afterwards detecting it.

Up to this point the Conservatives had been silent. But even Foster, Haggart, and Tupper had to laugh. Montague, still under the cloud of the letter scandal, refused to budge.

"For my part," Cartwright concluded, "I am prepared to grant the fullest consideration to the present First Minister, Sir Mackenzie Bowell, who, whatever his faults and sins may be, appears so far as we can see, to have acted straightforwardly under very difficult circumstances."

The House adjourned at ten to four, and the members on both sides of the chamber poured down onto the floor. It had been six months since they'd last been together and, despite their politics, they were happy to be back in their close fraternity.

Laurier was the first to greet Bowell. He sprang from his seat and extended a hand. As they chatted, a dozen or so other Liberals gathered around, each proffering their own hands and exchanging pleasantries. Even D'Alton McCarthy came over and warmly greeted the prime minister.

A few minutes later, Bowell crossed over to the Conservative side of the House. As he passed along the short end of the clerk's long, rectangular table that bisected the floor, someone on the Liberal side called out, "Come over to us and you will find no treachery here." Bowell chuckled and called back,

"No, thanks; matters are bad enough over here. They would be ten times worse over there."

On the Conservative side of the floor, Bowell was surrounded by another crowd of well-wishers. He glad-handed for a few moments and then made his way to where Hector Langevin was sitting. The two old colleagues spoke for a few minutes and then Bowell put his arm through Donald Smith's, who was standing nearby. The men bent their white-topped heads together for a few minutes to hear one another, and then Bowell was off again, spending some time with Nathaniel Clarke Wallace.

When he got to Caron and Ouimet, the two were trying to persuade Liberal Dr. George Landerkin to leave the opposition ranks and join them on the government benches. Another Liberal, from Quebec, asked Ouimet, now that he was acting minister of railways, if he'd build a railway in his county. Ouimet replied with a laugh, "Oh, you will build it yourself in a little while."

Bowell clearly had the room's sympathy. At one point, near the end of the impromptu party, one of the Liberals asked Bowell how well he felt. Bowell replied, loud enough to be heard by Lady Aberdeen at the speaker's desk and in the press gallery above, "Very well, considering that I have been living in a nest of traitors."

A rambunctious crowd waited outside the Senate doors for the evening session to begin. When the doors opened at eight, there was a rush for seats. In the crush, a lamp was broken. Not used to such pandemonium, one reporter said several senators were startled out of their chairs. Black Rod René Kimber took control of the situation with a stern glare.

The proceedings began with the introduction of the five new senators whom Bowell had just promoted — Hingston, Wood, O'Brien, Villeneuve, and Owens. Then, after reading out the same statement as Caron had made in the Commons earlier in the day, Bowell made a few extemporaneous remarks on Foster's statement.

I believe an explanation has been made in another place by one of the gentlemen who retired from the Cabinet, giving his reasons therefor. I have not yet had an opportunity of reading it, but only casually heard it, and am therefore not in a position to deal with it as I think its importance demands. I must therefore ask the indulgence of the House for at least twenty-four hours when I shall be in a much better position to deal with the statement as it deserves.

I shall add this, however: the declaration that I made in the House just before its prorogation last year, in reference to the future policy of the Government upon the great question which is agitating the people of this country, will, so far as I am concerned, and so far as my influence goes, be carried out to the letter. Having enunciated a principle, firmly believing as I did and as I suppose my colleagues did that it was a sound principle; that it was but doing justice to a portion of this Dominion and maintaining the provisions of the constitution, and giving to a portion of her Majesty's subjects who had been deprived of their rights that which the constitution and the highest court of the realm stated that they were entitled to, I feel it my duty, as far as in my power lies, to see that the remedy is given.

The senators gave Bowell as warm a reception as the commoners had earlier in the day.

Pressure Again

On Wednesday, January 8, Sir Charles turned up the heat on Bowell to resign by indelicately declaring his candidacy for the leadership of the Conservative Party in an interview published in the *Mail and Empire*. Tupper said that he'd met with the prime minister the previous Saturday and had "a very frank and confidential and thoroughly friendly" conversation. During the conversation, Tupper "did not hesitate to say" that he'd "infinitely prefer retiring from public life rather than to take the leadership of the Conservative Party. But both he and I felt and believed, that the control of public affairs by that party was essential in the best interests of Canada, and that it was the duty of every one of its members, irrespective of his own feelings, to take whatever position might be necessary in order to advance its welfare. I also said that, in the event of any changes being brought about, I would hope to have the same cooperation from him that I had been prepared to give him in the position that he had occupied."

Asked about the interview as he left East Block to meet with Aberdeen at Rideau Hall, Bowell told the Ottawa correspondent for the *Evening Telegram* that Sir Charles "draws $10,000 a year for looking after Canadian business in England" but "has now been in Canada for some weeks." He said the high commissioner ought to be "ordered to return to England forthwith."

At Rideau Hall, Bowell entered the drawing-room, took a piece of paper from his pocket, and made to hand it to Lord Aberdeen.

"What is that?" Aberdeen asked.

"It is my resignation, sir," Bowell replied.

"Then you had better put it back in your pocket," Aberdeen told him. The Governor General wasn't ready to accept Bowell's resignation because, once he did, he would need to have a plan in place for a new ministry. He'd started his due diligence but wasn't quite finished. And so, for the moment, Aberdeen told Bowell, "The Speech from the Throne, although delivered to Parliament, has not yet been considered; and it would be unfitting that the head of the administration responsible for the preparation of that Speech should not have full opportunity to review the situation, and should he so determine, to test the feeling of Parliament thereupon."

One issue Aberdeen had settled was whether there was a precedent for calling on someone, in this case, Sir Charles Tupper, without a seat in Parliament to form a ministry. He hadn't had to look far: In 1871, the leaders of Ontario's Liberal Party had recommended Lieutenant Governor Howland call on Oliver Mowat to form the government in Ontario. At the time Mowat was vice-chancellor of the Upper Canadian Court of Chancery (later part of the Superior Court). The day after he accepted the offer, he resigned his judicial appointment and sought a seat in the provincial legislature. Citing the precedent of Pitt the Younger, Mowat had said the Crown had the right to call to council any of its subjects "whether he happens to hold a judicial or any other office."

While precedent supported asking Tupper to form a new ministry if Bowell failed at reconstruction, it was, at least for Lady Aberdeen, the most distasteful option on the table. She remained steadfast in her dislike for the man and preferred that her husband call on Wilfrid Laurier to form a ministry, dissolve Parliament, "which has seen four Administrations without an appeal to the country," and call a general election post-haste. Her plan did lack precedent: nowhere in Canada, or anywhere else in the British Empire, for that matter, had a Governor General called on the leader of the opposition to form a new ministry while the existing ministry had not lost the confidence of the legislature. The plan would also put her husband in the untenable position of asking someone — Laurier — to form a government to carry out the very business of the Crown — pass remedial legislation — which that person was on the public record as opposing.

Nevertheless, Lady Aberdeen took it upon herself to begin discussions with Laurier, justifying to her diary that "it is well at such a juncture to have some means of communication with the leader of the Opposition." Through a confidential emissary (a mutual friend, *Globe* columnist Emily Cummings), Laurier pleaded his case to Her Ladyship that the most "cogent" reason for calling on the Liberals to form a ministry if Bowell failed at reconstruction was that he and the party intended to, as Her Ladyship told her diary, "deal fairly with the minority — i.e., the RCs in Manitoba. The fact of the Conservative party having pledged themselves to the remedial measure has educated the country & they are prepared for something & thus it will be comparatively easy for the Liberals to do something. But if a government under Sir Charles Tupper or any other against or lukewarm about remedial legislation came in, they would gather round them all the PPA [Protestant Protective Association] and all the anti-Catholic feeling in Ontario and then the two provinces of Quebec and Ontario would be face to face for a deadly combat." Laurier also apparently told Lady Aberdeen he was "confident of sweeping the country if they come into power now — but if Sir Charles comes into power and dissolves, he will not hesitate to use means fair and foul to bribe the country into returning him. This is not mere supposition — his past record is clear enough on this subject." Although she was already predisposed to liking Laurier and supporting the Liberals, Laurier's anti-Tupper rhetoric didn't hurt his efforts to convince Lady Aberdeen of his cause.

No Precedent

Bowell had promised to update the Senate on the status of reconstruction efforts by Wednesday, January 8. But just before the session started that evening, Senator Henry Kaulback died of a heart attack on his way into the chamber. A visibly shaken Bowell asked permission from the Senate to put the statement off, but only until the next day, so that "the country may no longer be held in suspense on a question of such a grave character and of such momentous consequences."

On Thursday, Bowell began his promised address about "what course the Government proposed to pursue under the present trying circumstances." He said,

> I need scarcely say that English history offers no precedent for the position we find ourselves today. There have been many occasions upon which Ministers of a cabinet have resigned their portfolios, and have broken up governments, but there is no precedent that I have been able to discover of a single instance in which a Cabinet apparently united, met Parliament and placed an address affirming the principles and policy of the Government in the hands of her Majesty's representative, and then, after having asked for an adjournment of three or four days, in the interim, or between the time of the delivery of the address and the assembling of Parliament again, seven members of the Cabinet sent in their resignations.

My late colleague, the Hon. Mr. Foster, states there that there has been no difference of opinion between us. That being the case, can any of you conceive why, after Parliament has met after the address has been promulgated, that you should find seven of the Cabinet coming to Parliament and sending in their resignations simply because they did not like the gentleman with whom they had been associating, some of them for eight or ten years, and whose ability or character they knew just as well as they do today?

How is it that the discovery was not made until we were in the beginning of a session, until it was impossible almost to proceed with the business of the country without having not only a disintegration of the Government itself but treating the people of this country with comparative contempt? Surely my colleagues knew my incapacity to govern, to rule and control, before the two days after the meeting of Parliament, when they sent in their resignations? Surely, they could not have come to the opinion that I was unfit to continue at the head of this Government in so short a period? What happened between the writing of that address, the placing it in his Excellency's hands, the meeting of Parliament, and the delivery of that address by his Excellency? What could have happened during the last two or three days to lead them to a conclusion which induced and impelled them to take so important a step as they have done? Had they come to me previous to the meeting of Parliament, had they met me in Council and said "We disagree with the policy you have laid down;" had they said in any single particular there was a difference of opinion upon the great issues that were agitating the people of this country and they could not by any possibility be a party to it or had they gone further and said, "After one year and a quarter's experience of you as head of the Government we have lost confidence in your ability to continue to administer the affairs of this country," then I would have said, "Take the reins of government. I will not stand in the way," and I never shall in the future stand in the way of the success of that great party to which I have had the honour of belonging from boyhood up, and towards which I have done something for its prosperity and continuance in office.

I hesitate to say that had I had that loyal support which every Premier ought to have in his endeavours to govern the country, that characterized the support that was given most loyally to my late chiefs, Sir John Macdonald and Sir John Thompson, that I would have been just as successful in carrying out the affairs of the Government as my predecessors, though not possessed of the same ability or political tact or stratagem as they were. Had not that same jealousy prevailed, and the ambition to destroy the usefulness of the Government been so firmly rooted in the breasts of those with whom I was associated, I flatter myself that we should have been as successful in carrying on the affairs of this country.

That is all I have to say upon this question. I leave it, and I leave myself, whatever may be my future state, in the hands of my countrymen, and I leave them to judge whether a life of some fifty years, to a greater or lesser extent spent in politics, and whether thirty years of Parliamentary life, justifies the position that my colleagues have taken, or the imputation which they have cast upon my character, or my reputation, as a politician, I leave that to the country and to those who know me, and to those who do not know me, to those who are directly my political opponents, to say whether my conduct has ever been otherwise than that of a straightforward, perhaps blundering, politician. All I claim for myself is this: A moral honesty, a firm conviction of what is right, and the determination, under all circumstances, whether it pleases the prejudices of one party or another, to endeavour to carry out the policy of the Government and put it in force.

I think I may close by stating what it is proposed to do. After several interviews with the Governor General respecting the resignation of seven of my colleagues from the Cabinet, I yesterday waited upon his Excellency for the purpose of tendering my resignation. His Excellency, however, intimated that he was not at that moment prepared to receive it. The chief reason for this attitude is that the speech from the throne, although presented to Parliament, has not yet been considered nor an expression of opinion given by Parliament upon it. It is regarded by his Excellency as unfitting that the Premier, as the head of the Administration and responsible for that speech, should not have a full opportunity of reviewing the situation and testing the feelings of Parliament thereon. Under these circumstances, I deem it my duty to endeavour as far as in me lies to reorganize the Government. I, therefore, move that when the House adjourns, it do stand adjourned until Tuesday, the 14th, at 3 p.m. If I cannot succeed in reorganizing the Administration within these three days, then I shall do that which is the constitutional duty of every Premier who finds himself in such circumstances, namely, place my resignation in the hands of his Excellency.

Let me say this, to close, that although I am not going to pledge myself publicly to the details of any measure which may be proposed in Parliament, I wish it distinctly understood that whatever Government is formed, if I am to be its leader, must be formed on the basis of the principles enunciated in the speech from the throne. Otherwise, I shall not consent to be connected with any body of men who are not prepared to carry out and hold inviolable the pledges which were then solemnly made to Parliament.

Reconstructed

Bowell's only success with reconstruction came on Friday, January 10, when he convinced Senator Alphonse Desjardins — the man who'd turned him down ten days earlier — to fill Angers's spot in cabinet. (Desjardins became amenable once Angers lifted his mandament on the position after being convinced by Archbishop Langevin that Bowell was truly committed to getting remedial legislation passed during the current session.) But the win came at a price: Desjardins forced Bowell to sign — in front of Daly, Caron, Ouimet, and Donald Smith — a lengthy memorandum with numerous conditions, including giving Catholic authorities and "other authorized friends of the Manitoba minority cause" the right to approve the terms of the bill before it was voted on, promising that the approved terms would not be changed to suit Tupper or any other of the new cabinet members, and promising that the bill would be passed even if Manitoba legislated separate schools back into existence on its own.

Meanwhile, rumours were flying that Lord Aberdeen was in talks with Laurier about forming a new ministry if Bowell failed at reconstruction. It was these rumours that brought Charlie Tupper to Rideau Hall to talk with Lady Aberdeen Friday afternoon. Tupper's primary motivation was to counter Bowell's assertion in the Senate the day before that he and the other dissentients had resigned without cause: He was worried the misrepresentation would impugn his good reputation.

Tupper said Bowell had been given "fair warning" by his cabinet to fill Angers's spot in cabinet by the beginning of the coming session or "they would not stand by him." At cabinet on Tuesday, December 31, Tupper said Bowell had told them not to worry, he was in the process of signing up Senator Masson. But finding no Senator Masson on Friday, the day after Parliament reconvened, the dissentients "resolved they could wait no longer." Saturday morning, Tupper said he and Dickey went to see Bowell and Bowell agreed to resign. By the afternoon, though, Bowell told Thomas Daly he'd changed his mind and "moreover did not believe in the sincerity of their intention to resign." That was the point at which Tupper said the others decided they'd had enough and submitted their resignations. Lady Aberdeen said she was relieved to hear Tupper's side of the story as her husband "did not see how they could be allowed to be included in any new Cabinet" for such "execrable conduct." On the topic of new cabinets, Tupper assured Lady Aberdeen "that his father would proceed with remedial legislation if he formed a Govt." He also said "a chief factor in helping Sir Mackenzie to reconstruct was the belief that the only alternative to Bowell was Laurier & that the Premier and Sir Adolphe were both promoting this idea & that rumour had it that some of the staff had made observations which corroborated the belief." Her Ladyship guaranteed Tupper "that such could not be the case, as nobody knew anything."

Despite the rumours, Lady Aberdeen continued her discussions with Laurier. At a skating party hosted by her National Council of Women at Rideau Hall Saturday afternoon, Her Ladyship introduced her secretary, Captain John Sinclair, to Laurier and his wife, Zoé, a Council vice-president and the reason the Lauriers were in attendance that afternoon. Lady Aberdeen asked Sinclair to take a walk with Laurier and get more details on his plans if he were asked to form a new ministry. Sinclair reported back: "Dissolution of course at once. And he says he could form his Cabinet in three days and he is very confident of the country if he is in power at dissolution — but if Sir Charles were in power, this might be different ... I had a little talk with him when he took me to tea."

Rumours of Aberdeen asking Laurier to form a new government increased the pressure on the Conservatives to patch up their differences over the weekend. Conservative whip George Taylor arranged another meeting between Bowell and Tupper as the skating party was under way. It didn't start — or end — well.

Tupper said he'd learned from Taylor that Bowell was now willing to include all seven dissentients and himself in a reconstructed cabinet and once the Speech from the Throne had passed Bowell would submit his resignation and recommend to Aberdeen that Tupper be asked to form a new ministry. Bowell said Taylor was mistaken. There was simply no way he'd serve in the same government as those three traitors. He was quite ready to take in the other four, including Tupper's son Charlie. "I have no fault to find with your son, Charlie, who has always been frank and candid with me," Bowell told Tupper. "Perhaps he should succeed you in London as High Commissioner?"

"With the great financial questions of the Fast Line Service and the Atlantic and Pacific questions ripe for settlement," Tupper said, he thought "a great capitalist would be the one best able to promote the interest of Canada in that position." Besides, Charlie had already decided that if his father were to form a new government it would not be in anyone's interest for him to be a member of it. Tupper said he agreed with that decision.

Tupper brought the conversation around to reconstruction again. He said in the interests of the party — and the country — the only way he'd re-enter the cabinet was if everyone were included, Bowell and dissidents alike. He told Bowell he "ought not to allow his personal feelings towards any gentleman to influence him." Tupper said the only thing inducing him to re-enter parliamentary life was "the belief that an overwhelming proportion of the Conservative party in Canada believed that I could be of great service to the country in the present emergency by taking the leadership." Tupper said he assumed Bowell was animated "by the same feelings, that of considering alone what the interests of the party demanded." But refusing to invite the dissidents back into the cabinet would entirely defeat the purpose of Tupper's re-entering cabinet: to present a common, unified front to the party, to the opposition and the country.

While that meeting ended there, the rumour mill persisted on into Sunday. Daly told Bowell that he felt "as satisfied as possible that if you cannot succeed in arranging matters by Tuesday His Excellency will call on Laurier, beyond a doubt." And then the rumours got back to Lady Aberdeen once again. In conversation with Senator Frank Smith on the state of negotiations between Bowell and Tupper on Sunday, Smith said he assumed — based on what he'd heard — that Lord Aberdeen would call on Laurier to form a new government if the negotiations failed. Lady Aberdeen told her diary that she "took care to utter no syllable which would lend colour to such a supposition." She went on:

> At least we can feel that all through this crisis, not a word has been breathed by either HE, B, or I (the only three who

have discussed the question) as to what course is likely to be pursued. Alone we three have indeed discussed it in all its bearings up hill & down dale night after night until every possible side of it has been looked at, & should Sir Mackenzie now fail, HE's mind is pretty well made up, as is shadowed forth by the enclosed Mem. by B. But no one can say they know or have reason to guess.

Smith had been in politics long enough to know that smoke did not rise on its own. He left Rideau Hall and headed to the Russell, where he persuaded Bowell and Tupper to sit down yet again. By 5:00 p.m., the three had worked out a deal where Bowell would remain as prime minister for the remainder of the parliamentary session and see the remedial bill through Parliament. At the end of the session, Bowell would resign, and Tupper would take his place. Until then, Sir Charles would enter cabinet as secretary of state. As for the dissidents, six of them — Dickey, Foster, Haggart, Ives, Montague, and Wood — would be offered their spots back in cabinet. Charlie Tupper had agreed to sit out for the moment, one Tupper in cabinet at any one time being sufficient.

Bowell presented his reconstituted ministry to Lord Aberdeen on Monday afternoon, along with the deal he'd made with Tupper. Aberdeen approved the ministry but declined "any sort of arrangement or understanding about a change of Premiership."

"And so the crisis ends — for the present," Lady Aberdeen signed off her diary on Monday, January 14.

Adolphe Caron presented the official version of the week's events to the House on Wednesday, January 15, the same day the new cabinet was sworn in.

> Mr. Speaker, the statement I am about to make has been submitted to the Governor General by the prime minister and I am authorized to say that it has His Excellency's approval.

Coup

Since reference was made, in this House, to the retirement from office of certain members of the Government, the prime minister has had an opportunity of carefully reviewing the circumstances connected with these resignations, and has satisfied himself that the best interests of the country would be served, notwithstanding any differences of opinion that exist respecting the importance of filling the portfolio made vacant by the resignation of the Hon. Mr. Angers, by the return to their former positions in the Cabinet of those who deemed it their duty to retire on account of that vacancy.

While it is true that this point was freely discussed between the prime minister and his colleagues, it is equally true that the prime minister did not regard that vacancy as sufficient reason for the resignation of any member of the Government. This view, however, was not concurred in by some of his colleagues who urged that a meeting of Parliament with a Quebec portfolio vacant might seriously imperil certain important measures to be presented during this session. He had reasonable hopes of being able to fill that position up to the very day when Parliament met and was disappointed when his efforts failed.

After the opening of Parliament, certain members of the Government sent their resignations to the prime minister, giving among other reasons the fact that "having failed to fill the portfolio" and, that he evidently "intended to go on with the transaction of public business with an incomplete Cabinet," they thought this course so great "a departure from sound constitutional practice and so weak, as a matter of policy," that they were "unwilling any longer to remain as members of an incomplete Government."

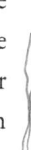

Since the receipt of the resignations referred to, the objections put forward by the Ministers who resigned have been removed by the acceptance of a seat in the Cabinet by the Hon. Alphonse Desjardins, a gentleman well known and esteemed in the province of Quebec for his ability and integrity of character, and by the acceptance to the Ministry of Sir Charles Tupper. Under these circumstances, and with these objections removed, the Ministers who resigned have deemed it consistent with the duty to their country to resume the positions they respectively held in the Government. It is gratifying, therefore, to be able to inform the House and the country that a Ministry has been formed which will command the support of the Majority in Parliament and enable us to proceed with the measures foreshadowed in the Speech from the Throne.

The Government as reconstructed is as follows:

President of the Council, Hon. Sir Mackenzie Bowell
Secretary of State, Hon. Sir Charles Tupper
Postmaster General, Hon. Sir Adolphe Caron
Minister of Marine and Fisheries, Hon. John Costigan
Minister of Finance, George Foster
Minister of Railways and Canals, Hon. John Haggart
Minister of Public Works, Hon. J.A. Ouimet
Minister of the Interior, Hon. Thomas Mayne Daly
Minister of Trade and Commerce, Hon. W.B. Ives
Minister of Agriculture, Hon. W.H. Montague
Minister of Militia and Defence, Hon. Alphonse Desjardins
Ministers without portfolio, Hon. Frank Smith, Hon. Donald Ferguson
Controller of Customs, Hon. J.F. Wood
Controller of Inland Revenue, Hon. E.G. Prior

8

Anew

Best Shot

The Conservatives' best shot at winning the 1896 general election was to face voters with a new leader, a new government, and a new policy platform, all free from the promises — and the scandals — of Prime Minister Mackenzie Bowell and his Sixth Ministry. And so, for the good of the party, Sir Charles Tupper entered cabinet on January 15 as secretary of state and Mackenzie Bowell agreed to stay on as prime minister until the end of the parliamentary session in April, when he'd hand over the reins to Tupper and a new ministry in time for an election in June.

The policy Tupper and his new ministry *had* to gain distance on was the separate school system proposed in the remedial bill. That policy was based on John Ewart's recommendations to recreate the system Manitoba had in place before 1890, in which Catholic schools were administered by Catholic-elected boards and supported by a combination of Catholic-based taxes and public monies. Distance was needed because the recommended policy had become politically intractable and practically unworkable. There were at least forty Ontario Conservatives and possibly another dozen from the Maritimes who were prepared to vote against such a remedial bill and trigger a loss of confidence in the government. Quebec's three Conservative ministers — Caron, Desjardins, and Ouimet — were set to resign if the bill wasn't passed, and Catholic authorities were clear that Conservatives would receive no electoral support from their pulpits if the bill wasn't passed by the end of the session. But even if, by some miracle, the remedial bill somehow made it through Parliament, Greenway's Manitoba government had made it clear on December 21 that it would neither operate nor fund a separate school system in the province ever again. And the results from the January 15 provincial election bolstered that position: Greenway's Liberals took thirty-two of the province's forty seats, nine by acclamation.

The easiest way for Tupper and the Conservatives to gain distance on Bowell's separate school policy would be to let the proposed remedial bill die in the House, blame the Liberals and Conservative anti-remedialists for its death, and socialize a more palatable alternative in time for the election. And right out of the gate Tupper made it clear he'd do everything in his power to help kill the bill as well, either by obstructing its passage outright or by indirectly running out the parliamentary clock. For example, instead of letting Bowell appoint him to the Senate in January, Tupper chose to enter Parliament by running for a Cape Breton seat in the House of Commons, the by-election for which was set for February 2.

The Cape Breton by-election also allowed Tupper to begin laying the groundwork for an alternative remediation policy. At a speech in Boisdale on January 22, Tupper reminded the audience that as premier of Nova Scotia he'd fought for "equal rights and justice for all without consideration of race or creed" and was committed to fighting for those same rights in Manitoba. He agreed with the Judicial Committee's ruling in *Brophy*, the Manitoba minority's right to appeal to the Dominion cabinet, and the Dominion's constitutional obligation to remediate the situation. "The Government," he said, "is pledged and will stand by that pledge." On the campaign trail, Tupper provided no further details on how he'd keep that pledge. Those would come in March when a special commission was sent to Manitoba to try one last time to negotiate a settlement with the Greenway government.

Anew

Enter Smith

On January 24, Tupper took a break from campaigning to attend McGill University's quinquennial dinner, hosted by its chancellor, Tupper's longtime colleague and friend Sir Donald Smith. A who's who of the Canadian political and business elite were there, including the Governor General and Lady Aberdeen. Her Ladyship reported afterward that Sir Donald was "very anxious for some compromise about the school question." So were the Aberdeens.

Despite the Governor General's public commitment in the Throne Speech to passing remedial legislation, the vice-regal couple was privately convinced that would not solve the schools issue. Lord Aberdeen wrote Colonial Secretary Chamberlain in January that "no measure compelling Manitoba to act can possibly satisfy in any permanent manner the two parties (Protestants and Catholics)." Accordingly, the Aberdeens had been actively lobbying key players to prevent, in Her Ladyship's words, "such a lamentable religious war." After the failure of Lord Aberdeen's exploratory conference with Greenway and Sifton in May 1895, Lady Aberdeen suggested to recently retired British prime ministers Gladstone and Rosebery that "confederation might be preserved through a tactful intervention by 'our leading men at home,' if someone was prepared to come out and deal with the matter." Both declined. In December, Lady Aberdeen implored Archbishop Langevin "to explore any avenue of compromise that might present itself." And then in January she asked Archbishop Walsh of Toronto if he might "ask if His Holiness the Pope could not intervene at this time in the interests of the Church and of peace?"[17]

Having gained little traction elsewhere on the issue, the Aberdeens pounced on Sir Donald's anxiety. Lord Aberdeen met with Smith the week following the McGill dinner "to see if something could not still be done to persuade the Manitoba Govt to do something & to persuade Archbishop Langevin to accept that something, which would give a loophole for the Dominion Govt to drop the remedial legislation to which it is now pledged." Lady Aberdeen thought Smith was exactly the right man for the job: "Sir Donald has more influence in Manitoba with all parties than anyone & he is prepared to go up there, ill as he is, as soon as his doctor will let him. But there is but faint hope of any compromise."

The plan Aberdeen and Smith came up with was for Smith to travel to Winnipeg "as a private citizen," meet "discreetly and unofficially" with Greenway and Langevin, and see if he might "pave the way for a reconciliation between the two Manitoba factions." Smith told Tupper about the plan on February 8 over lunch in Montreal and reported to Aberdeen afterward that Tupper was supportive.

Bill C-58

The historic remedial bill was introduced into the House of Commons on Tuesday afternoon, February 11. Even though based on a draft submitted by John Ewart back in March 1895, the bill still hadn't been finished by the time the new justice minister, Arthur Dickey, was sworn in on January 15. It took Dickey and justice officials until February 4 to get a good enough version together to send to Ewart, Archbishop Langevin, and the "other authorized friends of the Manitoba minority cause" for review (as per Bowell's arrangement with Desjardins to fill August-Réal Angers's spot in cabinet). Dickey gave a preview of Bill C-58 to the Conservative caucus on the morning of February 11.

At 11:00 a.m., Mackenzie Bowell strode into committee room 16 of Centre Block to loud cheers and hearty applause from the Conservative caucus. It had been months since caucus had met last and the whips from both chambers had been burning up the telegraph lines all weekend to ensure all Conservative parliamentarians would be in attendance. The prime minister shook a few hands, thanked everyone for their kind words, and then stepped back out into the hall. He came back in a moment later with the newly re-elected member for Cape Breton, Secretary of State (and newly appointed house leader) Sir Charles Tupper. This time, the applause was more formal, perfunctory; it lacked the warmth and goodwill afforded to Bowell a few minutes earlier.

Caucus chair William Roome (Middlesex) asked all to take their places and called the meeting to order. He said the agenda would be given over to considering "their position in regard to the remedial bill" and then turned the meeting over to Arthur Dickey. The justice minister's introduction to the bill that morning was much the same as he provided to the House that afternoon.

> I may say that in drafting the Bill the lines of the old legislation in Manitoba have been followed as closely as possible, in order that while restoring those rights which it was thought desirable should be restored, we should not transgress the lines of the jurisdiction of this Parliament.
>
> The general scheme, I may say, is this: It was found impossible to restore to the Roman Catholic minority in Manitoba those rights which it was thought they were entitled to under the constitution without establishing a system of separate schools. In order to make that workable, a Board of Education is to be established in the province for separate schools, composed of the same number of members as the Catholic section of the old Board of Education. This board will have the power to organize and carry on the schools.
>
> The persons who contribute to those schools are *prima facie* to be all Catholics in Manitoba. But the Roman Catholic who prefers that his children attend the public schools and decides that he will contribute to the public schools has the right to make that choice by giving certain notices outlined in the bill.
>
> The inspection is to be of a double kind. What I may call the every-day inspection of the schools for the practical working is to be carried on by inspectors to be appointed by the Board of Education. There is a further inspection to be made by inspectors to be appointed or authorized by the Manitoba Lieutenant-Governor in Council. These inspectors will inspect the schools simply for the purpose of certifying the efficiency of the teaching in them.

One very troublesome question dealt with by the Bill is the question of school books. That, I may say, gave a great deal of difficulty, but it was finally settled on this basis, that the Board of Education should be able to choose the school books, their choice, however, being limited to this, they should only select school books that have been the choice of the public schools of Manitoba, or the books in the public separate schools in Ontario.

These are the general lines of the Bill.

Someone asked for details about financing.

"The financial aspect of the measure is this," Dickey explained. He said,

> The Catholics who become adherents to this school system are allowed to tax themselves for separate schools in the district, and they are exempted from taxation for the public schools. The Bill enjoins the municipality to collect the whole municipal taxes over the whole of the property in the municipality and distribute it for the support of schools in the municipality: by property, I mean Roman Catholic property subject to be taxed for the support of separate schools.
>
> The Government did not feel that Parliament had any constitutional authority to deal practically with the question of the legislative grant, and so far as the difficulty was considered possible of a solution, it is solved in the Bill by adjudicating that the right to share in the legislative grant be one of the rights and privileges of the Catholic minority, taking it for granted that the province of Manitoba itself, will after the system is established, supply that fund to the separate schools.
>
> I do not know that I can say anything further just now as to the financial aspect of the case.

Anew

Dickey thanked his colleagues and asked for their support when he introduced the bill that afternoon. Someone asked why; someone else replied, "Because the Government will sink or swim with it."

Roome asked Tupper if he wanted to say a few words. Tupper stood, thanked the room, and asked for leave to read a letter of support he'd received from his good friend, and respected educator, McGill principal William Dawson. The former Nova Scotia school superintendent had written:

> Education should be fair for all, and it should not be regulated by feelings of religious jealousy. If this jealousy existed, justice and liberality would be the best means to make it disappear. The current difficulties with Manitoba schools will be profitable if they can educate parents about the importance of not only getting the best education for their children, but also helping others regardless of their religious beliefs so that they enjoy the same advantages, and if it makes us better appreciate the advantages which we enjoy under a constitution which also respects the religious convictions and the educational needs of people of any religion or origin, as the example of a great empire to which we belong and which everywhere protects the weak against the strong and grants civil and religious rights to all, without even excepting those who, when in power, deny these rights to others. This great empire thus resembles God, "who makes his sun rise on the wicked and on the good, sends rain on the just and on the unjust."

Tupper closed with the mantra he'd repeated during the Cape Breton by-election and would repeat again during debate on second reading: "No one who takes the trouble to examine the question can for a single moment consider that the question of separate schools is at issue at all. It is not a question of separate schools, it is a question of the constitution of the country."

The anti-remedialists from Ontario and the Maritimes dominated the rest of the meeting. In remarks like those he'd make at a rally two weeks later, Nathaniel Clarke Wallace (York West) asked his colleagues, "Who authorized this Government to thrust this policy upon the Conservative party of Ontario? If a poll were taken today in the Province of Ontario I am certain that nine out of every ten Conservatives would be found to be opposed to remedial legislation. I've made up my mind on this matter. Separate Schools are an unmitigated evil in this country, and they are unnecessary. And furthermore, if one-third of the people of Canada are to be dictated to by the church, parliamentary government is a farce. In the history of Canada, there was never such a bare-faced attempt to bulldoze the Parliament of Canada as there has been within the last few months."

Foreshadowing remarks he'd make on February 24, Thomas Dixon Craig (East Durham) declared that "on most of the great questions of the day I support the Conservative Government, but upon this question, I am obliged to withdraw my support. I admit that there are conditions under which interference might be necessary to the protection of a minority. I do not consider this such a case, and intend to vote against this bill because I am a Conservative and because I am a Canadian and do not wish to stir up race and sectarian hatred in Canada. I intend to oppose the bill because no injustice had been done to the minority of Manitoba. In the places in Ontario where there were no Separate Schools, the children of Catholics and Protestants alike go to public schools, and no injustice is done by it. The Separate Schools in Manitoba were poor schools, and no injustice was done in putting an end to them."

Dr. Richard Weldon (Albert) repeated comments he'd previously made in public and would make again during the debate on second reading. "Must I again be charged with being a Protestant bigot and taking an extreme view, when I say, that the happiest solution of the school question would be for the party to agree upon some such common ground as soon as we can, and get this unfortunate question out of politics? I profoundly regret that the Administration of today has taken a course on the school question which I cannot follow. I believe they are not reflecting the views of anything like one-half of the electors of the Conservative Party. Nevertheless, I confidently believe what I believe; and while it will give me no great personal pain to be drummed out of my county if that event were to happen, or to be drummed out of this House, I shall still remember with pride that I will vote against this bill."

John Haggart, the railway minister, got the last word, delivering a speech like the one he'd give during second reading. "The majority of the Protestant electors in Ontario believe that there should be religious exercises in the public schools. Why, then, should the people who hold this opinion object to a few Frenchmen on the banks of the Red River having schools for their children in accordance with their conscientious principles? I do not believe that, when the facts were laid before the people of Ontario, before my countrymen, that even a moiety of them would refuse to believe in the justice of the proposal. What interest is it to them to refuse religious training to Roman Catholics? No: this agitation is got up, not because of any objection to religious education in Manitoba, but because a few disappointed parties have not got the influence or precedence in the Conservative party which they think their abilities entitle them to. They desire to advance their own interest even at the price of stirring up strife in the community."

Second Reading

It took until February 21 for Ewart, Langevin, and "the other authorized friends" to review and tentatively approve the Sixth Ministry's remedial bill and two weeks after that (conveniently) for French translation to be completed. Finally, on the afternoon of Tuesday, March 3, Tupper led off on the historic debate. He said the remedial bill's importance transcended "any measure that has ever been submitted to this House during its existence." The rhetoric flowed, but Tupper made the same points he'd made at Boisdale back in January: the school issue was "not a question of separate schools [but] a question of the constitution of the country." Section 93 was unequivocal in its protection of minority education rights, the Judicial Committee of the Privy Council could not have been clearer ruling that those rights had been "invaded by the legislation of that province," and "the Parliament of this Dominion would be unworthy of the position it occupies if it turned deaf ears in a case made clear." And then he added something new: "Even down to the present hour the Government is open to any suggestion, from any quarter, of any means which will remove the necessity of their being compelled to take action of this kind."

Laurier went next. He said he'd never felt "so strong in the consciousness of right" as he did "opposing a Government which had outrageously misinterpreted the Constitution in the name of 'peace and harmony'... If this Bill were to become law, it would afford no protection whatever to the suffering minority in Manitoba, it would be a most violent wrench of the principles upon which our constitution is based." Laurier said these principles demanded that the government proceed based on evidence and only after the facts "alleged by the minority" had been ascertained could such remedy proposed by the government be applied. Investigation "was the first thing that they should have done, but they did not do it." In what had crystallized into the Liberal position on the issue, "there is in this Government the power to interfere, there is in the Parliament the power to interfere, but that power should not be exercised until all the facts bearing upon the case have been investigated and all means of conciliation exhausted. Holding these opinions, I move that the Bill be not now read the second time, but that it be read the second time this day six months."

Debate on second reading sprawled over the next two and a half weeks. Seventy-five members (forty-seven Conservatives, twenty-eight Liberals) spoke for a total of 140 hours, taking up 1,207 columns in Hansard (701 by Conservatives, 506 by Liberals). Six sittings adjourned after midnight, the last continuing for thirty-nine hours, from three in the afternoon on Wednesday, March 18, to six o'clock on Friday morning, March 20. Bill C-58 passed second reading with a majority of eighteen. One hundred and five Conservatives and seven Liberals voted for the bill, seventy-three Liberals, three Independents and eighteeen Conservatives voted against it. Seventeen of the eighteen Conservatives who voted against were from Ontario (Clarke Wallace, Craig, Sproule, et al.); only Richard Weldon from the Maritimes joined them.

The Conservatives might have lost the vote entirely had Tupper not, on March 9, promised that Sir Donald Smith would "conference with Mr. Greenway's government with a view to arriving at a settlement of this question on terms that will be satisfactory to his government and the minority of Manitoba." The only catch was that Conservatives would have to vote in favour of the remedial bill at second reading. If the conference wasn't successful, Tupper said they weren't bound to support the bill at third reading. But if it was, "there will be no Remedial Bill required from this House." The commission thus served three objectives: provide further evidence of Tupper's and the Conservatives' commitment to passing the remedial bill; give Conservative members a way to explain to voters their support of the remedial bill come election day; and permit Tupper to use the good name of Sir Donald Smith to socialize details of an alternative approach to resolving the Manitoba schools issue through the national media before the general election.

The Smith Commission

The Smith Commission began with Donald Smith's secret mission to Manitoba on Sunday, February 16. He spent five days shuttling between the Manitoba Hotel (a Smith holding), the legislative buildings, and the cathedral in Saint-Boniface, speaking with Greenway, Sifton, Langevin, Ewart, and other officials along the way. At some point, news got out that Smith was in town on government business. A reporter asked him on Thursday if that was true, but all Smith would admit to was being "deeply concerned for the future of Canada and would greatly regret to see it rent and torn by prolonging the agitation on the schools question." Greenway was also interviewed. He said he respected and was impressed by Smith's efforts but was clear the conversations they were having could only "contribute to success if no sacrifice of the principle of a national system of schools were involved."

Smith returned to Ottawa early on February 24 and told Tupper and Bowell that he'd made some progress: Greenway was willing to "consider proposition for conference if received from Dominion Government" and Sifton, while "not able to make any suggestion" on how the School Act could be amended to satisfy Roman Catholics, said his government would "be prepared to weigh carefully any suggestion that may be made to us." Smith told the Aberdeens that "Langevin is not in an impossible mood," news which gave Lady Aberdeen "some hope of this miserable question being adjusted at the last moment."

Of course, it took three weeks to iron out the conference details. On March 2, Greenway demanded that the Dominion issue an official invitation as "we are not to blame for the present situation." On March 6, an invitation was proffered, but Greenway insisted that Ottawa issue an Order in Council setting out "the object of the visit, and the subject matters intended to be discussed at the suggested conference." Enough was worked out by March 9 for Tupper to announce the commission in the House. It took until March 17 for cabinet to authorize Sir Donald Smith, justice minister Arthur Dickey, and militia minister Senator Alphonse Desjardins "to proceed to Winnipeg to hold a conference with the Government of Manitoba for the purpose of ascertaining whether legislation cannot be obtained from the Legislature of Manitoba during its present session which will deal in a manner satisfactorily to the minority in Manitoba with those grievances of the minority which are now before the House of Commons in connection with the remedial bill." The Dominion commissioners would leave for Winnipeg as soon as the remedial bill passed second reading.[18]

The Dominion commissioners arrived in Winnipeg on Wednesday, March 25. They met with the Manitoba delegates, Attorney General Clifford Sifton and Provincial Secretary John Cameron, on Thursday. After breakfast on Friday, the three went up to parlour room 25, adjacent to Sir Donald's suite, to prepare for the first session at ten thirty. Shortly before it was set to begin, a local reporter sent his card up asking for an interview. Sir Donald said they could spare a few moments before the conference started.

"We are very busy," Smith said, smiling and shaking hands with the reporter, "and anyway, we have practically nothing to say that is of interest."

With just the Dominion commissioners in the room, the reporter asked if any arrangements had been made for a stenographer to take notes.

"No, not as yet," Smith replied. "We are to hold the meetings in this room, but nothing in the way of selecting a Chairman or making other preliminary arrangements has been done."

Anew

The reporter then asked, "Can you remember any case in Canadian history that can be compared with the present conference?"

"Well, I cannot think of a parallel just now. It is a most important conference and will mark an epoch in Canadian history. We have come here to exhaust all the means in our power on behalf of the Dominion Government to effect a satisfactory settlement, not in the interests of any political party, but for the welfare of the country as a whole, and I believe, as I have before stated, that what I term the legitimate way of settling this question is by the Government of Manitoba and by this Legislature."

"That is right," Desjardins added.

"Have you any idea how long the conference will last?" the reporter asked the senator.

"Well, no," Desjardins said. "We are so very comfortable in this hotel that we are apt to prolong the enjoyment as long as possible. That is really all I can say on the matter."

At ten thirty, the Dragoon stationed outside the parlour door let the Manitoba delegates inside where, for the next ninety minutes, the Dominion commissioners presented their "Suggestions for Settlement of the Manitoba School Question." Based loosely on the Nova Scotia model the Tupper administration had put in place in 1865, the commissioners proposed that religious instruction take place within the framework of the public school system established in the *Public School Act, 1890*. Where numbers warranted (at least twenty-five Roman Catholic children in a town or village, fifty in a city), local school boards would provide a schoolhouse or a room where a Roman Catholic teacher could provide religious instruction. Textbooks would have to meet the educational standards of the provincial advisory board and not "offend the religious views of the minority." Catholics would be given representation on the advisory board and on the board of examiners that certified all teachers. Catholics would be given provincial assistance to maintain a normal school for their teachers. And existing Catholic teachers would be given two years to qualify for credentials.

The conference resumed Monday at four, with the Manitoba response. At bottom, Clifton said the province could not agree to a proposal that sought to "establish a system of state-supported separate schools for the

Roman Catholic people and would compel their support by the school taxes and legislative grants." Clifton then critiqued each of the Dominion's suggestions and finished with the contention that the people of Manitoba had rejected the separation principle underlying the Dominion's proposals in the January 15 election. "It is clear, therefore, that we are precluded from accepting the proposition which has been made. Such acceptance would ... be a direct breach of faith with the people of our province."

Clifton and Cameron then presented their counterproposal, to "completely secularize the public school system" by eliminating "religious exercises and teaching of every kind during school hours," permitting religious instruction by clergy of any faith on school premises between 3:30 p.m. and 4:00 p.m. and making religious instruction voluntary and subject to parental consent. It was pretty much the same "compromise" Greenway had submitted back in November. Monday's session adjourned at five.

On Tuesday, the Dominion team tried one last time to find common ground. They said the intent of their suggestions was merely to "put in general terms as a suggested basis upon which our future discussions might proceed with a view to a possible agreement of all parties interested." They said their "proposals very materially limit what is always considered the privileges essential in connection with a separate school system. The proposed schools would be controlled by trustees elected by the whole body of ratepayers under the provisions of your school law." But it was no use. The Manitobans were not interested in compromise, as they made clear in their final statement issued Wednesday morning:

"Your proposition aims at the legal recognition by the legislature of Manitoba of the right of the Roman Catholic people to separate for school purposes. Our proposition aims at removing every practical objection to the present system without giving a legal right to separate ... In a word, we are absolutely debarred from conceding a system of Roman Catholic and state-aided separate schools, while the representatives of the minority, and, as a consequence, the Federal Government will accept nothing less."

On Thursday, Smith pronounced the "conference has closed, and no settlement has been arrived at" and then he, Dickey, and Desjardins boarded their private car and returned to Ottawa.

Anew

Obstructed

The final act of the remedial bill drama began with committee review on Monday, April 6. As with debate on second reading, Tupper charged the House with sitting day and night. It was yet more proof of Tupper's and the Conservatives' supposed commitment to passing the bill: "I, for one, am prepared to exhaust every physical power I possess by staying here night and day in order to carry this measure through committee," said Tupper. "And failing that, to go to the intelligent electorate of this country to decide between the conduct of the Government in regard to this important measure and the public business of this country, and the unparliamentary means adopted by honourable gentlemen opposite to obstruct the public business." And exhausted the House became. The first sitting of clause-by-clause review lasted 129 hours, from Monday the sixth until Saturday the eleventh. The second lasted fifty-six hours, from Monday the thirteenth until Wednesday the fifteenth, when the bill was ultimately withdrawn.

Throughout committee review, Tupper's main goal was to make it look like he and the Conservatives were committed to passing the Sixth Ministry's remedial bill, but then do whatever could be done to obstruct its passage. One favoured tactic was to heap verbal abuse on a Liberal or Conservative anti-remedialist until the member would rise, indignant, on a point of order and sidetrack the committee into needless and lengthy debate about that. Tupper unleashed one particularly vitriolic diatribe against Wilfrid Laurier on April 8. Instead of doing his job as opposition leader and "promoting the interests of his party," Tupper charged that "every hour the honourable gentleman spends in this gross, palpable obstruction of the business of the House." In so doing, all Laurier was accomplishing was proving "his entire unfitness to occupy a position of responsibility in reference to the affairs of this country." In a rage, which grew over the course of the diatribe, Tupper continued:

> If he thinks by this means to turn the public attention away from the changing, chameleon-like policy he has pursued in the past, showing that he was ready to go east, west, north or south on the great fiscal and commercial questions before

the country if it would only afford the least chance of his obtaining power — if he thinks he is going to turn the public mind away from the incapacity to grasp the true interests of the country in those great matters which make for the progress and prosperity of Canada, he is entirely deceived. The position the honourable gentleman occupies today is one showing his utter incapacity to discharge the duties of a leader of a loyal, constitutional opposition....

And I can only say that the course the honourable gentleman is taking in this House is not only outraging the sense of justice of this Parliament but it is outraging the sense of justice and fair-play and sense of public duty of every right-minded man in this country. The honourable gentleman knows that he is taking unfair advantage of the fact that the duration of this Parliament is so limited to endeavour to prevent those of his own race and his own religion receiving justice, after long years of suffering, after long years of being deprived of the privileges enjoyed under the law and constitution of the country … he cares not who suffers, he cares not what race they are of, he cares not what religion they are of, he cares not what their sufferings may be; in a vain attempt to grasp power in this country, he is willing to let them suffer, and to let them take the consequences.

Laurier, as expected, took exception to Tupper's harangue, called it "a sorry and sad exhibition of impotent and unseemly rage", and demanded that Tupper retract the term "obstruction" as unparliamentary. Tupper claimed there was no other word for what Laurier was doing, citing precedent from New Zealand and Pakistan. Eventually, under pressure from the chair, Tupper relented and retracted the term. That tussle took up the better part of an hour.

While Laurier wouldn't admit it outright, Tupper was right on one count: the Liberals were indeed waging a classic filibuster campaign against the remedial bill. On April 8, for example, John Charlton said the only way to demonstrate what "religious teaching actually is" was to "refer to the selections themselves." The member for Norfolk North then proceeded to read sixty-six selections from the Old and New Testaments, the first being "the first eighteen verses of John, Chapter 1." One reporter said "the Conservative benches began to resound with amens and laughter. Mr. Charlton, without heeding the jeers and jokes, proceeded to examine the Bible selections. Mr. Wallace asked the reading of the chapter about Joseph and his brothers. Mr. Charlton acquiesced, and as he read, the House became noisy with jeers and laughter again." On April 10, Dr. Frederick Borden (Kings) advised the committee that he wished "to speak of the effect of these long sittings upon the health of the members of this House." Borden said, "everybody knows that a supply of fresh air is absolutely necessary for health, [but] most everybody didn't know that when the same air is breathed for several hours, it is turned into actual poison." Borden then reached down and picked up Kirk's *Handbook of Physiology* from the pile of medical textbooks he'd stacked beside his desk. Borden "read copiously ... causing amusement in the committee, but when he pursued in his reading of the terrible effect of members continuing in session in an atmosphere heavy with carbonic acid poison, the amusement turned to expressions of mock terror." Charlton's Sunday school lesson lasted two hours, Borden's tutorial an hour and a half.

Even without the filibusters, it is unclear if committee review would have proceeded much faster. The bill was in such poor shape that even when substantive debate occurred it focused on drafting rather than intent. For example, section 2 (3) authorized: "The Department of Education may also make from time to time such regulations as they may think fit for the general organization of the Separate Schools." Section 4 (A), by contrast, said, "It shall be the duty of the Board of Education to have under its control and management the Separate Schools and to make from time to time such regulations as may be deemed fit for their general government and discipline and the carrying out of the provisions of the act." For eighteen hours, Liberals James Edgar, David Mills, and Richard Cartwright hounded the government for an answer on how the two provisions should be reconciled. Thomas Daly finally admitted on April 3 "that there does seem to be an anomaly between subsection 2 of section 3, and section 4. The matter is of such serious importance that it seems to me that the Government will have to consider whether they will press subsection 2 of section 3 as a part of the Bill. This is a matter that I should like some time to consider; and if you will leave the discussion of that over, I will undertake that opportunity will be given for discussion before the third reading." The bill died before Daly could provide clarification.

Another example was section 7, which gave Manitoba's Lieutenant Governor in Council the authority to "appoint one of the members of the board to be the superintendent of the separate schools, and the superintendent shall be the secretary of the board." On April 9, Liberal François Langelier (Quebec-Centre) said, "I do not see any provision for paying the superintendent. If you want a good man of ability you must give him a good salary."

Tupper told him, "I will have to ask the honourable gentleman not to interpose an objection of that kind at this stage. The question of payment will rise later."

"This is the proper place to provide for it, otherwise the clause will be useless," said Langelier. "We have the right now to know what the Government proposes to do."

"If the honourable gentleman wants to interpose difficulty in the way of getting the Bill through I cannot prevent him," Tupper told him. "But if he is disposed to assist in carrying the Bill through it is not desirable to raise this question now."

"I do not see in any other part of the Bill a provision for the pay of the superintendent, and I do not see when the question can be raised if not now."

"We will have to leave that as it is. The matter has been carefully considered, and I do not see any possible difficulty in asking the Lieutenant Governor to make the appointment."

The gruelling schedule also took a toll on parliamentary decorum and etiquette. Early on April 7, "strange noises" began emitting from the backbenches. "Jokes were played and applause interspersed at inappropriate periods through the Doric speech of the member for South Huron. Girouard borrowed a harmonica from Turcotte and played bits of tunes as obbligato accompaniment of the speech-making." Late on April 11, Independent member John Ferguson (Renfrew South) stomped over to Thomas Craig Sproule's seat with a view to "intimidate Sproule and to force him to alter his policy." Ferguson shook his fist in Sproule's face, and "poured forth a torrent of abuse, among which profane adjectives accompanying the words 'liar' 'Boodler' and 'fool' could distinctly be heard." Sproule held his ground. He "brought his fist down on his desk with the air of a man who is not to be coerced by any means." McAllister got to the quarrelling couple first and pushed the by-then flailing Ferguson out of the chamber. Sproule evaded capture by another member and followed McAllister and Ferguson out into the hallway but returned when others showed up to separate the combatants. Back in the chamber, Sproule suggested that "the bar downstairs has been helping to bring about this unseemly and disgraceful spectacle. This is a great reason why this committee should rise until some of the members on the opposite side are sober."

Debate on Bill C-58 drew to an ignominious conclusion on Wednesday, April 15, with only 15 of 112 clauses passed. The Governor General had sent a note to cabinet the day before, warning that "Parliament had but a week more to run and the Supplementary Estimates had yet to be passed." Many government employees, including parliamentary staff, hadn't been paid in over a month. In moving adjournment, Tupper said how deeply he regretted, "owing to the persistent obstruction of the advantage taken of the limited character of this session, that it had been in our power to do no more … I only express my regret that we have not been able to carry this measure to its fruition, and especially as there has not been an opportunity of taking the opinion of Parliament upon some important questions arising in connection with it."

Laurier asked if Tupper was withdrawing the bill.

Tupper said no, he was merely suspending "proceeding with the bill in order to take the necessary supply to provide for the absolute necessities of the public services, leaving the question open to be resumed the moment supplies are obtained."

After the marathon sittings, Laurier was understandably punchy. "I think I understand well that this is his way of covering his retreat. At all events, I protest against the assertion of the honourable gentleman that if he does not proceed any further with this measure at the present time it is due to the obstruction with which, as he says, this bill had been met."

"We have had nine hours of persistent obstruction now," Tupper said.

"You have had nine hours discussion upon a motion to adjourn, which was made at two o'clock in the morning at a very proper time," Laurier charged.

"It was made at four o'clock," Tupper said.

The usually unflappable Laurier had had it.

> It matters not whether it was made at four o'clock or two o'clock. The motion was made at a time when the House should no longer have been in session and when the Government should have acceded to the motion because it was fair and reasonable. Besides, whose fault is it if today this bill is not proceeded with? Who has had charge of this question? Why, they are upon the Treasury benches. Whose fault is it if the honourable gentlemen, who sit on the Treasury benches for five long weeks did not dare to take up this question? Whose fault is it if after they took hold of it they did it with an Order in Council, which was drastic and violent in its tone, which instead of inviting conciliation on the part of Manitoba, almost forced Manitoba to a hostile action? Whose fault was it after calling a session last year to deal with the other business and with this question, this question was never brought up? Whose fault was it? I want to know if there was wrangling between the rival factions of the Government when the only man who was endowed with courage and conviction was forced to withdraw from the Cabinet? Whose fault was it that in July last they undertook to invite negotiations with Manitoba, and six months passed, and no

negotiations took place? Whose fault was it if, when we met on January 2, purposely to deal with this question, we found the Cabinet divided into two factions, one member speaking of the other as an imbecile and the other calling his colleagues traitors? Whose fault was it when they had patched up their differences, when they were more or less a united family, that the bill was not introduced? Whose fault was it that instead of the bill being introduced, we proceeded with the budget debate? Whose fault was it if sixty days elapsed before the bill was introduced? Whose fault was it that the bill was not introduced for discussion until we had come to the dying days of the session when the life of this Parliament can only go on until the 24th of this month? It was not the fault of anybody but the honourable gentlemen on the Treasury benches. They say they have had to withdraw this bill from the committee at the present time, that it is due to obstruction. It is a statement which, for my part, I am quite willing to leave to the judgment of the impartial electors of this country.

The curtains lowered on the great remedial bill debate at 2:30 a.m. when the House, finally, adopted a motion to adjourn and everyone went home to bed.

Resignation

Prime Minister Mackenzie Bowell arrived at Topley's Ottawa photography studio for a special sitting late Monday morning, April 27. Bedecked in full Windsor kit, he wanted to have a special portrait of himself done for Lord and Lady Aberdeen as a token of thanks for the advice and support the Aberdeens had given him, "which enabled him now to retire with dignity after having pressed the remedial policy to which he had pledged himself."

Afterward, Bowell went to Rideau Hall to have lunch with the Aberdeens and tender his resignation. Lady Aberdeen said Bowell made it clear he didn't want the Governor General to "ask his advice as to whom to send for & H.E. did not." Aberdeen, though, told Bowell he "only saw one alternative & that was Sir Charles Tupper." Bowell said Tupper had asked him if he'd join Tupper's cabinet, "or take the Lieutenant-Governorship of Ontario, or the High Commissionership in London," but he had declined. Bowell said he accepted being named commissioner to negotiate the fast Atlantic ferry service, only because "he has always been interested in it." The Aberdeens asked what Bowell thought about the Conservatives' electoral chances. Bowell said he didn't "think that the Conservatives will win in the election unless the policy of obstruction of the Liberals has given them a chance."

At four thirty, Bowell left Rideau Hall and the Governor General sent Captain Sinclair to summon Tupper — "the old Cumberland war-horse," as Lady Aberdeen called him. Tupper arrived at five thirty and agreed to undertake the commission to form Canada's Seventh Ministry. Aberdeen asked if Tupper would "summon Parliament together as early as possible [and] press forward the supplies" as there was "no public money granted now for public service after June 30th." Tupper agreed to summon Parliament back on July 16, after the June 23 election.

Mackenzie Bowell gave his last public speech as prime minister at the annual St. George's Society dinner on April 23, 1896. In reply to a toast to "the Parliament of Canada," Bowell said that august body "had not added much to its reputation during the past three or four years. Truly it was unique in its character, but unfortunately for us, we have lost three Premiers, three of the most brilliant men that ever lived in Canada. There never had been a Parliament, however, that had had so many sleepless nights and done so little work as the present one!" Bowell said he was "relieved from anxiety and worry being placed in the easier position as a member of the Senate." However, he hoped that "never in Canada would we witness a session of Parliament that would be in the remotest degree a parallel to the one just closed. We have had enough for once, and we should hope to have no more." Bowell said it was doubtful whether he would go to England to sit on the Pacific Cable Commission, as "my ability to act would perhaps be doubted by my confreres."

9

Coda

Sir Charles Tupper and Canada's Seventh Ministry were sworn into office on May 1, 1896, and spent their sixty-eight-day term on the campaign trail. While Tupper insisted that the "real issue" of the campaign was "our fight to protect the industries of Canada," neither he nor his ministers backed down from their commitment to protect the denominational school rights of Roman Catholics in Manitoba. Tupper told a rally in London on June 13 that "we have nothing to do with the question of separate schools; the Government of Canada have to deal with one point only, and that is to maintain the law and constitution of the country." Details on exactly how the Conservatives proposed to deliver on that commitment were never provided.

Sir Wilfrid Laurier and his Liberals won a twenty-three-seat majority in the June 23 general election, largely on the back of a landslide victory in Quebec (the Liberals took forty-nine of sixty-five seats there, up from thirty in 1891). Senator Alphonse Desjardins said the Conservative defeat in Quebec boiled down to "the desire of French Canada to have a French-Canadian prime minister, and, secondly, to the superior organization of the

Liberal Party." Bowell agreed that nationalism had triumphed over religion. In a letter he wrote to Tupper shortly after the results came in, "I have not yet recovered from surprise and astonishment at the returns from Quebec. What does it mean? Have the people in that province thrown off the influence of the Church, or did the desire for a French Premier counterbalance all other considerations? I am somewhat inclined to the latter opinion, race having had more influence with the people than creed."

Throughout the 1896 election, Laurier maintained his "investigation and conciliation" policy on the Manitoba schools question, and once in office began discussions with the Manitoba government on a solution to the schools issue. In November 1896, the so-called Laurier-Greenway Compromise was announced. No separate school system was created. Instead, thirty minutes of clergy-led denominational instruction were to be permitted at the end of each school day, where parents requested and numbers warranted (ten children in rural areas, twenty-five in urban). School boards were to employ at least one certified Roman Catholic teacher to deliver instruction in rural districts having at least twenty-five Catholic children, forty in urban areas. Instruction was to be delivered in both French and English in any school with ten or more students who spoke French. And while no specific details were announced, there was to be Catholic representation in school administration (inspectors, advisory council, etc.) and textbooks were to be mutually acceptable.

The Aberdeens returned to Great Britain at the end of their term in 1898 and proceeded to throw themselves into the anti–Boer War cause as part of the International Crusade for Peace. When the Liberals came back into power in the U.K. in 1906, the couple moved to Dublin once again, when Lord Aberdeen was reappointed Lord Lieutenant of Ireland in 1906, a position he held until 1914.

After the 1896 election, Sir Charles Tupper let himself be convinced to stay on as opposition leader — "the party can have no other leader than yourself," said one party official. The decision put an end to Charlie Hibbert Tupper's leadership ambitions. Even though Charlie retained his Pictou seat in the 1896 and 1900 elections, there was simply no room for a second Tupper to share the leadership spotlight in the Dominion cabinet. Tupper

Coda

père served as opposition leader until early 1901. He resigned after leading the Conservatives to a second general election loss, in November 1900. He was seventy-nine years old.

Mackenzie Bowell sat out the 1896 election in London, England. He did accept Tupper's nomination to join his friend Sandford Fleming there as Canada's official representatives on the Pacific Cable Commission (none of his confreres objected). The two men left Ottawa on May 9, 1896. Bowell returned to Canada in the fall and took up duties as leader of the opposition in the Senate, a position he held until 1906.

Outside of Parliament, former prime minister Bowell maintained an active life. In 1896, he returned to work in Belleville at the *Intelligencer*, the newspaper where he'd started his career, making regular contributions there until 1913. He also continued to travel extensively. In 1897, he and Sir Charles Tupper took a cross-country trip, with an extensive tour of the Kootenay region where both men owned property. A decade later, Bowell and son John visited Dawson City, where the elder Bowell insisted on taking a dip in the Yukon River.

In 1912, Bowell had a close brush with death. While coming down the stairs of the Albany Club in Toronto, he slipped and fell. Fearing the worst, friends moved the unconscious octogenarian to an adjacent room, made him comfortable, and called for a doctor.

"Is he dead?" one of Mack's friends asked when the doctor arrived.

At this point, Mack opened his eyes and saw above him pictures of Sir John A. Macdonald, Sir Charles Tupper, and Robert Borden hanging on the wall.

"If I'm dead, I'm in very good company," Bowell said drolly, to the doctor's surprise and his friends' relief.

Five years later, Bowell wasn't so lucky. After contracting pneumonia at a friend's funeral, Canada's fifth prime minister died on December 10, 1917, seventeen days short of his ninety-fourth birthday. His funeral at the Bridge Street Methodist Church was well attended by hundreds of Belleville residents, with local business suspended for the afternoon while the long cortège of family and friends travelled from the church to Belleville Cemetery. Ottawa did not send a delegation.

Notes

1 Abbott didn't think much of Thompson's plan. "I am sorry I cannot agree with you [wrote Abbott] as to the recommendation to be given on [my] resigning. I do not think the choice you suggest would be to the advantage of the country, and I am convinced also it would cause great difficulty in the Cabinet. Foster agrees with me entirely in both of these views, and deprecates very strongly any such step on my part. In fact, I am convinced not only that the feeling of the party points directly and unmistakably to yourself, but that the interest of the country will be best served by your assuming power."

2 Solicitor General John Curran, Controller of Customs Nathaniel Clarke Wallace, and Controller of Inland Revenue John Wood were part of the ministry but were not "of cabinet." Modelled after the British undersecretary position, those portfolios were created by Macdonald in 1887 as "training grounds" for "younger members of Parliament" who, after some period of probation, might prove eligible for promotion to cabinet minister. The solicitor general was responsible for managing Crown prosecutions and reported to the attorney general/minister of justice. The customs controller oversaw the administration of tariffs, and the inland revenue controller oversaw the administration of taxes and duties. The controllers reported to the minister of trade and commerce.

3 On December 12, Tupper was on his way from Vancouver to Westminster on the government ferry *Quadra* when he noticed that all the flags had been lowered at the landing. He thought it was the canners playing a joke because they didn't think that he, the minister, was listening to them. When the *Quadra* docked, the harbour master handed Tupper a mittful of telegraphs announcing Thompson's death. Tupper said it was like "being hit in the stomach. I could barely catch my breath." He grabbed the next ferry back to Vancouver and got on the first train east that afternoon.

4 It would be another eight months before Laurier would enunciate his party's official position on the issue: "investigation and conciliation."

5 On July 26, 1894, the Dominion had sent a memorandum to the lieutenant governors of Manitoba and the Northwest Territories advising them of the petitions it had received about education from their Roman Catholic minorities. The memo expressed the hope that "they would take speedy

measures to give redress in all the matters in relation to which any well founded complaint or grievance be ascertained to exist." The Greenway government replied in October 1894 that there was no grievance and that "the executive of the province see no reason for recommending the legislature to alter the principle of the legislation complained of."

6   Bowell had a long history of supporting the constitutional rights of minorities. In his first effort to win public office, in 1863, Bowell was defeated for failing to denounce the incorporation of a Catholic welfare charity, the Ladies of Loretto. According to Payne, Bowell "took the high and patriotic ground, that in a country like this, occupied by a heterogenous population, it was impossible to govern successfully along narrow lines. He argued that it would be unjust to take away rights and privileges which had been acquired by law, and contrary to what he understood to be the principles of the Conservative Party. Prejudices were actively aroused, and a deaf ear was turned to the voice of reason and toleration. Bowell was defeated." Thirty-two years later, and despite his long association with and participation in the Orange Order in-between, the defining feature of Bowell's time as prime minister was once again his effort to take "the high and patriotic ground" and defend minority rights.

7   It wasn't a hollow threat. The influential Bishop of Trois-Rivières, Louis-François Laflèche, was advising Archbishop Adélard Langevin (who'd succeeded Taché at Saint-Boniface) along similar lines: "If it happened that the federal government did not follow through on this decree, it would be, in my humble opinion, the duty of all Catholic and French Canadian ministers to resign and leave such a ministry, by striving to form a new party whose program would be to maintain and respect the constitution which guarantees freedom of conscience and education to all members of the confederation and to render justice equal to all the Power, without distinction of nationality, language and religion."

8   Resignation, or the threat to resign, was one of Charlie Tupper's favourite tactics. In June 1891, Tupper told his father he'd resign from cabinet if John Thompson became prime minister instead of his father. In March 1893, both Tuppers resigned in a dispute with George Foster over the terms of a trade treaty with France that Tupper Sr. had negotiated. In June 1893, Charlie Tupper threatened to resign over his dissatisfaction with John Costigan's management of his fisheries portfolio while he was in Paris as part of the Bering Sea arbitration delegation. And in November 1893, Tupper threatened to resign if Thompson did not withdraw the Dominion government's patronage from the *Halifax Herald* after it made disparaging comments about him and his father. Tupper Sr. convinced Charlie to remain in cabinet in the first instance; Thompson talked Charlie off the ledge in the others.

9   Hugh Sutherland understood what was happening and wasn't pleased. He wrote Haggart on April 24 to say he was appointing new contractors.

Notes

William Mackenzie warned Haggart two days later that any such move would invalidate the terms of his and Mann's contracts with Sutherland and also the Court of Manitoba's 1891 judgment. Haggart wrote a one-liner back to Sutherland on April 27: "I may inform you that the Government cannot recognize these contractors in the matter."

10   Thomas Daly said he'd "as soon saw wood at fifty cents a cord and board myself than go through another round of estimates with Foster right now."

11   As minister of customs in 1890, Bowell had conducted a wagon train inspection tour of customs houses along a 750-mile stretch of the Canada-US border between Deloraine, Manitoba, (the terminus of the CPR) and Milk River, Alberta. The next summer, Bowell toured the Kootenay region of southeast British Columbia. He left Fort Macleod on August 29 on a NWMP pack train of "eleven horses and eleven pack animals," and travelled almost 600 miles through the Crowsnest Pass, reaching Revelstoke on September 18.

12   The Crosby Home for Girls was established in 1879, the Crosby Boys' Home in 1890. Both facilities began receiving government funding in 1893. A 1905 inspection report concluded that the students were being harshly treated and underfed. University of British Columbia. The Indian Residential School History and Dialogue Centre. "Port Simpson (B.C.)," accessed March 24, 2021. collections.irshdc.ubc.ca/index.php/Detail/entities/51.

13   The Kuper Island School opened in 1889. Students set it ablaze when holidays were cancelled in 1896. A survey that year reported that of 264 former students, 107 had died. It is unclear if "James," referred to below, was among them. University of British Columbia. The Indian Residential School History and Dialogue Centre. "Kuper Island (B.C.)," accessed March 24, 2021. collections.irshdc.ubc.ca/index.php/Detail/entities/48.

14   The Duck Lake Residential School had been established by Roman Catholic missionaries in 1894. Tuberculosis was epidemic in the school's early years. In 1910, an Indian agent estimated that 50 percent of the children sent to the school had died. Later rebuilt as St. Michael's, the residential school was one of the last to close in Canada, in 1996. University of British Columbia. The Indian Residential School History and Dialogue Centre. "St. Michael's (S.K.)," accessed March 24, 2021. collections.irshdc.ubc.ca/index.php/Detail/entities/1229.

15   Bowell also had a hand in approving Canada's first Métis colony in present-day northeast Alberta. In December 1895, Bowell's cabinet approved Father Lacombe's request for four townships for settlement by destitute Métis families and four sections to the Catholic Church to build an industrial school and church. Saint-Paul-des-Métis became operational in the summer of 1896, with forty families settled by 1901. Financial irregularities, crop failures, and mismanagement caused the colony to be opened to general settlement in 1909.

16. The Manitoba government was equally dug in. Asked by a *Daily Tribune* reporter "if negotiations were proceeding between Ottawa and Winnipeg looking to a compromise on the school question," an unnamed member of Greenway's cabinet took out his pencil, "swept it round a few circles on the pad in front of [the reporter], and tore off the written answer — 'No Compromise' it said."

17. Crunican says "There is no record of Walsh's reply to Lady Aberdeen. It seems clear that he did not make the request to Rome, but did write to Lacombe and Langevin to urge moderation. More significantly, Walsh also wrote to Laurier, opposing the latter's plan for an inquiry in Manitoba and suggesting instead the meeting of all principles. The same suggestion was sent to Lacombe, Begin, and Langevin" (180).

18. Of course, Lady Aberdeen couldn't help inserting herself into the mix to "soften the wheels" for the conference. In Quebec City the week of March 22, she asked Archbishop Begin in Montreal to see if he could get Archbishop Langevin "to agree to an agreement with the federal delegates in Winnipeg." Begin did write Langevin but encouraged him not to concede the principle of separate schools enshrined in the remedial bill. Langevin replied to Lady Aberdeen through Begin on March 30, saying "I will do my utmost to get along with these gentlemen," even though the Dominion commissioners had offered "an arrangement which is the extreme limit of concessions." Knowing the relationship between Her Ladyship and Laurier, Langevin added for good measure that he hoped "the angels of peace will use their influence over the Hon. Laurier and the liberal deputies who follow him so that they urge the Government to prove its goodwill by passing the remedial law." The correspondence was indeed passed on to Laurier, who replied to Lady Aberdeen that "at a later day, your kind influence may prevail upon them to accept an honourable compromise, which would practically give them all that they want, without any violence to the express will of the majority."

Sources

Chapter 1: Sans Souci

Faith Fenton provided these rare glimpses into the notoriously private lives of prime ministers Sir John Sparrow Thompson and Sir Mackenzie Bowell in "At Sans Souci," *Empire*, September 1, 1894: 11.

I have taken some liberty including Bowell's Edward Blake story here. Although it was one of Bowell's favourites, Fenton makes no mention of Bowell telling it at Sans Souci. The story is from "Sir M. Bowell Passes Away," *Globe*, December 11, 1917: 1.

Chapter 2: Black Day

WEDNESDAY, DECEMBER 12, 1894
Writing for the Conservative Party's official newspaper, the *Empire*'s Ottawa correspondent Fred Cook had unparalleled access to Bowell and his ministers throughout this period. Cook's account of Bowell receiving the news of Thompson's death, as well as the telegrams, are from "Ottawa in Gloom," *Empire*, December 13, 1894: 1. The account of Haggart et al. hearing the news is from "Heard News from Listowel," *Globe*, December 13, 1894: 2; "Like A Thunderbolt," *Globe*, December 13, 1894: 11; and "Grief in the City," *Globe*, December 13, 1894: 1.

Bowell's account of Thompson's death is based on a telegram from Tupper and interviews Tupper gave to the British press. These are in "Canada Again Mourns," *Empire*, December 13, 1894: 2; and "All Canada Mourns," *Globe*, December 13, 1894: 1.

Bowell's conversation with Cook is from "Canada Again Mourns," *Empire*, December 13, 1894: 5.

ASCENSION
Lady Aberdeen's diary is a key source for this period, although her observations must be taken with a grain of salt and fact-checked for veracity. For example, in

writing about a conversation she had with Charlie Tupper in July 1895, Lady Aberdeen said Tupper told her that Thompson thought Bowell was not fit for cabinet office and had determined to retire him. Thompson, in fact, said exactly the opposite in 1892 when, in discussing Abbott's succession in 1892, he wrote that "Mr. Bowell has the respect of all of us and that any of us would follow him while we could agree with his policy." Lady Aberdeen also said Tupper told her the reason he and his colleagues had agreed to serve under Bowell in the first place was out of fear Lord Aberdeen was about to ask Laurier to form a government. "They were talking over this plan one evening some days after Sir Mackenzie had been commissioned to form a Govt, when it was heard that a paragraph in the papers, or rather a telegram to one of the Ministers, stated that an A.D.C. of H.E. had been seen with M. Laurier. 'We all turned in like sheep into the fold, at the very rumour. We thought it quite on the cards that H.E. would say, "Well you have had nearly a week — you evidently cannot form a Government. I will send for someone who can.""' As this chapter documents, nine of Thompson's fourteen cabinet ministers had agreed to serve under Bowell within twenty-four hours of Aberdeen asking him to see if he could form a government, and thirteen of fourteen had agreed to serve within seventy-two hours. As for the "talking over this plan one evening," Tupper wasn't even in Ottawa until Monday, December 17. He arrived mid-morning, met with Bowell midday, and then agreed to join Bowell's government an hour or so later — the last minister, in fact, to come aboard. For this conversation, see Ishbel Gordon, *The Canadian Journal of Lady Aberdeen, 1893–1898* (Toronto: Champlain Society, 1960), 247.

Lady Aberdeen's thoughts on Foster, Haggart, and Bowell, the account of her conversation with Annie Thompson, and her account of Lord Aberdeen's conversations with Bowell are at ibid., 165–66.

For more on the Aberdeen's relationship and their "very modern" marriage, see Veronica Strong-Boag, *Liberal Hearts and Coronets: The Lives and Times of Ishbel Marjoribanks Gordon and John Campbell Gordon, the Aberdeens* (Toronto: University of Toronto Press, 2015), especially chapter 3; and Doris Shackleton, *Ishbel and the Empire: A Biography of Lady Aberdeen* (Toronto: Dundurn Press, 1996), especially chapter 6.

The story of George and Addie Foster is from P.B. Waite, *The Man from Halifax: Sir John Thompson, Prime Minister* (Toronto: University of Toronto Press, 1985), 391; and Robert Craig Brown, "Foster, Sir George Eulas," *Dictionary of Canadian Biography*, accessed April 22, 2021, biographi.ca/en/bio/foster_george_eulas_16E.html.

For more on Haggart, see Ron W. Shaw, "Bohemian — John Graham Haggart (1836–1913)" (Perth & District Historical Society, 2019), accessed March 12, 2021, perthhs.org/documents/Bohemian-John-Haggart.pdf.

For more on Foster, see J.W. Dafoe, "The Political Career of Sir George Foster," *Canadian Historical Review* 15, no. 2 (June 1934): 191–95.

Sources

The "lecherous instinct" is from R.F. Armstrong to Thompson, 1 November 1892, Thompson Papers, Public Archives Canada (PAC), Ottawa. Quoted in Lovell Clark, "A History of the Conservative Administrations, 1891 to 1896" (PhD diss., University of Toronto, 1968), 326.

The text of Aberdeen's December 12, 1894, cable to Lord Ripon is at Shackleton, *Ishbel*, 166.

Tupper's statement that he is "too old" and that Thompson had left no succession plan is from "Canada Again Mourns," *Empire*, December 13, 1894: 2.

Shackleton says Ripon's December 13 reply to Aberdeen is "a most significant cable, one which unfortunately has missed the eye of those recounting these events. It appears never to have been read by Canadian historians, perhaps because it was unavailable in the Public Archives in Ottawa, although on record in London. It is not an endorsement of Bowell [as Lady Aberdeen suggests in her journal and Lord Aberdeen suggests in *We Twa*]. It said plainly that Aberdeen ought to get advice from the cabinet, through Bowell, and Aberdeen ought *not* to make his own decision" (167).

Thompson's recommendation of Bowell is from Thompson to Senator Perley, 14 October 1892, Thompson Papers, Letter Book, 33. Abbott's reply is from Abbott to Thompson, 10 November 1892, Thompson Papers, 166. Both reprinted in Clark, "A History," 117.

Tupper's correspondence from this period was published in E.M. Saunders, *The Life and Letters of the Rt. Hon. Sir Charles Tupper* (Toronto: Cassell and Company, 1916).

The insolvent estate analogy is from "Bowell," *Globe*, December 14, 1894: 1.

Smith's statement is from "As to the Cabinet," *Empire*, December 15, 1894: 1.

For coverage of Bowell's invitation to form Canada's Sixth Ministry, see "Mr. Bowell's Selection," *Empire*, December 13, 1894: 2.

The story of Bowell writing his own press release is from Betsy Boyce, *The Accidental Prime Minister: The Biography of Sir Mackenzie Bowell* (Hastings County: Kirby Books, 2001). The release itself is carried in "Bowell," *Globe*, December 14, 1894: 1.

SIXTH MINISTRY

The construction of Canada's Sixth Ministry is based on "Hon. Mr. Bowell," *Globe*, December 15, 1894: 29; "As to the Cabinet," *Empire*, December 15, 1894: 1; "Latest Cabinet Gossip," *Empire*, December 17, 1894: 1; "Slate-making in Ottawa," *Empire*, December 18, 1894: 1; "Just About Completed," *Empire*, December 19, 1894: 1; "Mr. Bowell's Ministry," *Empire*, December 20, 1894: 4.

For the parliamentary debate on the role of the controllers, see *Debates of the House of Commons of the Dominion of Canada* (hereafter, *House of Commons Debates*), 6th Parliament, 1st Session (10 June 1887) starting at 863.

A VERY CANADIAN COUP

Macdonald and Thompson's exchange on Charlie Tupper is from Waite, *Man from Halifax*, 245–46.

Charlie Tupper's account of hearing the news of Thompson's death is from "Sir Charles H. Tupper," *Globe*, December 18, 1894: 5.

OLD PARTY, OLD POLICY
Bowell and his ministers' trip to Montreal is from "The New Cabinet," *Globe*, December 21, 1894: 1; "The New Cabinet" *Globe*, December 22, 1894: 1; "To Be Sworn in Today," *Empire*, December 21, 1894: 1; "Ministers Gone to Take the Oath of Office," *Empire*, December 21, 1894: 1; "They Have Sworn," *Empire*, December 22, 1894: 2.

The first published interview with Canada's fifth prime minister is in "To Be Sworn in Today," *Empire*, December 21, 1894: x.

Chapter 3: Halifax

KNIGHT COMMANDER
Bowell's illness is covered in "Eighteen Ministers," *Globe*, December 25, 1894: 1; "On Tuesday Night at Ten," *Empire*, December 27, 1894: 1; "Premier Bowell," *Globe*, December 28, 1894: 6; "Notes from Ottawa," *Empire*, December 29, 1895: 3; "In His Native City," *Empire*, January 2, 1895: 1; "Preparations," *Globe*, January 3, 1895: 1.

The account of Bowell becoming a Knight Commander of the Order of St. Michael and St. George is from "Royally Honored," *Empire*, January 1, 1895: 1.

Dr. Reid's order for Bowell to remain at home is from "In His Native City," *Empire*, January 2, 1895: 1.

HOME
Coverage of the Blenheims' arrival at Halifax is from "In His Native City," *Empire*, January 2, 1895: 1; "Remains Brought Home," *Globe*, January 2, 1895: 1.

FAREWELL
Thompson's funeral is based on "For the State Funeral," *Empire*, December 31, 1894: 1; "Halifax is Ready," *Empire*, January 1, 1895: 1–2; "Lying in State," *Empire*, January 3, 1895: 1–2; "Consigned to Mother Earth," *Empire*, January 4, 1895: 1–2; "Preparations," *Globe*, January 3, 1895: 1; "In the Tomb," *Globe*, January 4, 1895: 2; "The State Funeral," *Globe*, January 26, 1895: 7.

The Empire has the prime minister in the cathedral and in the parade. Other papers (the *Globe*, the *Toronto World*, and the *Fredericton Herald*) say he did not attend. According to the *Herald*, "all the Dominion Cabinet Ministers excepting Premier Bowell (who was indisposed)." "Sir John Thompson's Remains," *Herald*, January 5, 1895. The *World* reported similarly that "Premier Bowell did

Sources

not attend either service at the Cathedral or funeral, being confined to the house by sickness," *Toronto World*, January 4, 1895: 1.

Cameron's comments to Lady Aberdeen are from Lady Aberdeen's diary, 181.

Thompson's funeral sermon is extracted from Cornelius O'Brien (Archbishop of Halifax), *Funeral Sermon on Sir John Thompson* (Halifax: E.P. Meagher Limited, 1906).

Chapter 4: Ides

Coverage of Bowell's illness is from "The News from Ottawa," *Empire*, January 8, 1895: 2; "The Premier's Illness," *Globe*, January 11, 1895: 8; "The News from Ottawa," *Empire*, January 17, 1895: 1.

Cabinet business in January is from "Cabinet Questions," *Globe*, January 9, 1895: 1; "The General Elections," *Globe*, January 15, 1895; 4; "Question of the Hour," *Globe*, January 17, 1895: 1; "Election Probabilities," *Globe*, January 19, 1895: 13; "His Excellency Sounded," *Globe*, January 25, 1895: 1; "Manitoba Schools," *Empire*, January 10, 1895: 1; "The News from Ottawa," *Empire*, January 17, 1895: 1; "Meeting of the Cabinet," *Empire*, January 19, 1895: 1.

BROPHY

The law and history of the Manitoba school question here is based on Gordon Bale, "Law, Politics and the Manitoba School Question: Supreme Court and Privy Council," *Canadian Bar Review* 63, no.3 (September 1985); and "Quebecers, the Roman Catholic Church and the Manitoba School Question: A Chronology," Marianopolis College, faculty.marianopolis.edu/c.belanger/QuebecHistory/chronos/manitoba.htm.

The Macdonald quote is from correspondence between Macdonald to Chevrier, 25 March 1890; cited in Clark, "A History," 249.

Taché's affidavit is included in *Barrett v. The City of Winnipeg*, part 1, chapter 2, 8. In John Ewart, *The Manitoba School Question. Being a Compilation of the Legislation, the Legal Proceedings, the Proceedings before the Governor-in-Council* (Toronto: Copp, Clark, 1894).

HE'S ALL RIGHT

Laurier's speech at Massey Hall is from "Laurier at Massey Hall," *Empire*, February 6, 1896: 1.

Bowell's first public comments as prime minister were made at the Annual Convention of the Canadian Press Association on February 1, 1895. See "Gathering of Pressmen," *Empire*, February 1, 1895: 2. Bowell's first formal public address as prime minister, as well as Tupper's speech, is from "Their New Home," *Empire*, February 8, 1896: 1–2; "Five Ministers," *Globe*, February 8, 1895: 1.

A VERY CANADIAN COUP

PRELIMINARY CANTER

Ouimet's quote in *La Minerve* is reprinted in "The School Question," *Empire*, February 12, 1895: 2.

Bowell's statement to the press is from "At the Capital," *Empire*, February 18, 1895: 8.

Charlie Tupper described his position to his father in Sir Charles H. Tupper to Tupper, 29 January 1895, Tupper Papers, 18, PAC. Reprinted in various sources.

The French ministers' position is from Ouimet's remarks to the Conservative Club in St. Hyacinthe, "Doings in Montreal," *Globe*, February 25, 1895: 2; and "At St. Hyacinthe," *Globe*, February 25, 1895: 1.

The Bowell-Schultz correspondence is from Bowell to Schultz, 7 March 1895, Bowell Papers, PAC, Ottawa. Reprinted in various sources.

Lafleche's letter to Langevin is reprinted in Paul Crunican, *Priests and Politicians: Manitoba Schools and the Election of 1896* (University of Toronto Press, Scholarly Publishing Division, 1974), 49.

The Bowell-Aberdeen correspondence is from Aberdeen to Bowell, 16 February 1895, Aberdeen Papers, PAC, Ottawa; Bowell to Aberdeen, 17 February 1895. Reprinted in various sources.

On the state of the Dominion voters' lists and its impact on election timing, see "Notes from Ottawa," *Empire*, January 9, 1895: 1; "The Premier's Illness," *Globe*, January 11, 1895: 1; "Election Chances," *Globe*, January 23, 1895: 2; "His Excellency 'Sounded,'" *Globe*, January 25, 1895: 1; "At St. Hyacinthe," *Globe*, February 25, 1895: 1; "Voters' Lists Almost Finalized," *Globe*, February 28, 1895: 1.

The Dominion's July 1894 memorandum is from House of Commons. Sessional Papers (20B), 1895, at 341. Manitoba's response is in ibid. at 347. Both are quoted in Clark, *A History*, 321.

APPEAL

Full text of the Roman Catholic appeal to the Dominion cabinet is in *Proceedings in the Manitoba School Case, Heard Before Her Majesty's Privy Council for Canada, February 26th to March 7th, 1895*, ed. Gerald Brophy (Ottawa: Government Printing Bureau, 1895).

For newspaper coverage of the appeal, see "The School Case," *Globe*, March 5, 1895: 1; "The School Case," *Globe*, March 6, 1895: 1; "M'Carthy's Argument," *Globe*, March 7, 1895: 2; "Manitoba School Case," *Globe*, March 8, 1895: 1; "The School Case," *Daily Mail and Empire*, March 5, 1895: 5–8; "The School Case," *Daily Mail and Empire*, March 6, 1895: 5; "The School Case," *Daily Mail and Empire*, March 7, 1895: 1; "The School Case," *Daily Mail and Empire*, March 8, 1895: 1.

On Ewart and his role in the Manitoba school issue, see Douglas Lowell Cole, *The Better Patriot: John S. Ewart and the Canadian Nation* (PhD diss., University of Washington, 1968), accessed March 12, 2021. archive.org/details/betterpatriotjoh0000cole/page/n3/mode/2up.

Sources

On McCarthy's role in the Manitoba school issue, see J.R. Miller, "D'Alton McCarthy, Equal Rights, and the Origins of the Manitoba School Question," *Canadian Historical Review* 54, no. 4 (March 1973).

MICAWBERS
Minutes for cabinet meetings of the Sixth Ministry are not available — except for two scraps of paper related to the July 3 cabinet meeting (see Clark, *A History*, 391). Cabinet proceedings described in this book generally are derived from newspaper accounts, usually written by Ottawa correspondents based on private conversations with those "in the room." (Former *Globe* editor John Willison said his relationship with "a Conservative member" enabled him as Ottawa correspondent in the late 1880s to "occasionally forecast ministerial policy and even to announce impending Cabinet changes in advance of official organs … But if I got, I had to give. Neither of us committed any venal offence, and there was mutual advantage in the understanding." Sir John Willison, "Reminiscences Political and Personal," *The Canadian Magazine* 51, no. 5 (September 1918), 233. canadiana.ca/view/oocihm.8_06251_307/4.

The Dominion cabinet debate on the Roman Catholic appeal is based on "The Cabinet's position," *Globe*, March 14, 1895: 2; "Cabinet Council Today," *Globe*, March 16, 1895: 8; "Manitoba School Question Unsettled," *Globe*, March 18, 1895: 1; "The Cabinet Appears to be Floundering," *Globe*, March 19, 1895: 1; "The Order Made," *Globe*, March 20, 1895: 1; "His Excellency Signs the Order in Council," *Globe*, March 21, 1895: 1; "Remedial Order," *Globe*, March 22, 1895: 1; "From the Capital," *Daily Mail and Empire*, March 12, 1895: 2; "From the Capital," *Daily Mail and Empire*, March 15, 1895: 8; "The School Case," *Daily Mail and Empire*, March 16, 1895: 1; "From the Capital," *Daily Mail and Empire*, March 18, 1895: 2; "From the Capital," *Daily Mail and Empire*, March 19, 1895: 1; "From the Capital," *Daily Mail and Empire*, March 20, 1895: 1; "From the Capital," *Daily Mail and Empire*, March 21, 1895: 1; "School Question," *Daily Mail and Empire*, March 22, 1895: 1; "From the Capital," *Daily Mail and Empire*, March 25, 1895: 8.

This iteration of Bowell's position on separate schools is from *Debates of the Senate of the Dominion of Canada* (hereafter, *Senate Debates*), 7th Parliament, 5th Session (11 July 1895) at 669.

Payne's account of Bowell's unsuccessful run for office in 1863 is from J.L. Payne, "Sir Mackenzie Bowell, Premier of Canada," *The Canadian Magazine* 6, no. 3 (Jan 1896): 233.

The Lafleche letter to Langevin is quoted in Crunican, *Priests and Politicians*, 49.

The account of Aberdeen attending the Privy Council chamber is from "School Question," *Mail and Empire*, March 22, 1895.

The Bowell-Tupper March correspondence is from C.H. Tupper to Bowell, 21 March 1895, Bowell Papers, PAC; Bowell to Tupper, 23 March 1895, Bowell

A VERY CANADIAN COUP

Papers; Tupper to Bowell, 25 March 1895, Bowell Papers. Reprinted in various sources.

Charlie Tupper's resignations are documented in Clark, *A History*, at 52, 144, 146, and 168.

Tupper's letter to Daly is from Tupper to Daly, 26 March 1895, C.H. Tupper Papers, PAC. Reprinted in various sources.

The advice Smith and Drummond give Charlie Tupper is adopted from Tupper Sr.'s advice to Charlie in a letter dated January 1895. Smith offered this advice to Tupper Sr. when meeting with him in London.

Drummond's note to Aberdeen is from Lady Aberdeen's diary, 213.

Charlie Tupper's conversation with the *Globe* is from "Tupper Back at Work," *Globe*, April 3, 1895: 1.

WORD INVIOLATE
The opening of the Fifth Session of Canada's Seventh Parliament is from "Parliament," *Globe*, April 19, 1895: 1.

The full text of Aberdeen's April 18 Throne Speech begins at *Senate Debates*, 7th Parliament, 5th Session (18 April 1895) at 3.

The full text of Bowell's maiden speech as prime minister begins at *Senate Debates*, 7th Parliament, 5th Session (22 April 1895) at 16.

Chapter 5: Blazing Heather

FIRST SPIKE
The history of the Hudson Bay railway presented here is based on Howard Fleming, *Canada's Arctic Outlet: A History of the Hudson Bay Railway* (Berkeley: University of California Press, 1957).

As Fleming suggests, there is only "circumstantial evidence that sometime late in April or early May [1895] a plan was devised by Mackenzie and Mann and the Bowell ministry to outwit the bloodhounds of the Opposition with the object of securing the construction of [a railway to Hudson Bay]. The combination of business and parliamentary manoeuvres which unfolded in the next few months is so contrived and devious that it is inconceivable that it should be the outgrowth of mere chance. The chain of events set in motion in the late spring of 1895 was the result of either the most careful planning or a whole series of remarkable coincidences [which] led to the most amazing saga of Canadian railway building, the construction of the giant Canadian Northern system that ultimately pushed northward to the Saskatchewan River and provided the first leg in the modern Hudson Bay route" (46). Similarly, only circumstantial evidence exists to support Liberal charges of Conservative boodling in connection with the Hudson Bay railway. Saywell, for example, cites this letter from James Edgar to Wilfrid Laurier: "Yesterday my friend of Montreal was here and called to see me. He told

Sources

me, most confidentially of course, that the reason the Session was called at the last moment was because the Hudson Bay Ry people refused to accept an Order in Council for their $2½ million load. The reason they were able to insist is because 10%, that is $250,000, is to be set apart for an election fund, besides something that Sir Adolphe rakes in for himself! This quite agrees with what I heard from another source — and we may accept it as true I think." Edgar to Laurier, 28 March 1895, Laurier Papers, PAC, Ottawa. Cited in John Saywell, "Introduction," *The Canadian Journal of Lady Aberdeen*, xlviii.

Official correspondence related to the HBR is reprinted in "The Hudson Bay Railway Papers," *Globe*, May 6, 1895: 1.

For newspaper coverage of the relationship between the Sixth Ministry and the Hudson Bay railway, see "The Hudson Bay Railway," *Globe*, April 13, 1895: 12; "Hudson Bay Road," *Globe*, May 2, 1895: 1; "The Hudson Bay Railway," *Globe*, July 25, 1895: 4; "The Mysterious Subsidy," *Globe*, August 20, 1895: 4.

Details of Caron's boodling can be found in Canada, House of Commons, *Royal Commission in Reference to Certain Charges Made Against the Honourable Sir. A.P. Caron, K.C.M.G.* Sessional Papers (no. 27), 1893.

For newspaper coverage of Aberdeen's sit-down with Greenway and Sifton, see "Coming to Ottawa," *Globe*, May 11, 1895: 5; "At the Capital," *Globe*, May 25, 1895: 8; "At the Capital," *Globe*, May 28, 1895: 1.

Bowell's comments on Aberdeen's May sit-down with Greenway and Sifton were included in a letter from Langevin to Begin, May 26, 1895, reprinted in Crunican, *Priests and Politicians*, 92.

For newspaper coverage of Manitoba's response to the March remedial order, see "The Answer," *Globe*, June 14, 1895: 1; "At the Capital," *Globe*, June 14, 1895: 5; "Manitoba Schools," *Daily Mail and Empire*, June 17, 1895: 2; "Manitoba Schools," *Daily Mail and Empire*, June 18, 1895: 1; "Manitoba Schools," *Daily Mail and Empire*, June 20, 1895: 1.

Manitoba's reply is in "Manitoba Schools," *Daily Mail and Empire*, July 3, 1895: 1.

ABLAZE

For newspaper coverage of Ottawa's response to Manitoba, see "From the Capital," *Daily Mail and Empire*, July 4, 1895: 1; "At the Capital," *Globe*, June 15, 1895: 5.

Cabinet members' positions leading up to the cabinet meetings on July 4 and 5 are based on "Factions in the Cabinet," *Globe*, June 11, 1895: 1; "At the Capital," *Globe*, June 20, 1895: 7; "The School Crisis," *Globe*, June 21, 1895: 1; "Many Troubles in the Tory Camp," *Globe*, June 22, 1895: 8; "At the Capital," *Globe*, June 24, 1895: 1; "At the Capital," *Globe*, June 26, 1895: 2; "At the Capital," *Globe*, July 1, 1895: 1; "At the Capital," *Globe*, July 3, 1895: 1; "At the Capital," *Globe*, July 4, 1895: 7.

Proceedings of the cabinet meetings on July 4 and 5 are based on "In a Quandary," *Globe*, July 5, 1895: 1; "No Remedial Bill," *Globe*, July 6, 1895: 17; "A

Wide Breach," *Globe*, July 8, 1895: 8; "From the Capital," *Daily Mail and Empire*, July 5, 1895: 1; "From the Capital," *Daily Mail and Empire*, July 6, 1895: 16.

The Bowell-Clark Wallace exchange is from a July story in the *Ottawa Evening Telegram* reprinted in "A Wide Breach," *Globe*, July 8, 1895: 8.

Haggart's "spoiled children" comment is quoted in "Dominion Parliament," *Daily Mail and Empire*, July 9, 1895: 8.

GROWING DIFFERENCES
Bowell's correspondence with Aberdeen is from Lady Aberdeen's diary, 233–39.

The account of Foster's statement in the House — and the statement itself — is from "Dominion Parliament," *Daily Mail and Empire*, July 9, 1895: 8. The Commons lobby after Foster's statement is based on "From the Capital," *Daily Mail and Empire*, July 8, 1895: 1–2. Ouimet's *Gazette* quote is from here as well.

PRESSURE
The account of Bowell's efforts to get Caron and Ouimet back is based on "Cabinet Crisis," *Daily Mail and Empire*, July 10, 1895: 1; "Still Suspense," *Daily Mail and Empire*, July 11, 1895: 1; "They Came Back," *Daily Mail and Empire*, July 12, 1895: 1; "A Pledge Given," *Globe*, July 9, 1895: 1; "A Grave Crisis," *Globe*, July 10, 1895: 1; "The Ragged Cabinet," *Globe*, July 11, 1895: 1; "At the Old Stand," *Globe*, July 12, 1895: 7.

Smith's statement is from *Senate Debates*, 7th Parliament, 5th Session (11 July 1895) at 664.

The Foster-Laurier exchange is from *House of Commons Debates*, 7th Parliament, 5th Session (9 July 1895) at 4056.

Aberdeen's contribution to the Bowell-Caron-Ouimet conversation is from Lady Aberdeen's diary, 237.

Bowell's statement to Cook is from "Still Suspense," *Daily Mail and Empire*, July 11, 1895: 1.

BATS
The Foster-Laurier exchange is from *House of Commons Debates*, 7th Parliament, 5th Session (11 July 1895) starting at 4187.

The Bowell and Angers speeches are adopted from *Senate Debates*, 7th Parliament, 5th Session (11 July 1895) beginning at 657.

Daly's comment on Foster is from a letter, Daly to Thompson, 23 February 1894, Thompson Papers, PAC, 201. Reprinted in Clark, *A History*, 336.

MILKMAIDS
Laurier's "flagrant constitutional outrages" comment is from *House of Commons Debates*, 7th Parliament, 5th Session (18 June 1895) at 2890.

Dawson's milkmaids comment is from *House of Commons Debates*, 7th Parliament, 5th Session (10 May 1895) at 1451.

Sources

Debate on the W&GNR Bill is adapted from *House of Common Debates*, 7th Parliament, 5th Session (20 July 1895) beginning at 4864; and *Senate Debates*, 7th Parliament, 5th Session (20 July 1895) beginning at 769.

Bowell's discussion with Daly et al. during Powell's speech on the W&GNR is from "Put off the Show," *Globe*, July 22, 1895: 5.

Chapter 6: Friendly Negotiations

Official correspondence between the Dominion and Manitoba on the school issue is included in *Sessional Papers of the Dominion of Canada*, 7th Parliament, 5th Session, vol. 11, no. 39 (1896).

The account of Aberdeen's July 29 chat with Greenway, and his update to Bowell, is from Lady Aberdeen's diary, 254.

The few details of Bowell's 1890 trip west are from *Sessional Papers of the Dominion of Canada*, vol. 10; Annual Report of Commissioner L.W. Herchmer, NWMP, 1890; Sessional Paper no.13, A 1890"; and "Annual report of Inspector Sanders Commanding 'A' Division (Maple Creek)," Sessional Papers no.13A, 1890. 6th Parliament, 4th Session.

Bowell's *Quadra* voyage is based on "The Premier at Vancouver," *Daily Colonist*, August 4, 1895: 5; "Premier Bowell's Party," *Daily Colonist*, August 13, 1895: 1; "The City," *Daily Colonist*, August 14, 1895: 5; "The Visiting Ministers," *Daily Colonist*, August 16, 1895: 5; "Sir Mackenzie Bowell," *Daily Colonist*, August 18, 1895: 5; "News of the Province," *Daily Colonist*, August 22, 1895: 2.

Bowell's prairie swing is based on *Annual Report of the Department of Indian Affairs for the Year Ended 30th June 1896* (Ottawa: Dawson): 324, 528; "Regina's Great Fair," *Mail and Empire*, August 5, 1895: 2; "Formally Opened," *Mail and Empire*, July 31, 1895: 1; "The Premier's Party Visit a Farm and See for Themselves," *Daily Nor'Wester*, August 29, 1895: 4; "The Premier," *Prince Albert Times*, September 10, 1895: 3; "The Premier," *Daily Colonist*, September 10, 1895: 1; "Bowell at Fort Saskatchewan," *Daily Colonist*, September 12, 1895: 1; "Premier Bowell's Tour in the West," *Winnipeg Daily Tribune*, September 12, 1895: 1.

The account of Bowell at the Battleford Industrial School is based on Jane Griffith, "News from School: Language, Time, and Place in the Newspapers of 1890s Indian Boarding Schools in Canada" (PhD diss., York University, 2015), 173–75.

Payne's account of the Bowell's western tour is from J. Lambert Payne, "The Premier on the Prairie," *Montreal Daily Star*, November 9, 1895: 4.

Bowell's meeting with Geraldine Moodie is from "The Ministers' Visit," *Saskatchewan Herald*, September 13, 1895: 1. See, as well, Donny White, *In Search of Geraldine Moodie* (Regina: Canadian Plains Research Center, 1998).

Bowell's return to Winnipeg after his prairie swing is based on "Winnipeg," *Globe*, August 27, 1895: 1; "A Conference Probable," *Globe*, August 28, 1895:

2; "Premier Bowell's Intentions," *Globe*, September 2, 1895: 1; "The Premier at Winnipeg," *Globe*, September 14, 1895: 9; "Winnipeg," *Globe*, September 16, 1895: 1; "At the Capital," *Globe*, September 20, 1895: 2; "Dismissal or Surrender," *Winnipeg Daily Tribune*, August 23, 1895: 1; "Premier Greenway Seen," *Winnipeg Daily Tribune*, August 27, 1895: 4; "Bowell and Greenway," *Winnipeg Daily Tribune*, August 29, 1895: 1; "Ottawa can Suggest but Cannot Command," *Winnipeg Daily Tribune*, September 3, 1895: 1; "Doings About Town," *Daily Nor'Wester*, September 7, 1895: 8; "Premier Bowell's Tour in the West," *Winnipeg Daily Tribune*, September 12, 1895: 1; "The Premier Departs," *Daily Nor'Wester*, September 14, 1895: 5; "Premier Returns," *Daily Nor'Wester*, September 12, 1895: 1.

Bowell's meeting with Greenway is from "Premiers Meet," *Winnipeg Daily Tribune*, September 14, 1895: 1. The *Montreal Daily Herald* reported on the meeting as well but had it taking place Saturday morning. "Met by Accident," *Montreal Daily Herald*, September 16, 1895: 1.

The history of Saint-Paul-des-Métis is from Emeric Drouin, "La Colonie Saint-Paul-Des-Metis, Alberta" (PhD. diss., University of Ottawa, 1962); George F.G. Stanley, "Alberta's Half-Breed Reserve Saint-Paul-des Métis 1896–1909," in *The Other Natives: The — Les Métis*, vol. 2, A.S. Lussier and D.B. Sealey, eds. (Winnipeg: Manitoba Métis Federation Press, 1978), 75–107. Truth and Reconciliation Commission of Canada, *Canada's Residential Schools: The Métis Experience* (Kingston: McGill-Queen's University Press, 2015): 16–19. See, as well, Library and Archives Canada (LAC), RG15, D-II-1, vol. 708, file 366530, part 1, Albert Lacombe, "A Philanthropic Plan to Redeem the Half-Breeds of Manitoba and the Northwest Territories," 25; and LAC, RG15, D-II-1, vol. 708, file 360530, PC no. 3723, "Extract from a Report of the Committee of the Honourable the Privy Council, Approved by His Excellency on the 28th December, 1895"; Annex "A" to PC no. 3723, 12 December 1895.

BACKLOGGED

Crunican describes Angers's efforts to frustrate Bowell in chapter 5 of *Priests and Politicians*. See, as well, *Le Moniteur de Lévis*, November 4, 1895: 1, reprinted in "A Meeting of Cabinet this Afternoon," *Globe*, November 5, 1895: 1.

Dickey's letter to Tupper is at Dickey to Tupper, 1 November 1895, Tupper Papers, PAC. Reprinted in various sources.

The Curran appointment is based on "At the Capital," *Globe*, October 18, 1895: 2; "Mr. Justice Curran," *Globe*, October 19, 1895: 12.

The November 4 cabinet meeting and its aftermath is based on "A Meeting of Cabinet this Afternoon," *Globe*, November 5, 1895: 1; "At the Capital," *Globe*, November 5, 1895: 6; "At the Capital," *Globe*, November 7, 1895: 9; "At the Capital," *Globe*, November 8, 1895: 1; "At the Capital," *Globe*, November 11, 1895: 1.

Bowell's efforts to recruit Pelletier, Chapleau, Meredith, and Masson are based on "At the Capital," *Globe*, October 8, 1895: 7; "At the Capital," *Globe*, November 11, 1895: 9; "At the Capital," *Globe*, November 12, 1895: 1; "Quebec

Sources

Politics," *Globe*, November 26, 1895: 7; "At the Capital," *Globe*, December 2, 1895: 9. For additional background, see Crunican, *Priests and Politicians*, chapters 4 and 5; Blair Neatby and John Saywell, "Chapleau and the Conservative Party in Quebec," *Canadian Historical Review* 27, no. 1 (March 1956).

RECKONING

On Bowell and the remedial bill in November, see Crunican, *Priests and Politicians*, chapter 4. The *Daily Tribune* quote is from "No Compromise Negotiations," *Winnipeg Daily Tribune*, November 28, 1895: 1.

The Bowell–Clark Wallace exchange and the latter's resignation is based on "Clark Wallace," *Globe*, December 12, 1895: 1; "Resist Coercion," *Globe*, December 19, 1895: 8; "Wallace at Home," *Globe*, December 20, 1895: 5; "Hon. N.C. Wallace," *Evening Star*, December 30, 1895: 1.

The B.C. caucus revolt and Prior's appointment is based on "A New Minister," *Mail and Empire*, December 16, 1895: 1; "At the Capital," *Globe*, December 17, 1895: 1; "Col. Prior's Position," *Daily Colonist*, December 18, 1895: 1–2; "Col. Prior's Standing," *Globe*, December 19, 1895: 1; "At the Capital," *Globe*, Jan 1, 1896: 1.

The Bowell-Dewdney correspondence is included in "Col. Prior's Standing," ibid.

The *Globe* controller quote is from "At the Capital," *Globe*, December 20, 1895: 8.

Manitoba's December 21 response to the July 27 order is in Clark, *A History*, 422. Greenway's characterization of the election is in Joseph Hilts, "The Political Career of Thomas Greenway" (PhD diss., University of Manitoba, 1974), 239.

Cabinet's treatment of the *Shortis* case is based on Saywell, "Introduction," lxx–lxxi; "At the Capital," *The Globe*, January 4, 1896: 18. For more on *Shortis*, see Martin Friedland, *The Case of Valentine Shortis: A True Story* (Toronto: University of Toronto Press, 1988).

SESSION OPEN

For the opening of the Seventh Session of Canada's Sixth Parliament, see "A Dull Opening," *Globe*, January 3, 1896: 2; and "Dominion Parliament," *Daily Mail and Empire*, January 3, 1896: 3.

Chapter 7: Coup

COMETH THE HOUR, COMETH THE RAM

On newspaper coverage of the coup in general, see "Conspiracy," *Globe*, January 8, 1896, 1; "Tupper," *Globe*, January 9, 1896, 1; "Sir Charles Tupper and the Premiership," *Globe*, January 23, 1896, 2; "At the Capital," *Globe*, February 21, 1896, 3.

Dickey's letter to Tupper is at Tupper Papers, PAC, November 1, 1895. Reprinted in various sources.

Tupper's relationship with Macdonald and his roles in the 1887 and 1891 elections is from Alan Macintosh, "The Career of Sir Charles Tupper in Canada, 1864–1900," vol. 2 (Franklin, 2018), chapters 8–10; and Phillip Buckner, "Tupper, Sir Charles," in *Dictionary of Canadian Biography*, biographi.ca/en/bio/tupper_charles_14E.html.

Tupper's January, 1895, visit with Smith is recounted in Macintosh, *Career of Sir Charles Tupper*, 413–14.

C.H. Tupper to Tupper, 29 January 1895, Tupper Papers, PAC. Reprinted in various sources.

C.H. Wood to Tupper, 21 March 1895, Tupper Papers, PAC. Reprinted in various sources.

Tupper's November 1895 telegrams to Bowell and Bowell's reply are included in Saunders, *Life and Letters*, 187.

CABALLING

On Tupper's December 16 meetings in Ottawa, see his January 6, 1896, letter to Van Horne included in Saunders, *Life and Letters*, 190. Macintosh, *Career*, 413 provides additional background on the meeting.

For newspaper coverage of cabinet difficulties prior to the January 4 resignations, see "At the Capital," *Globe*, January 2, 1896: 10; "A Dull Opening," *Globe*, January 3, 1896: 2; "Cabinet Shuffles," *Globe*, January 4, 1896: 5; "At the Capital," *Globe*, January 4, 1896: 18; "Cabinet Crisis," *Daily Mail and Empire*, January 4, 1896: 1.

Bowell's meeting with Haggart and Montague, including the "pistol to his head" quote is from "One to Smash," *Globe*, January 6, 1896: 1.

There is no definitive evidence that Bowell or Caron leaked the anonymous letters. On January 6, Fred Cook wrote that "The story was printed on Saturday in the *Ottawa Citizen*, as a dispatch from Toronto, and in the *Toronto World* as a dispatch from Ottawa. On the face of it this was a ruse to deceive. The story as published in Ottawa presumably originated in Toronto, whereas the story as published in Toronto presumably originated in Ottawa." See "Cabinet Crisis," *Mail and Empire*, January 6, 1896: 1. On January 9, Bowell told the Senate that on January 2, "a member of Parliament came to my residence and asked me about the letters. He told me what he had heard, and I asked him how he obtained such information. The answer was that it was common talk in the Albany Club in the city of Toronto. I then came to the conclusion that it would ultimately get into the press, and that my duty to my colleague [Montague] was to inform him of the fact; and, after consulting Sir Adolphe Caron, I did so the next day. There is the whole history, so far as I am concerned of that transaction." *Senate Debates*, 7th Parliament, 6th Session (9 January 1896) at 15.

Sources

The Governor General's meetings with Bowell, Foster, and Haggart on Friday, January 3, are based on Lady Aberdeen's diary, 299–300.

HACKLES
The timing of events on Saturday, January 4, is from "Cabinet Crisis," *Daily Mail and Empire*, January 6, 1896: 1–2, 8; "One to Smash," *Globe*, January 6, 1896, 1; and George Foster's memorandum to Governor General Aberdeen included in Wallace Stewart, *The Memoirs of the Rt. Hon. Sir George Foster* (Toronto: Macmillan, 1933), 92–95.

Daly's comments are from a letter to Bowell. Daly to Bowell, 4 January 1896, Tupper Papers, 18. Reprinted in various sources.

The January 4 meeting between Tupper and Bowell is based on an interview Tupper gave in "Cabinet Crisis," *Daily Mail and Empire*, January 6, 1896: 1–2.

RECONSTRUCTION
Bowell's meeting with Aberdeen on Sunday, January 5, is based on Lady Aberdeen's diary, 299–300.

The cabinet crisis and Bowell's reconstruction efforts on January 5–6 are based on "Cabinet Crisis," *Daily Mail and Empire*, January 7, 1896: 1–2; "Dissolution," *Globe*, January 7, 1896, 1; "What He Would Do," *Daily Mail and Empire*, January 8, 1896: 5.

Bowell's January 6 note to Aberdeen is quoted in Shackleton, *Ishbel and the Empire*, 199.

The Laurier-Caron exchange, Foster's January 7 statement on the resignations, and Cartwright's observations are from *Senate Debates*, 7th Parliament, 6th Session (7 January 1895) beginning at 10.

TRAITORS
Bowell's reception in the House on January 7 is based on "In the Gallery," *Globe*, January 8, 1896, 7; and an *Ottawa Citizen* account reprinted in "The Cabinet Crisis," *Sydney Morning Herald*, February 12, 1896: 8. Both reference Bowell's "nest of traitors" comment.

Bowell's January 7 comments in the Senate are from *Senate Debates*, 7th Parliament, 6th Session (7 January 1896) beginning at 4.

UNDER PRESSURE
The Tupper interview is in "Cabinet Crisis," *Daily Mail and Empire*, January 8, 1896: 1–2, 4.

The January 8 meeting between Bowell and Aberdeen is based on Lady Aberdeen's diary, 303–4.

Bowell's comment to the *Evening Telegram* is reprinted in "Cabinet Crisis," *Daily Mail and Empire*, January 9, 1896.

A VERY CANADIAN COUP

The Mowat precedent is from Paul Romney, "Mowat, Sir Oliver," *Dictionary of Canadian Biography*, biographi.ca/en/bio/mowat_oliver_13E.html.

The Lady Aberdeen–Laurier exchange is based on Her Ladyship's diaries; Saywell, "Introduction"; Shackleton, *Ishbel and the Empire*, chapters 14 and 15.

NO PRECEDENT
Bowell's January 9 statement is based on *Senate Debates*, 7th Parliament, 6th Session (9 January 1896) starting at 10.

RECONSTRUCTED
Bowell's efforts at reconstruction are based on "Cabinet Crisis," *Daily Mail and Empire*, January 10, 1896: 1–2, 8; "Cabinet Crisis," *Daily Mail and Empire*, January 11, 1896: 1–2; "Cabinet Crisis," *Daily Mail and Empire*, January 13, 1896: 1–2; "Will Hold On," *Globe*, January 10, 1896, 7; "Waiting," *Globe*, January 11, 1896, 5; "Struggling," *Globe*, January 13, 1896, 1; "The Strike," *Globe*, January 14, 1896, 1.

The terms of Desjardins's entry into cabinet are set out in Memorandum by Alphonse Desjardins, 15 January 1896, Desjardins Collection, ACSM. Quoted in Crunican, *Priests and Politicians*, 156.

The meeting between Charlie Tupper and Lady Aberdeen is based on Her Ladyship's diary, 310–11.

Tupper and Bowell's January 12 meeting is based on an interview with Tupper in "Cabinet Crisis," *Daily Mail and Empire*, January 13, 1896: 1–2.

Daly's warning is from a letter to Bowell. Daly to Bowell, 12 January 1896, Bowell Papers, PAC. Reprinted in Clark, *A History*, 437.

For newspaper coverage of the resolution to the January crisis, see "Trouble Abating," *Daily Mail and Empire*, January 14, 1896: 1–2; "Again Put Off," *Globe*, January 15, 1896: 5; "Booked to Burst," *Globe*, January 15, 1896: 1; "Reunited," *Globe*, January 16, 1896: 2; "The New Cabinet," *Globe*, January 16, 1896: 4; "Ottawa Trouble," *Daily Mail and Empire*, January 15, 1896: 1–2; "The New Cabinet," *Daily Mail and Empire*, January 16, 1896: 1–2; "Political Notes," *Daily Mail and Empire*, January 18, 1896: 1–2.

Caron's January 15 statement is from *House of Commons Debates*, 7th Parliament, 6th Session (15 January 1896) beginning at 70.

Chapter 8: Anew

ANEW
Tupper's Boisdale speech is in "In Cape Breton," *Globe*, January 23, 1896: 1.

Sources

ENTER SMITH

Aberdeen's letter to Chamberlain is in Aberdeen to Chamberlain, 25 January 1896, PAC. Reprinted in Crunican, *Priests and Politicians*, 179.

Lady Aberdeen's letters to Gladstone and Rosebery are reprinted in Shackleton, *Ishbel and Empire*, 192. Her letter to Langevin, 22 December 1895, AASB; her letter to Walsh, February 3, 1896, AAB. Both are reprinted in Crunican, *Priests and Politicians*, 179–80.

The "plan" Aberdeen and Smith settled on and Tupper agreed to is from Donna McDonald, *Lord Strathcona: A Biography of Donald Alexander Smith* (Toronto: Dundurn Press, 2002), 397.

BILL C-58

The February 11 caucus meeting is based on "A Challenge," *Globe*, February 11, 1896: 7; and "At the Capital," *Globe*, February 12, 1896: 2.

I have taken some liberties in reconstructing the February 11 caucus presentations. The two *Globe* stories describe only who spoke and what the general tenor of their remarks were. The full text of Dawson's letter is in "Sir William Dawson," *La Presse*, February 12, 1896: 2; Tupper's mantra is from his speech during debate on second reading. Dickey's presentation is the one he gave in the House on the afternoon of February 11; I assume his remarks to caucus would have been similar. Clark Wallace and Craig's comments are based on speeches they gave at Massey Hall at a rally held on February 24, 1896. These, in turn, are similar to speeches they gave during debate on second reading. I assume their remarks in caucus would have been similar. For their full addresses at Massey Hall, see "Toronto Stands by Manitoba," *Globe*, February 24, 1896: 1. Weldon and Haggart's remarks are adapted from their speeches during second reading debate on Bill C-58 (Weldon on March 31 at 4985; Haggart on March 17 at 3778).

SECOND READING

Crunican, *Priests and Politicians* (187), provides details on Ewart and Langevin's review and approval of Bill C-58.

Tupper's remarks on Bill C-58 are from *House of Commons Debates*, 7th Parliament, 6th Session (3 March 1896) beginning at 2720; Laurier's remarks begin at 2736.

Tupper's promise of a conference is at *Debates* (9 March 1896) at 3098; the "catch" is explained by Smith at 4135.

THE SMITH COMMISSION

Smith's secret February mission to Manitoba is based on "Sir Donald Smith's Winnipeg Mission," *Globe*, February 25, 1896: 2; "At the Capital," *Globe*, February 26, 1896: 1.

Smith's report to Tupper and Bowell is based on telegrams he'd sent to both. These are reprinted in "At the Capital," *Globe*, March 27, 1886.

All official correspondence between Smith and the Manitoba government, and the text of the March 17 OIC are reprinted in "At the Capital," *Globe*, March 27, 1896.

Lady Aberdeen's efforts to "soften the wheels" are recounted in Crunican, *Priests and Politicians*, 229.

In addition to official documentation, the Smith Commission is based on "A Tupper Fall," *Globe*, March 10, 1896: 2; "The Second Day," *Globe*, March 20, 1896: 1; "The Winnipeg Conference," *Globe*, March 23, 1896: 4; "A Mass of Inconsistencies," *Globe*, March 25, 1896: 4; "School Commission," *Globe*, March 26, 1896: 9; "The Conference," *Globe*, March 28, 1896: 13; "More Hopeful," *Globe*, March 30, 1896: 1; "At Winnipeg, *Globe*, April 1, 1896: 1; "No Settlement," *Globe*, April 2, 1896: 1; "The Whole Case," *Globe*, April 3, 1896: 1.

OBSTRUCTED

Tupper's "every physical power" remark is from *House of Commons Debate*, 7th Parliament, 6th Session (31 March 1896) at 4961. Tupper's attack on Laurier is from *Debates* (8 April 1896) at 5694; Charlton's Bible lesson begins at 5665; and Borden's medical tutorial begins at 5915.

Debate on sections 2 and 4 of Bill C-58 begins at *Debates* (4 April 1896) at 5243; debate on section 7 begins at *Debates* (9 April 1896) at 5847.

The "strange noises" episode is from "Cannot Answer," *Globe*, April 7, 1896: 2; additional colour on Charlton's Bible lesson is from "The Leaders," *Globe*, April 9, 1896: 2; additional colour on Borden's tutorial is from "Sixth Day Begun," *Globe*, April 11, 1896: 5; and the Ferguson v. Sproule match is from "The Whole Week," *Globe*, April 13, 1896: 9.

Aberdeen's note to cabinet about supply is in Saywell, "Introduction," lxix.

The Tupper-Laurier exchange on April 15 is from *Debates* (15 April 1896) at 6458.

RESIGNATION

Bowell's resignation and Tupper's ascension is based on "Sir Mackenzie Bowell to Resign Today," *Globe*, April 27, 1896: 7; "The Premier Resigns," *Globe*, April 28, 1896: 3.

Bowell and Aberdeen's April 27 meeting is based on Lady Aberdeen's diary, 340–41, as is Aberdeen and Tupper's conversation.

Bowell's remarks at the St. George's Society Dinner are in "At the Capital," *Globe*, April 27, 1896: 7.

Sources

Chapter 9: Coda

Tupper's "Manifesto" is reprinted in "The Manifesto," *Globe*, May 6, 1896: 1; and "Tupper at London," *Mail and Empire*, June 13, 1896: 1. The Desjardins interview is in *Mail and Empire*, June 25, 1896: 1.

Bowell's comment is from a letter he wrote to Tupper after the election in June: Bowell to Tupper, 30 June 1896, Tupper Papers, 10, PAC. Reprinted in Clark, *A History*, 539.

For coverage of the Laurier-Greenway Compromise, see Crunican, *Priests and Politicians*, Epilogue; and O.D. Skelton, *The Life and Letters of Sir Wilfrid Laurier*, vol. 2 (Toronto: Oxford University Press, 1921), 13–21.

On the Aberdeens' post-Canadian life, see Shackleton, *Ishbel and Empire*, chapters 18–20.

On Tupper's decision to stay on as party leader and subsequent history as opposition leader, see Macintosh, *Career of Sir Charles Tupper*, chapter 13.

The story of Bowell swimming in the Yukon River is from "Sir M. Bowell Passes Away," *Globe*, December 11, 1917: 1.

The account of the funeral is from "Sir Mackenzie Bowell Honored in Death," *The Intelligencer*, December 14, 1917: 2.

Image Credits

7   Library and Archives Canada, C-010111.
17   Library and Archives Canada, PA-027331. Photograph by William James Topley.
19   Library and Archives Canada, PA-027853. Photograph by William James Topley.
23   Library and Archives Canada, PA-025663. Photograph by William James Topley.
35   Nova Scotia Archives, N-1994.
42   Nova Scotia Archives, Notman Studio, 1983-310, N-1395.
102   Library and Archives Canada, C-044604. Photograph by John Lambert Payne.
104   Library and Archives Canada, C-044608. Photograph by John Lambert Payne.
105   Library and Archives Canada, C-044606. Photograph by John Lambert Payne.
106   Parks Canada, BT5/JB676.2.7. Photograph by Geraldine Moodie.
107   Library and Archives Canada, C-044603. Photograph by John Lambert Payne.

Index

Aberdeen, Lady Ishbel Marjoribanks, ix
   clandestine discussions with Laurier, 135–37, 142–44
   efforts to help resolve schools crisis, 149
   January Throne Speech, 116–17
   meets with Annie Thompson, 19–21
   meets with Charlie Tupper, 141–42
   returns to Britain, 172
   and *Shortis*, 115
Aberdeen, Lord John Hamilton Gordon, ix
   accepts Bowell's resignation, 168
   appoints Bowell PM, 26–28
   appoints Tupper PM, 168
   approves reconstructed Sixth Ministry, 144
   considers appointment of new ministry, 135–36
   decides *Shortis*, 123
   delivers April Throne Speech, 65–67
   discussions with Donald Smith, 149–50
   February meeting with Bowell, 54–56
   January 5 meeting with Bowell, 125
   January Throne Speech, 116–18
   July crisis, 78–79
   meeting with Frank Smith, 25
   meets with Caron and Ouimet, 84
   meets with Greenway, 74–75
   notifies Bowell of KCMG, 34
   prorogues Parliament, 97
   receives Thompson's body, 37
   refuses Bowell's resignation, 135
   returns to Britain, 172
   second meeting with Greenway, 100
   signs March remedial order, 61
   swears in Sixth Ministry, 31–32
   at Thompson's funeral, 38
   on Thompson's successor, 21–25
Albany Club, 172, 189
Angers, Auguste-Réal, ix
   appointed to Sixth Ministry, 28
   April Throne Speech, 66
   July cabinet meeting and resignation, 76–78
   mandament, 110, 113, 141
   March cabinet meeting, 54, 60
   Senate statement, 90

Barrett v. The City of Winnipeg, xvii, 46–48
Batoche, 106
Bering Sea conference, 11, 29, 196
Bill C-58, *The Remedial Act (Manitoba)*, xxiii
   committee review, 160–65
   introduction, 150–55
   second reading, 155–57
   suspension, 165
Blake, Edward, 3–4
Blenheim, 25, 35–37
Bowell, Mackenzie
   appointed KCMG, 34
   appointed member of Pacific Cable Commission, 173
   appointed PM, 27
   BC caucus revolt, 114–15
   Clarke Wallace resignation, 114

Commons reception, 132–33
death, 173
effort to fill vacancies, 109–10
February cabinet meeting, 53–55
first meeting with Sir Charles, 125
first speech as PM, 50–51
forms Sixth Ministry, 28–30
"friendly negotiations" memo, 99
Haggart and Montague meeting, 122–23
illness, 33, 45
invites Sir Charles to Canada, 120
July cabinet meeting, 75–79
July crisis, 79–90
last public speech, 168–69
maiden speech as PM, 67–69
March cabinet meeting, 58–61
March crisis, 61–65
meets Greenway, 109
ministry reconstruction, 125–27
November cabinet meeting, 111–12
Pacific Coast tour, 100–101
passage of the *W&GNR Act*, 93–98
prairie tour, 101–9
resignation, 167–68
Roman Catholic appeal, 56–58
at Sans Souci, 3–7
second meeting with Sir Charles, 142–43
Senate update, 137–40
third meeting with Sir Charles, 144
and Thompson's death, 9–16
Brophy v. The Attorney General of Manitoba, xviii, 48–49, 53, 57, 73, 148
Burd, R.J., 107–9

Cameron, John, 100, 109, 158–60
Cameron, John (Bishop), 38–42
Canadian Northern Railway, xx, 71–74, 92, 183
Carling, John, 24, 126
Caron, Adolphe, ix
    announces reconstructed Ministry, 144–45

appointed to Sixth Ministry, 28
Commons statement, 87
Desjardins deal, 141
efforts to reconcile, 83–85
February cabinet meeting, 54
January Throne Speech, 117
July cabinet meeting, 76–77
Montague-Caron affair, 122–23
replaces Ouimet as chief wire-puller, 113
resignation, 77–78
response to Greenway, 75–76
statement to Commons, 128
on *Shortis*, 116
Cartwright, Richard, 49, 131–32, 163
Chapleau, Joseph-Adolphe, 1, 110
Coldstream Ranch, 101
Cook, Fred, x, 2, 10, 16, 27–29, 31, 33, 35–36, 84
Costigan, John, 10–11, 28–29, 31–32, 42, 59, 75–76, 81–82, 124, 127, 146
Craig, Thomas Dixon, 154, 156
Curran, John, 27–28, 36, 58, 81–82, 110–11

Daly, Thomas, x
    appointed to Sixth Ministry, 28
    counsels Bowell, 124–25
    debate on Bill C-58, 163–64
    Desjardin appointment, 141
    in Halifax, 33–36
    Hudson Bay railway loan, 73
    July cabinet meeting, 76
    Laurier rumors, 143
    letter to Charlie Tupper, 63
    March Cabinet meeting, 59–60
    Pacific Coast tour, 100–101
    prairie tour, 101–9
    Thompson's death, 13
Dawson, William, 153
Desjardins, Alphonse, 116, 141, 146, 148, 150, 158–60, 171
Dewdney, Edward, 114
Dickey, Arthur, x
    appointed to Sixth Ministry, 29, 31–32

Index

introduces Bill C-58, 150–53
letter to Sir Charles, 110–11, 119
March cabinet meeting, 59
meets with Bowell, 124
meets with Sir Charles, 121
part of Smith Commission, 158, 160
resignation, 125, 141
return to cabinet, 144
Drummond, George, 25, 64
Duck Lake, 106–7

Equal Rights Association, 57, 116
Ermineskin, 102
Ewart, John, xi, 46–48, 56–58, 113, 155, 157

Fenton, Faith, 5–7
Ferguson, Donald, 5, 13–14, 28, 59, 127, 156
Fifth Ministry, 11, 18, 28
Fleming, Sandford, 9–10, 173
Forget, Amédée-Emmanuel, 103–4
Fort Rupert, 101
Foster, George, ii
   with Annie Thompson, 14
   appointed to Sixth Ministry, 28
   Commons address, 129–31
   March cabinet meeting, 59–60
   meets with Aberdeen, 123
   meets with Sir Charles, 121
   possible successor, 22
   reconciliation with Caron and Ouimet, 82–84
   resigns, 125
   return to cabinet, 144–46
   statement on Caron and Ouimet, 85–86
   statement on July crisis, 79–80
   Thompson pallbearer, 42
   and Thompson's death, 10–11
   and *W&GNR Act*, 92–93
Frog Lake, 105

Girouard, Désiré, 110
Gladstone, William, 102, 149

Gordon, Arthur, 24, 26–27
Greenway, Thomas, xi
   agrees to Smith Commission, 158
   appeals *Barrett*, 47
   discusses Bowell meeting, 102
   discussions with LG Schultz, 55
   first meeting with Aberdeen, 74
   Hudson Bay railway bonus, 72
   issues formal response to July 27 order, 115
   issues schools compromise, 113
   Laurier-Greenway Compromise, 172
   meets Bowell, 109
   meets with Smith, 157
   second meeting with Aberdeen, 100
Griesbach, Arthur, 103–4

Haggart, John, xi
   appointed to Sixth Ministry, 28
   December cabinet meeting, 116
   February cabinet meeting, 55
   July cabinet meeting 76, 78
   March cabinet meeting, 59–60
   meets with Bowell with Montague, 122
   meets with Sir Charles, 121
   November cabinet meeting, 112
   possible successor, 20–21
   resignation, 125
   resumes cabinet position, 146
   speech on Bill C-58, 155
   and Thompson's death, 11–14
   and *W&GNR Act*, 92–93
Hayter Reed, 100, 102, 104
Herchmer, Lawrence, 103
Holt, Herbert, 72–73

Ives, William, xii
   appointed to Sixth Ministry, 28–32
   April Throne Speech, 66
   in Halifax, 34, 36
   March cabinet meeting, 59
   meets with Sir Charles, 121
   November cabinet meeting, 111–12
   questions Ewart, 57

resignation, 125
return to cabinet, 144
Thompson's pallbearer, 42

Jesuit Estates Act, 1888, 46
Judicial Committee of the Privy
  Council (JCPC)
  in *Barrett*, 45–48
  in *Brophy*, 48–49

Kenny, Thomas, 34, 48, 81, 126
Kimber, René, 66–67, 117, 133
Kuper Island, 101

Lake Manitoba Railway & Canal
  Company (LMR), 72–73, 92
Langevin, Adélard, 64, 113, 133, 141,
  149–50, 155, 157–58
Laurier, Wilfrid, xii
  April Throne Speech, 65
  with Bowell in Commons, 132
  Caron-Ouimet resignations, 79–89
  clandestine discussions with Lady
    Aberdeen, 136–44
  Hudson Bay railway subsidy, 91
  introduction of Bill C-58, 156
  Laurier-Greenway Compromise, 172
  response to Tupper's harangue, 162
  return of Caron and Ouimet, 128–29
  speech at Massey Hall, 49–50
  suspension of Bill C-58, 166–67
  W&GNR Act, 92–93
  wins 1896 election, 171
  withdrawal of Bill C-58, 165–67
Laurier, Zoé, 142
Laurier-Greenway Compromise, 172
Lawlor, James, 107, 109
Leduc, Hippolyte, 103

Macdonald, Agnes, 22
Macdonald, Hugh John, 64, 111
Macdonald, John A., 1, 10, 16, 20, 25,
  29, 46, 52, 56, 72, 110, 119, 139,
  173

Mackenzie, William, plan for CNR,
  71–75
Mackintosh, Charles, 107
Magurn, Arnott, xiii, 2, 28, 65, 78, 81,
  120, 127
Manitoba Act, 1870, 46–48, 57, 60, 68
Manitoba schools question, 2, 45, 48,
  52–56, 68, 78, 99, 102, 110, 113,
  157, 172
Mann, Donald, 71–74
Mann, George, 71–75
McCarthy, D'Alton, xii, 56–58, 116, 132
McGee, John, 31–32
McKay, Joe, 106–7
Meredith, William Ralph, 111, 126
Montague, Walter, xii, 12, 29, 31, 59,
  60, 78, 82, 110, 112
  meets with Bowell and Haggart, 122
  resignation, 125, 132
  return to cabinet, 144
Moodie, Geraldine, 105
Mowat, Sir Oliver, 49, 135–36

National Council of Women, ix, 142
Northwest Mounted Police, 100, 109
Northwest Rebellion, x, xiii, 46, 104–6
Northwest Territorial Exhibition, 100

O'Brien, Cornelius (archbishop of
  Halifax), 33, 39–42
Onion Lake, 105–6, 108
Orange Order, 26, 76
Ouimet, Joseph-Aldric, xiii
  appointed to Sixth Ministry, 28
  Commons statement, 87–88
  efforts to reconcile, 83–85
  February cabinet meeting, 54
  July cabinet meeting, 76–78
  March Cabinet meeting, 59
  November cabinet meeting, 112–13
  resignation, 77–78
  response to Greenway, 75–76
  on *Shortis*, 116, 133
  witness to Desjardins deal, 141, 148

Index

Pakan, Chief, 104–5
Patterson, James, 11–14, 26, 29, 42, 50, 55, 59, 109
Payne, John, 9–11, 24, 61, 100, 101–4, 122, 125
Poe, Edmund, 36–37
Princess Louise Dragoon Guards, 66, 96
Prior, E.G., 114–25
Public Schools Act, 1890, 45–48, 57

Remedial Order (March 1895), 61, 75, 77–80, 90, 98–99, 114
Ripon, 1st Marquess of (George Robinson), 14–16, 21–22, 24, 26
Ross, James, 72–73,
Ross, John Jones, 66, 93, 98, 117
Russell House, 16, 27, 31, 64, 79, 83, 144

Sanford, William, xiii, 3–7, 16, 36–37
Scott, Richard, 67, 89, 93–37
Seventh Ministry, x, 125, 168, 171
Shortis, Valentine, 115–16, 123
Sifton, Clifford, xiii, 74–77, 145, 157–58
Sinclair, John, 142, 168
Sixth Ministry
 formed, 28–30
 January 15 reconstruction, 146, 147
 January 6 reconstruction, 127
 sworn in, 31–2, 49, 71, 83, 90, 99
Smith, Donald, xiii, 25, 64, 119, 141
 meets with Aberdeen, 149, 156
 secret mission, 157–58
 Smith Commission, 158–60
Smith, Frank, xiii
 appointed to Sixth Ministry, 28
 defends delay of remedial legislation, 82, 95, 117, 127
 facilitates meeting with Bowell and Tupper, 144
 February cabinet meeting, 54
 in Halifax, 33–34, 36
 July cabinet meeting, 76
 March cabinet meeting, 59
 meeting with Aberdeen, 26, 27
 meeting with Lady Aberdeen, 143–44
 Thompson's pallbearer, 42
Smith Commission, 157–60
Stewart, Douglas, 11–12, 14, 18
Supreme Court of Canada, 47–48, 57, 110
Sutherland, Hugh, 72–73, 197

Taché, Alexandre-Antonin, xiv, 46–48
Taylor, George, xiv, 76, 81, 121–22, 142
Thompson, Annie, 2–3, 6, 11, 13
 conversation with Bowell, 14–16
 conversation with Lady Aberdeen, 18–21
 at Thompson's funeral, 38, 43
Thompson, Helena, 16
Thompson, Joe, 5, 18, 36
Thompson, John, Jr., 5, 18, 36
Thompson, John Sparrow David, xiv, 1
 assessment of Bowell, 24
 assessment of Charlie Tupper, 29
 death of, 9–12, 14–16
 fall out with Chapleau, 110
 legality of *Public Schools Act, 1890*, 46
 mourned in Commons, 65, 66, 99
 promise to promote Curran, 110
 refers *Brophy* to Supreme Court, 48, 53, 54
 return to Halifax, 35–38
 in Sans Souci, 3–7
 state funeral, 38–43
 strikes cabinet committee to hear Roman Catholic appeal, 48
Tupper, Charles Hibbert, xiv
 appointed to Sixth Ministry, 29–30
 end of leadership ambitions, 172
 in Halifax, 36, 42
 meets with Dickey and Bowell, 124
 meets with Sir Charles, 121
 not included in reconstructed cabinet, 144

November telegram to Sir Charles, 120
resignation and March crisis, 61–65, 125
and *Shortis*, 115–16, 123
speech in Toronto, 52–53
talks with Lady Aberdeen, 141–42
warns Ewart about cabinet troubles, 113
Tupper, Sir Charles, xv
committee review of Bill C-58, 161–62
announces Smith Commission, 156–58
appointed prime minister, 168, 171
Cape Breton by-election, 148
caucus address, 150
Dickey letter, 110, 119
enters Sixth Ministry, 147
first meeting with Bowell, 125
Globe interview published, 134–35
introduces debate on Bill C-58, 155–56
loses 1896 election, becomes opposition leader, 171
meets with caballers, 121
meets with Smith, 149–50
possible successor, 20
role in previous elections, 119
second meeting with Bowell, 142–43
suspends Bill C-58, 165
telegram exchange with Bowell, 120
third meeting with Bowell, 144
and Thompson's death, 10–11, 13, 16, 18

Van Horne, William, 25
Victoria, Queen, 15–16, 34, 37, 39, 45

Wallace, Nathaniel Clarke, x, 28, 50, 53, 76, 82, 110
position on Bill C-58, 153–54, 156
resignation, 114
Weldon, Richard, 126, 127, 154, 156

White, Frederick, 103
White, Peter, 65, 79, 85, 92–93, 117, 127–29, 128
Winnipeg & Great Northern Railway Act (*W&GNR Act*), 92
Winnipeg & Hudson Bay Railway (WHB), 72
in the Commons, 90–93
in the Senate, 93–98

About the Author

Ted Glenn is an author, educator, and cyclist who divides his time between the bicycle paths of Toronto and the rolling hills of Grey County, Ontario. For the past twenty years, he's managed the graduate program in public administration at Humber College and written about Canadian legislatures, professional communications, and statecraft. Ted spends much of his spare time writing about forgotten interstices in Canadian history. This work includes *Riding into Battle: Canadian Cyclists in the Great War* (Dundurn, 2018), "Lawrence of Canada: How the Legend of the Dashing British First World War Hero Went Through a Test Run in Toronto" (*Canadian History*, December 2020), and *Embedded: Two Journalists, a Burlesque Star, and the Expedition to Oust Louis Riel* (Dundurn, 2020).